BRAHMS
and the PRINCIPLE
of DEVELOPING VARIATION

California Studies in

19TH CENTURY MUSIC

Joseph Kerman, General Editor

BRAHMS
and the Principle
of Developing Variation

Walter Frisch

University of California Press

BERKELEY · LOS ANGELES · LONDON

University of California Press
Berkeley and Los Angeles, California
University of California Press, Ltd.
London, England
© 1984 by
The Regents of the University of California

Library of Congress Cataloging in Publication Data

Frisch, Walter.
Brahms and the principle of developing variation.

(California studies in 19th century music; 2)
Bibliography: p.
Index: p.
1. Brahms, Johannes, 1833–1897.   Works.   I. Title.
MT92.B81F7 1983   780′.92′4   82–13675
ISBN 0–520–04700–1

Printed in the United States of America

1 2 3 4 5 6 7 8 9

For my parents

Would you be interested in a talk on Brahms? Here I'd probably have something to say that only I can say. For though my exact contemporaries, and those who are older than I, also lived in Brahms's time, they aren't "modern." But the younger Brahmsians can't know the Brahms tradition from first-hand experience, and anyway they mostly tend to be "reactionary." But: what I have in mind is the theory of composition, not anecdotes!

Letter from Arnold Schoenberg to Hans
Rosbaud, 7 January 1933, in response
to an invitation to give a radio talk

Contents

List of Longer Musical Examples

(Longer musical examples are found in the Appendix;
shorter examples accompany text discussion)

Preface

Yes, you have completely conquered me with your music! Not for a long time has any first impression affected me to such a degree. I feel the symphony belongs to those few exalted works that grab hold of a man mercilessly, embrace him with the first note, and refuse to release him with the last—instead pursuing him further and making him feel they have taken possession of him for all time. One even forgets admiration (which is otherwise a nice thing) and is easily carried along on magnificent waves. I need not tell you by what means of enchantment you manage this, from the tenderest and sweetest to the stormiest and most powerful.

Ernst Rudorff, a composer and teacher in Berlin, wrote thus to Brahms on 5 January 1884 after having heard one of the first performances of the Third Symphony. Anyone who has been "possessed" by a Brahms work will probably appreciate the sincere, if high-flown, sentiments. But if at all familiar with the literature on Brahms, he will also be aware how few commentators have succeeded in the difficult task hinted at (but distinctly avoided) by Rudorff, that of articulating how Brahms works his special magic. Musical analysis and criticism too often fall short of communicating the *Bewunderung* or the *Bezauberung* evoked in a listener (to use Rudorff's categories)—either the more conscious, intellectual "admiration" for technical achievement, or the less voluntary "enchantment" at the aesthetic experience.

In discussing Brahms's procedures of thematic continuity and economy—for which he coined the term "developing variation"—Arnold Schoenberg came closer than any other critic to unveiling the most compelling qualities of this music. Schoenberg's analyses, however, are frustratingly brief, normally covering only a few bars of music: they provide flashes of insight rather than sustained illumination. This book attempts to show that a careful clarification, refinement, and enlargement of Schoenberg's concept of developing variation can yield a valuable tool for examining not just brief themes by Brahms, but larger portions of movements, and even entire works.

I have made no attempt to treat every piece or genre, concentrating instead on about eighteen important works that allow us to trace Brahms's increasingly sophisticated use of the techniques of developing variation during his compositional career. I also assess what these techniques might owe to the music of Beethoven, Schubert, Schumann, and Liszt, and how they find their way into Schoenberg's early compositions. By adopting an approach that is both chronological and comparative, I have sought to avoid the common shortcoming of analytical studies—that of viewing works in isolation, ignoring their relationships to other pieces by the same composer and to those by significant predecessors, contemporaries, and followers.

I deal mainly with the larger instrumental works of Brahms—chamber, piano, and symphonic—because it is here that we see the composer at his most ambitious; he attempts to reconcile the procedures of developing variation and of his beloved sonata form, thus applying on an impressively large scale what was defined by Schoenberg as a more local, lower-level principle. But I have also included analyses of several songs that reveal these methods at work in the smaller dimensions of the Lied.

Ideally, the reader of this book should have a basic familiarity with the music discussed, and have as well a score with bars numbered (although the publishers have allowed me to be generous with musical examples and to include substantial portions of pieces). I hope that even without these resources the main points of my arguments and analyses can be followed. Even the densest writing about music should never become opaque; it should not retreat behind needlessly technical jargon or intricate graphic representations.

Although Brahms and Schoenberg provided inspiration and raw material for this study, I am indebted to many others for its realization. I am grateful to the Department of Music at the University of California, Berkeley, for its support and encouragement. My thanks go especially to Professor Joseph Kerman, whose editorial judgment—at once firm, sensitive, and diplomatic—remains the *Bewunderung* of all whose words pass under his pen. Professor Michael Senturia suggested, and then helped me to implement, the methods of rhythmic and metrical analysis used here; his highly original ideas on the structure of the Third Symphony stimulated my own account of that piece. Professor Edward Cone of Princeton made helpful suggestions that induced me to reformulate several of my analyses.

I want also to thank the staffs of the Music Library at Berkeley and the Arnold Schoenberg Institute in Los Angeles, especially Jerry McBride. The Schoenberg manuscript reproduced as Figure 1 was brought to my attention by the late Clara Steuermann.

My editors at the University of California Press, Doris Kretschmer, Marilyn Schwartz, Mary Lamprech, and Ann Basart, have all helped make the production of this book very smooth. I am also grateful to Mel Wildberger for preparing the musical examples and to Clovis Lark for the index.

Throughout this project, and the years of graduate school that led up to it, my father, mother, and sister have been both materially and spiritually supportive. My wife Anne has been this and more—more sensible, good-natured, and affectionate than any moody author has a right to expect.

1

Prologue: Brahms and
the Schoenberg Critical Tradition

I

In 1946 Robert Maynard Hutchins, chancellor of the University of Chicago, sought Arnold Schoenberg's advice on the creation and organization of a music department. Schoenberg recommended, as one of several possibilities, "a clean-cut Musicological Department" whose sole function should be research. He provided Hutchins with "Some Problems for the Department," a list of a few subjects "with which classes could become busy." As might be expected, Schoenberg included mainly compositional and analytical topics, such as "methods of transition" and a "systematic cataloguing of features of rhythm." He also proposed a subject with the suggestive title "developing variation."[1]

Although Schoenberg discussed developing variation in his published writings only sporadically, and often aphoristically, he clearly considered it one of the most important structural principles of Western art music since about 1750. Perhaps the clearest single definition is one of the last he attempted, in a 1950 essay entitled "Bach":

> Music of the homophonic-melodic style of composition, that is, music with a main theme, accompanied by and based on harmony, produces its material by, as I call it, *developing variation*. This means that variation of the features of a basic unit produces all the thematic formulations which provide for fluency, contrasts, vari-

[1] Arnold Schoenberg, *Letters*, pp. 240–42.

ety, logic and unity on the one hand, and character, mood, expression, and every needed differentiation, on the other hand—thus elaborating the *idea* of the piece.[2]

Here and elsewhere Schoenberg stresses that this is primarily a thematic or melodic procedure, distinct from the techniques characteristic of contrapuntal, polyphonic music, where "the theme is practically unchangeable and all the necessary contrasts are produced by the addition of one or more voices" (p. 109). In polyphonic music, development, or *Entwicklung*, takes place less by means of variation within a single voice than by alteration of "the mutual relationship of the simultaneous sounds," or parts.

The concept of developing variation appears in a number of different locutions in Schoenberg's writings. As early as the 1923 essay "Twelve-Tone Composition" (pp. 207–8), he discusses development and variation in the sense adumbrated above. In "For a Treatise on Composition" (1931), he states that "repetition is the initial stage in music's formal technique, and variation and development its higher developmental stages" (p. 265)—a viewpoint later elaborated in *Fundamentals of Musical Composition*. In 1933 he writes similarly of "development through variation."[3]

These terms can be misleading, for they do not refer to specific formal structures—to the "development" section (*Durchführung*) of a sonata form or to a set of discrete "variations" on a theme (although both kinds of structures can make use of the techniques).[4] Rather, developing variation represents a broad principle of thematic composition, one that Schoenberg formulates most polemically (and characteristically) in the 1931 essay "Linear Counterpoint." "Whatever happens in a piece of music is nothing but the endless reshaping of a basic shape," he argues. "Or, in other words, there is nothing in a piece of music but what comes from the theme, springs from it and can be traced back to it; to put it still more severely, nothing but the theme itself. . . . The various characters and forms [arise] from the fact that variation is carried out in a number of different ways" (p. 290).

[2]Arnold Schoenberg, *Style and Idea*, ed. Leonard Stein, p. 397. All further references to *Style and Idea* in this chapter will be to the Stein edition and will be included in the text. For a bibliography of all Schoenberg's published writings, see Walter B. Bailey, "Schoenberg's Published Articles."

[3]Arnold Schoenberg, "Neue und veraltete Musik, oder Stil und Gedanke," in *Stil und Gedanke*, p. 468. This is the original German version of the essay-lecture that Schoenberg revised and translated in 1946 and then included in the original *Style and Idea* (1950). Most of Schoenberg's remarks on developing variation are conveniently assembled as an appendix in Rainer Wilke, *Brahms, Reger, Schönberg Streichquartette*, pp. 193–98.

[4]Schoenberg felt the English term "development" was a misnomer for the central segment of sonata form: "It suggests germination and growth which rarely occur. The thematic elaboration and modulatory 'working out' (*Durchführung*) produce some variation, and place the musical elements in different contexts, but seldom lead to the 'development' of anything new." See Arnold Schoenberg, *Fundamentals of Musical Composition*, p. 200, fn. 1.

Schoenberg's essays do not spell out the ways that the basic shape—what he sometimes called a *Grundgestalt*—can be varied. (I return to that topic below.) But they do suggest how he viewed the historical evolution of the principle. J. S. Bach was at once the greatest master of the contrapuntal art and, in his "fluent and well-balanced melodies," the originator of developing variation; this technique was then taken up and refined by the Viennese classicists (p. 118). Schoenberg gives no specific examples of how Bach employed developing variation, but in one well-known example seeks to demonstrate its use by the pre-eminent Viennese classicist, Beethoven: he describes the second subject in the first movement of the Fifth Symphony as deriving "from a reinterpretation of the two main notes [of the first subject] E♭ and F as tonic and dominant of E♭ major, surrounded by B♭s" (p. 164). This is, unfortunately, not one of Schoenberg's more persuasive analyses.[5] He had greater success (and more interest) in his investigations of Brahms, who he felt brought developing variation to its most advanced state in the nineteenth century.

In "Criteria for the Evaluation of Music" (1946), Schoenberg compares Brahms with Wagner, who, "in order to make his themes suitable for memorability, had to use sequences and semi-sequences, that is, unvaried or only slightly varied repetitions differing in nothing essential from first appearances, except that they are exactly transposed to other degrees" (p. 129). Schoenberg gives two examples from *Tristan*, the first seven bars of the Prelude and the two bars of Isolde's command to Brangäne in Act I, scene 2, "*Befehlen liess dem Eigenholde.*" In each, a brief phrase is repeated sequentially (though *not* exactly). Dismissing this technique as "primitive" and "inferior," Schoenberg points admiringly to Brahms, who avoided exact repetition and "repeated phrases, motives and other structural ingredients of themes only in varied forms, if possible in the form of . . . *developing variation*" (p. 129).

Schoenberg does not analyze Brahms's music from this viewpoint here, but he does so on several other occasions, most notably in two lectures given over Radio Frankfurt in 1931 and 1933. The first accompanied a broadcast performance of his own Orchestral Variations, op. 31. The second was read in honor of the centenary of Brahms's birth; in 1947 Schoenberg expanded and translated it for inclusion in *Style and Idea*, and provided the well-known title "Brahms the Progressive."

In the earlier talk, Schoenberg adduces a late Brahms theme in order to defend the theme of the Orchestral Variations against charges of ugliness and incomprehensibility. "New music is never beautiful on first acquaintance," he

---

[5]Treating only a few bars of music, the analysis is too brief to demonstrate how developing variation shapes Beethoven's movement as a whole. Furthermore, Schoenberg misconstrues the main theme; as Schenker demonstrated and as basic musical perception tells us, the "two main notes" are not E♭ and F, but the two analogous downbeats, E♭ and D, which Schenker analyzes as the basic "two-note motive" of the movement. See Heinrich Schenker, ["Analysis of the First Movement"].

explains. "The reason is simply this: one can only like what one remembers; and with all new music that is very difficult."[6] The greatest popular composers, like Johann Strauss, made their melodies "memorable" by using exact or parallel repetition, Schoenberg observes, citing the first part of the *Blue Danube* and numbering from one to seven the parallel restatements of the simple four-bar phrase. As we have just seen, even Wagner (in Schoenberg's view) relied heavily on sequential repetition. "But a stricter style of composition must do without such convenient resources," Schoenberg claims. "It demands that nothing be repeated without promoting the development of the music, and that can only happen by way of far-reaching variations." He then evokes Brahms:

Here is a theme that develops rapidly:

You are certainly expecting me to quote something modern and extreme, but you are wrong: It is the opening of Brahms's F major Cello Sonata [op. 99].

Young listeners will probably be unaware that at the time of Brahms's death this sonata was still very unpopular and was considered indigestible. . . . At that time the unusual rhythm within this $\frac{3}{4}$ time, the syncopations which give the impression that the third phrase is in $\frac{4}{4}$:

and the unusual intervals, the ninths contained in this phrase [bar 5], made it difficult to grasp. I felt all this myself, so I know how seriously it must be taken! To make matters worse, the theme develops too quickly, and its motivic evolution is very difficult for the ear to trace, without the help of the written page. It is only there that one sees that the opening fourth is inverted into a fifth:

[6]Arnold Schoenberg, "The Orchestral Variations, Op. 31: A Radio Talk," p. 28. The original German version of the talk is included as "Vortrag über Op. 31" in Schoenberg's *Stil und Gedanke*, pp. 255–71. At the archives of the Arnold Schoenberg Institute in Los Angeles there is a partial tape recording of the broadcast.

but this is hard for the ear to grasp, if only because the initial phrasing in two-note groups then switches to groups of three:

So those who did not understand at the time, were right.[7]

The developmental features that Schoenberg admires involve the intervals, rhythms, meter, and note groupings of Brahms's theme. Schoenberg's analysis of the first element is, alas, almost as elliptical as the theme itself. We do not learn precisely where or how the opening fourth is inverted to a fifth: the D–G figure never appears on the "written page" in the initial rhythm, as Schoenberg notates it in his third example. Nor is the figure easy to discern among his parentheses and grace notes.

More important and "memorable," I think, is the rhythmic and metrical evolution of the opening two-note motive. In his last example, Schoenberg suggests that the Bb–G figure of bar 4 represents a developmental variation of the head motive, whose unequal rhythmic values are now equalized in two quarter notes. Bars 5–6 constitute a further development, in which the two notes become three. Schoenberg's second example implies that variation of the basic motive also obscures the notated meter, creating the illusion of a $\frac{4}{4}$ measure in bars 3–4. He might have suggested further that in the second half of the theme there is an analogous or corresponding metrical extension, here implying $\frac{5}{4}$ (ex. 1). Despite its rapid and fluid motivic development, Brahms's theme comprises two nearly symmetrical phrases of four and five measures.

EXAMPLE 1: Brahms, Violoncello Sonata, op. 99, I.

By slightly refining Schoenberg's analysis, then, we can begin to understand his view of developing variation in Brahms. Brahms builds a theme by means of a very free, but recognizable, reinterpretation of the intervals and rhythms of a brief motive. Although the process can result in considerable metrical ambiguity, the phrase structure remains essentially conventional and symmetrical on a higher level.

[7]Schoenberg, "Orchestral Variations," pp. 28–30.

EXAMPLE 2: Schoenberg's analysis of Brahms's String Quartet, op. 51, no. 2. Examples 2–4 are reprinted by permission of Faber and Faber, Ltd., from *Style and Idea*, edited by Leonard Stein.

In "Brahms the Progressive," his most celebrated essay, Schoenberg reveals these same procedures at work in other themes of Brahms's. Here he evokes the older composer not simply to justify his own music, but to demonstrate that Brahms, so often branded pejoratively as "the classicist, the academician," was in fact "a great innovator in the realm of musical language" (p. 401). Much of the discussion consists of brief examples of asymmetrical phrase structures in Brahms (and other composers)—combinations of phrases of differing lengths and numbers of measures not divisible by eight, four, or two. But Schoenberg gives a lengthier and more persuasive account of how two themes of Brahms are generated by the process of developing variation: those from the Andante of the A-Minor String Quartet, op. 51, no. 2, and from "O Tod," the third of the *Four Serious Songs*, op. 121.

EXAMPLE 3: Schoenberg's rewriting of the Brahms theme.

The quartet theme, Schoenberg notes, "contains exclusively motive forms which can be explained as derivatives of the interval of a second" (p. 431) (see ex. 2). The multiple staves in Schoenberg's example do not represent any hierarchy of structural levels (as they might in Schenker); they serve only to display clearly the numerous motive forms that Brahms develops from the basic interval, the second, labeled *a*. Schoenberg explains:

> *b* then is the inversion upward [*sic*] of *a*;
> *c* is *a* + *b*;
> *d* is part of *c*;
> *e* is *b* + *b*, descending seconds, comprising a fourth;
> *f* is the interval of a fourth, abstracted from *e*, in inversion.
> *(p. 431)*

Schoenberg anticipates criticism of this kind of intervallic analysis: skeptics "might reason that steps of a second or even fractions of a scale are present in every theme without constituting the thematic material" (p. 431). But he defends himself by analyzing "O Tod," which displays a "similar secret" based on another single interval, a third. (This analysis will be discussed in Chapter 6.) Schoenberg then returns to the metrical-rhythmic aspects of the quartet theme, which, as in op. 99, are intimately bound up with the intervallic processes.

The theme has a conventional length of eight bars, which divide into two roughly symmetrical halves, an "antecedent" extending through the half cadence on V on the second beat of bar 5 and a "consequent" beginning on the next beat and continuing to a tonic cadence in bar 8. As Schoenberg demonstrates, however, the six component "phrases"—for convenience I shall retain his term for the groupings—evolve quite freely, often overriding the notated meter. The first three phrases and the last occupy one and one-half bars each, the fourth and fifth a single bar. This design wreaks havoc with the written bar line:

> This first phrase ends practically on the first beat of measure 2. In order to appreciate fully the artistic value of the second phrase's metrical shift, one must realize that even some of the great composers, Brahms' predecessors, might have continued as in [example 3], placing the second phrase in the third measure.
> *(p. 435)*

But Brahms eschews any such symmetry, preferring to let his theme evolve more flexibly.

EXAMPLE 4: Schoenberg's rebarring of the Brahms theme.

In his next example (ex. 4), Schoenberg preserves Brahms's phrases intact, but rebars them in order to have analogous accents appear in the same part of a measure. The result is that the first three phrases fall into $\frac{3}{2}$, the fourth and fifth into $\frac{4}{4}$. But Schoenberg also indicates with an asterisk above bar 6 that the last phrase would not be represented adequately by this plan "if all the preceding phrases had their main accents placed on first beats" (p. 435).

In his perceptive commentary on this analysis, Carl Dahlhaus challenges Schoenberg's assumption (in example 4) that melody and meter must correspond at every point. Brahms's notation of the theme is more accurate than Schoenberg's, Dahlhaus says, for, although it seems at first to give unusual emphasis to the concluding D of phrase 1, it represents phrase 2 properly by placing on a downbeat the note E, which is strong because of its dotted-quarter value and its harmonization by the tonic triad.[8] Schoenberg ultimately agrees that Brahms's notation is the more sensible, since it contains the motivic development within a rational eight bars: "In Brahms' notation these subcutaneous beauties are accommodated within eight measures; and if eight measures constitute an aesthetic principle, it is preserved here in spite of the great freedom of construction" (pp. 435–36).

As in the cello sonata theme, then, Brahms develops his motive forms fluidly within an outwardly regular phrase structure. The developmental process involves not only intervals (fourths and seconds), but also rhythm and meter. Indeed, manipulation of the latter, temporal sphere constitutes one of Brahms's most powerful tools of developing variation. As we shall see later in the F-Minor Piano Quintet, op. 34, and in the Third Symphony, Brahms also displaces meter for longer periods and on a higher structural level.

Schoenberg characterized themes like those of opp. 51 and 99 as "musical prose"—that is, music that does not fall into regular, predefined or predictable patterns. The *Blue Danube* theme, with its repeated symmetrical phrases, would be "musical verse." Musical prose, however, is "a direct and straightforward presentation of ideas, without any patchwork, without mere padding and empty repetitions" (p. 415). Developing variation and musical prose are, in a

[8]Carl Dahlhaus, "Musikalische Prosa," p. 137.

sense, two different ways of describing the same process. Developing variation—the principle according to which ideas are continuously varied—provides the grammar by which the musical prose is created.

I have quoted at length from Schoenberg's radio talks and essays not only because his ideas seem intimately linked with his crusty prose style and thus resist paraphrase, but also because the analyses reveal the nature and significance of developing variation in Brahms. To summarize: by "developing variation," Schoenberg means the construction of a theme (usually of eight bars) by the continuous modification of the intervallic and/or rhythmic components of an initial idea. The intervals are "developed" by such recognized procedures as inversion and combination (e.g., two consecutive seconds make a fourth), the rhythms by such devices as augmentation and displacement. Schoenberg values developing variation as a compositional principle because it can prevent obvious, hence monotonous, repetition—the kind of repetition found in Johann Strauss and Wagner (composers whom Schoenberg nevertheless admired greatly). And Brahms's music stands as the most advanced manifestation of this principle in the common-practice era, for Brahms develops or varies his motives almost at once, dispensing with small-scale rhythmic or metrical symmetry and thereby creating genuine musical prose.

II

Because they are generally polemical, Schoenberg's analyses tend also to be idiosyncratic and selective. He concentrates only on the more progressive aspects of motivic development in themes by Brahms (and other composers), often with the goal of defending his own musical techniques. But fortunately Schoenberg did leave a more careful, even-handed account of developing variation, of the basic premises behind what often seem to be impulsive analytical or critical judgments. This discussion is found not in essays or radio talks, but (logically enough) in a textbook, *Fundamentals of Musical Composition*.

In 1932, Schoenberg claimed that "for nearly twenty years I have been collecting material, ideas and sketches for an all-inclusive textbook of composition. When I shall finish it, I do not know."[9] As with so many of his projects, this textbook was never really "finished"; but it assumed several different shapes.[10] The more broadly theoretical and philosophical concepts were published in 1931 in a brief essay entitled "Zur Kompositionslehre" (included as "For a Treatise on Composition" in *Style and Idea*); they were then reformulated and expanded in a series of unpublished manuscripts, the largest of which (199 pages) dates from the summer of 1934 and bears the title "Der musikalische

[9]Cited in Josef Rufer, *The Works of Arnold Schoenberg*, p. 140.

[10]Schoenberg's completed and uncompleted theoretical works are inventoried and briefly described in Rufer, *Works*, pp. 133–39.

EXAMPLE 5: Schoenberg's developing variations of a motive based on a broken chord. Examples 5–9 and 11 are reproduced by permission of Faber and Faber, Ltd., from *Fundamentals of Musical Composition*, edited by Gerald Strang and Leonard Stein.

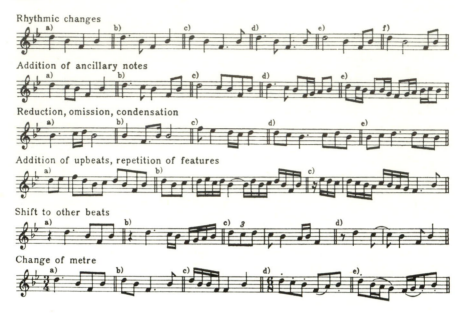

Gedanke und die Logik, Technik und Kunst seiner Darstellung" (often referred to as "Gedanke").[11] This document contains numerous outlines and definitions of such topics as motive, basic shape, development, variation, coherence, and comprehensibility. Schoenberg later gave these concepts a more practical, concrete expression, first in the concise *Models for Beginners in Composition*, published in 1942, and then in the more comprehensive *Fundamentals of Musical Composition*, written during the years 1937–48 and edited and published posthumously in 1967.

Both these books—as well as *Preliminary Exercises in Counterpoint* and *Structural Functions of Harmony*—grew out of Schoenberg's courses at the University of California at Los Angeles. Not surprisingly, Schoenberg wears a very different hat here than in *Style and Idea* or "Gedanke": no longer the ardent polemicist or musing philosopher, he is now the pragmatic didact, explaining to the student composer how to expand a small motive into an entire, if small-scale, composition by the application of developing variation. As I hope to show, Schoenberg's instruction in *Fundamentals* can prove equally helpful to

---

[11]This manuscript is discussed and partially transcribed and translated in Alexander Goehr, "Schoenberg's *Gedanke* Manuscript."

the musicologist—the historian and analyst—at the other end of the creative process.

The composer's basic tool is the motive, whose features are "intervals and rhythms, combined to produce a memorable shape or contour."[12] Schoenberg stresses that the coherence of a composition depends not on the motive's initial form but on its "treatment and development." The composition grows by the continuous repetition of a motive, a repetition that can be exact or modified—and thus developed:[13]

> *Exact repetitions* preserve all features and relationships. Transpositions to a different degree, inversions, retrogrades, diminutions and augmentations are exact repetitions if they preserve strictly the features and note relations.
>
> *Modified repetitions* are created through variation. . . .
>
> Some variations, however, are merely local "variants," and have little or no influence on the continuation.
>
> Variation, it must be remembered, is repetition in which some features are changed and the rest preserved.
>
> All the features of rhythm, interval, harmony and contour are subject to various alterations . . . but such changes must not produce a motive-form too foreign to the basic motive.
>
> *(p. 9)*

In a set of made-up musical examples entitled "Developing variations of a motive based on a broken chord" (ex. 5), Schoenberg demonstrates just how these features (rhythm, meter, interval, contour, etc.) can be modified. These motive forms do not "develop" successively from one another, of course, but simply constitute different individual alternatives of development. Schoenberg soon advances, however, to a higher structural level at which continuous elaboration takes place.

After demonstrating how to build single phrases by connecting the varied motive forms (see his Chapter 4), Schoenberg moves on to the musical sentence, which "not only makes a statement of an idea, but at once starts a kind of development." He explains:

---

[12]Schoenberg, *Fundamentals*, p. 8. Further references in this chapter will be included in the text. For a helpful summary and synthesis of Schoenberg's statements on motivic development, see David Epstein, *Beyond Orpheus*, pp. 207–210.

[13]It is significant that despite their disagreement on many theoretical issues, Schoenberg and (the early) Schenker concur on the importance of repetition in generating and perceiving musical form. In his treatise on harmony (1906), Schenker claims that a motive is defined or created by repetition: "Only by repetition can a series of tones be characterized as something definite. . . . Repetition is thus the basis of music as an art" (*Harmony*, p. 4). Schoenberg underlined this very passage with red crayon in his own copy of Schenker's book and added some comments of approval in the margin. See Jonathan M. Dunsby, "Schoenberg and the Writings of Schenker," p. 28.

The practice form will consist, in simpler cases, of eight measures, of which the first four comprise a phrase and its repetition. The technique to be applied in the continuation is a kind of development, comparable in some respects to the condensing technique of "liquidation." Development implies not only growth, augmentation, extension and expansion, but also reduction, condensation and intensification.

(p. 58)

EXAMPLE 6: Schoenberg's analysis of Beethoven's Piano Sonata, op. 2, no. 1.

The *locus classicus* for such an eight-bar sentence is perhaps the opening theme of Beethoven's F-Minor Piano Sonata, op. 2, no. 1, which Schoenberg parses as in example 6. The first two-bar phrase is repeated sequentially on the dominant; the continuation, an indivisible four-bar unit (5–8), "reduces" the initial phrase by separating off and developing motives b and c. Beethoven also intensifies the harmonic rhythm, which accelerates from one harmony per two bars (in bars 1–4), to one per bar (in 5–6), finally to two harmonies in bar 7.

Schoenberg provides numerous other examples from the classical and romantic literature, including an eight-measure sentence of Brahms's, the second theme from the first movement of the E-Minor Violoncello Sonata, op. 38 (ex. 7). At first glance this theme bears little resemblance to Beethoven's; it has no clear tonic and dominant statements and no distinctly developmental continuation. Schoenberg admits that the Brahms "has little in common with the practice form" except for the small-scale repetitions in bars 5–6 (analogous to Beethoven's bars 5–6) and the cadential process in bars 7–8, where the one-bar groupings of bars 3–4 are "reduced" to half-bar "residues." But Schoenberg cites the Brahms as a clear illustration of developing variation: "The analysis shows that all the motive-forms and phrases of this melody develop gradually out of the first three notes, or perhaps even out of the first two notes" (p. 62). Schoen-

EXAMPLE 7: Schoenberg's analysis of Brahms's Violoncello Sonata, op. 38.

berg is certainly right about the first two measures, where motive *a* grows into *b*, which is then repeated and varied. His derivation of motive *c* is less persuasive, however; *c* is apparently a purely rhythmic motive (dotted quarter note plus eighth note), derived from the conjunction of the two statements of *a*.

Anyone hoping to learn how Brahms transforms his classical models by the use of developing variation will be disappointed in Schoenberg's analysis of the op. 38 theme. Far more instructive for this purpose are the "model" sentences Schoenberg composes as examples 54 and 55 of his textbook, given here as examples 8 and 9. He provides no clue as to their musical idiom, but when studied in succession these examples comprise—better than any possible verbal account—an extraordinary capsule history of developing variation from the classical composers to Brahms (hence my epithets "classical" and "Brahmsian").

On the first staff of example 8, Schoenberg shows the three-stage process (a, b, c) of constructing a theme from a broken-chord figure similar to the one examined above in example 5. The theme has three little motives, which in the second system (d) are labeled as motives *a*, *b*, and *c* and developed into a full eight-bar sentence according to the "practice form"—that is, a two-bar phrase, its varied repetition, and a four-bar continuation or development. The repetition (bars 2–4) is essentially a sequential reiteration of the original phrase, now on

EXAMPLE 8: Schoenberg's "classical" sentence.

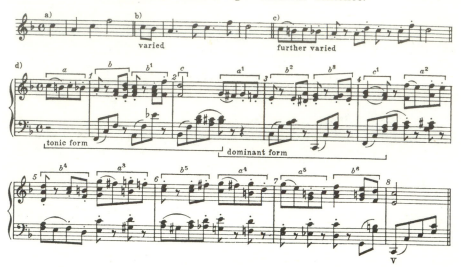

the dominant: the accompaniment pattern and the succession of motive forms (a, b, c) remain constant. In the continuation (5–8), as Schoenberg remarks, the motive forms still retain their original order, but are now reduced or "condensed"; the cadential c is eliminated, and at each occurrence b is heard only once, not twice as in bars 1 and 3.

The developing variation here is quite simple, involving only small, insignificant changes in the intervallic content of motives a and b, whose rhythmic profile and basic contour do not change. Schoenberg's procedure thus closely follows that of Beethoven's F-Minor Sonata. Indeed, although Schoenberg does not specify any musical style, the clearly articulated phrase structure and limited motivic development suggest late-classical procedures—perhaps those of Hummel, Weber, or Schubert. (The harmony, however, betrays the real composer's late nineteenth-century sensibility.)

Schoenberg now recomposes the entire sentence with the very same motives, but in a different meter (ex. 9). The proportions of the original "model" are intact but are doubled, so that the sentence is now 16 bars long instead of 8. The initial phrase has 4 bars, the repetition 4, and the continuation or development 8. Again Schoenberg fails to indicate the style, but our eyes and ears could, I think, take it for none other than Brahms's. Most strikingly Brahmsian are the Viennese waltz rhythms and the piano writing—in particular the broken-chord figuration of the right hand in bars 3 and 7–13. (See, for example, the piano part from the Vivace of Brahms's A-Major Violin Sonata, op. 100—also in triple meter—which Schoenberg has quoted earlier in his book, on p. 57.)

More revealing, however, are the actual structural features. For example,

EXAMPLE 9: Schoenberg's "Brahmsian" sentence.

motive b is immediately varied in bar 3 (though Schoenberg does not give it a superscript number), where the original rhythmic pattern of bar 2 is changed to a quarter and four eighths. At the analogous spot in the "classical" sentence (bar 2 of example 8, which becomes two bars in example 9 because of the increased proportions), motive b was repeated exactly. The continuation section of example 9 is also much freer than in example 8, where it had closely followed the original sequence of motives (a, b). In example 9, as Schoenberg points out in his commentary, the continuation abandons motive a, beginning instead with c (bar 9)—the same motive that has just concluded the previous phrase (bar 8). In the "classical" sentence, motive c (which presumably includes the left-hand figuration) serves only as an unobtrusive cadential figure to close off the first two phrases; but in example 9 the cadential c^1 generates the first motive form of the next phrase, c^2 (bar 9).[14]

This technique, by which a "new" idea evolves spontaneously from a preceding one, is a distinctly Brahmsian one, which Schenker called *Knüpftechnik*,

[14]As printed on p. 65 of *Fundamentals*, the "Brahmsian" example has no motive c^1. The motive of bar 8 is labeled c^2, that of bar 9 c^3, and that of bar 11 c^4. This is undoubtedly an error and has been corrected in my example, where the c superscripts have been lowered by one number to bring them into accord with Schoenberg's discussion.

EXAMPLE 10: Brahms, Symphony No. 2, op. 73, III.

or linkage technique.[15] One well-known example is the theme from the Allegretto of the Second Symphony (ex. 10). In bar 11, Brahms reinterprets the
preceding cadential motive, E–D, to initiate a new phrase. The motive is unchanged; only its harmonic support is altered. In "Brahms the Progressive,"
Schoenberg provides an exquisite example of Brahms's linkage technique on a
smaller scale. In the Andante from the String Quartet (see my ex. 2), the tail of
each "phrase" immediately generates the succeeding phrase. Observe, for example, how motive form b ends the first phrase and initiates the second. Or, as
Schoenberg indicates on the third staff, motive form d genuinely "links" the
two phrases: its third note, D, serves both as conclusion and beginning.

To return to the "Brahmsian" sentence in *Fundamentals* (ex. 9): the juncture
between phrases displays not only the linkage technique but also a typically
Brahmsian moment of ambiguity. In bar 8, the left hand breaks in upon the right
hand's cadential c^1 with a statement of the same motive, and this stretto-like
entrance makes us momentarily uncertain where the phrase ends. The ambiguity is then compounded in bar 9 as the right hand gives out c^2, which we
initially take for still another echo of c^1 and an extension of the first phrase,
although it in fact begins the next phrase. The subdominant harmony at bar 9
enhances the ambiguity, for it is not the conventional starting point of a continuation phrase: neither Schoenberg's "classical" sentence nor any of his other
examples begins its "development" on IV.

Brahms's Allegretto (ex. 10) contains the same kind of ambiguity at the
juncture between phrases. The E–D cadential motive appears first in bar 8 and
is echoed an octave higher in bar 9. It returns to the original register in bar 10
and appears to be echoed once again in bar 11, but this last statement in fact

---

[15]See Schenker, *Harmony*, pp. 9–10 and fn. 10. For further discussion and more examples of
Schenker's concept, see Sylvan Kalib, "Thirteen Essays from the Three Yearbooks *Das Meister-
werk in der Musik*," 1: 89–92. See also Oswald Jonas, *Introduction to the Theory of Heinrich
Schenker*, pp. 7–10. Jonas remarks on Brahms's predilection for the linkage technique.

EXAMPLE 11: Schoenberg's continuation of Example 9.

initiates the new phrase. Precisely as in the Schoenberg example, the successive motivic repetitions make us uncertain where one phrase ends and the other begins. Here as well, the harmony obscures the phrase juncture. The first phrase concludes on a dominant seventh $(D^7$, bars 8–10); the first bar of the second phrase then resolves that chord to *another* dominant seventh $(G^7$, or $V^7/IV)$. The tonic arrives only on the third beat of the bar.

The motivic nature of Schoenberg's accompaniment in example 9 also evokes Brahms. In the "classical" example, the left-hand part consists mostly of conventional figuration that attracts little attention, except in bars 2, 5, and 6 where the bass imitates motive a. In the "Brahmsian" sentence, however, the rhythmic patterns—which Schoenberg labels d and e—undergo an independent developmental process. Schoenberg comments, "Observe also the treatment of the motive of the accompaniment, 'e,' which . . . is shifted from the weak to the strong measure in m. 9–10" (p. 60). That is, e moves from its initial position across bars 2–3 of a four-bar phrase to a new position within the first two bars $(e^2$, bars 9–10).

Schoenberg goes on to provide two alternative continuation sections for the "Brahmsian" sentence. The second (ex. 11) betrays a further characteristic device—Brahms's beloved hemiola, which here serves to develop the rhythmic aspects of motive c (bars 13–14).

In these "model" sentences, then, Schoenberg has in effect demonstrated how Brahms's methods of developing variation evolve from and extend those of classical composers. In Brahms, motivic treatment becomes freer and more fluid. Where an earlier composer would repeat a motive form exactly, Brahms avoids repetition. Motivic development and variation permeate all parts of Brahms's texture, including the accompaniment; they even begin to break down or obscure the phrase structure, as in the ambiguity created at the juncture of the two halves of the "Brahmsian" sentence. Motivic development can also affect the metrical framework, as in the hemiola, where a $\frac{3}{2}$ pattern momentarily supersedes the notated $\frac{3}{4}$. Although the goal of *Fundamentals of Musical Composition* is ostensibly to give the student composer several ways of developing motive forms, Schoenberg has in fact presented a shrewd account—expressed in purely musical terms—of how different would be the results if both Brahms and one of his classical forbears were to write a composition with the same motivic material and formal structure.

III

Hans Keller has claimed that Schoenberg's analyses and analytical concepts "represent perhaps the most revolutionary event in the history of music criticism." He adds, "There is no really musical analyst whom Schoenberg has not helped to rethink in creative terms."[16] However exaggerated, such statements reflect the fact that within the past forty years a large number of commentators have been attracted by Schoenberg's ideas on thematic procedure—especially the procedure he called developing variation. Unlike the followers of Schenker, they have made no attempt to build or apply a systematic theory; indeed, their approaches are remarkably, and refreshingly, diverse. Some commentary focuses on specific composers, most often on Beethoven, Brahms, or Schoenberg himself, while some of it covers a wide range of music from the common-practice period. Several writers were students or direct disciples of Schoenberg; others had little or no personal contact with him (and occasionally fail even to acknowledge his authority). Yet, because of a fundamental similarity in outlook, they can be said to constitute a Schoenberg critical or analytical tradition.

One common endeavor is to go beyond Schoenberg by showing how the techniques of developing variation—techniques that are given a variety of names—can shape entire movements or compositions. Schoenberg confined his analytical remarks almost exclusively to the level of the individual theme. The largest proportion of any composition he accounted for in detail is about one-third, in his analysis of the first twelve bars of Brahms's song "O Tod." In the section on "Large Forms" that comprises the final chapters of *Fundamentals*, Schoenberg has few compelling thoughts on more expanded structures. The sonata form, for example, is divided into its traditional segments and sub-segments and is illustrated with numerous citations from the musical literature. But Schoenberg's discussion lacks the conviction and originality of the preceding chapters on thematic construction. He remarks that the "greatest merit" of sonata form

> is its extraordinary flexibility in accommodating the widest variety of musical ideas, long or short, many or few, active or passive, in almost any combination. The internal details may be subjected to almost any mutation without disturbing the aesthetic validity of the structure as a whole.[17]
>
>   (p. 200)

[16]Hans Keller, "The Chamber Music," p. 93.

This seems to give the student composer or analyst *carte blanche*—but no real guidelines—for applying the methods of developing variation.

One of the first and most forceful commentators to claim a role for developing variation in the larger dimension was Theodor Adorno, whose intimate acquaintance with Schoenberg and his music extended over many years, both in Europe and the United States. In a long essay written in 1940–41 and later incorporated in *Philosophy of New Music*, Adorno elevates Schoenberg's technical observations to a more abstract level. His principal goal is to show how Schoenberg was the first twentieth-century composer to grasp and carry out the "historical tendencies" of Western art music. One of those tendencies is the continuous transformation or reshaping of musical material (an activity equated with the "autonomous aesthetic subjectivity" of a composer), which begins to dominate the external form (equated with objectivity).

Adorno is no more a real music historian than is Schoenberg; but in an important paragraph entitled "Total Development" ("Totale Durchführung"), he too claims that the tendency of continuous transformation is manifested strongly by Beethoven, then by Brahms. Whereas before Beethoven, conventional form had governed the thematic material, with Beethoven "the development—subjective reflection upon the theme which decides the fate of the theme—becomes the focal point of the entire form."[18] In Beethoven's music, development becomes associated with variation techniques, which had heretofore been only "among the more superficial technical procedures"; but now "variational [*variative*] development is extended over the entire sonata." Brahms's music embodies the next stage in this process:

> In Brahms the development—as the execution and transformation of the thematic material—took possession of the sonata as a whole. Subjectification and objectification are intertwined. . . . While still composing within the total framework of tonality, Brahms by and large rejects conventional formulae and fundamentals, producing a unity of the work which—out of freedom—is constantly renewed at every moment. He consequently becomes the advocate of universal economy, refuting all coincidental moments of music, and yet developing the most extreme multiplicity—the result from thematic materials the identity of which has been preserved. This indeed is his greatest accomplishment.[19]

---

[17]Gerald Strang, the editor of *Fundamentals*, notes in his preface that the chapter on sonata-allegro form (Chapter 20), the last in the book, "was incomplete and required reorganization" for publication (p. xiii). It is not surprising, then, that this is one of the least successful parts of the book.

[18]Theodor W. Adorno, *Philosophy of Modern Music*, p. 55.

[19]Adorno, *Philosophy*, pp. 56–57.

Here is an unmistakable *Nachklang* of Schoenberg's ideas on Brahms—the Brahms whose musical prose avoids all predefined or "coincidental" patterns, yet is coherent because of its thematic-motivic economy. (As a resident of Frankfurt, Adorno would undoubtedly have heard Schoenberg's radio talk on Brahms in February 1933.) But Adorno amplifies the notion: not confining himself to the structure of a single theme, he sees a "total" development that spans an entire movement or piece.

Adorno never spelled out just how such a process might work in either Beethoven or Brahms. His interest in these composers was ultimately ideological, not analytical. (As both analyst and ideologue, Schoenberg proves the more effective critic.) In the early 1950s, however, two former Schoenberg pupils from Europe, Erwin Ratz and Josef Rufer, attempted to elaborate upon these concepts in a more practical and technical fashion. Both Ratz and Rufer studied with Schoenberg in Vienna in the years following World War I; in 1926 Rufer became Schoenberg's assistant at the Prussian Academy of the Arts in Berlin.

Ratz's *Einführung in die musikalische Formenlehre* (1951) is neither a textbook nor a history of an analytical tradition, but (as its subtitle implies) a detailed study of music by Bach and Beethoven. Although Ratz would surely have known and drawn upon such writers as Koch, Marx, and Riemann, his direct source is Schoenberg. Indeed, Schoenberg is the only authority he explicitly acknowledges, noting in his preface that "the method of musical analysis Schoenberg used in his teaching forms an essential prerequisite [*Voraussetzung*] for the following investigations."[20] As the first example of an eight-bar *Satz* or sentence, we are given the familiar opening theme of Beethoven's F-Minor Sonata, op. 2, no. 1; like Schoenberg, Ratz labels the two-bar tonic and dominant statements, then the "Entwicklung" of bars 5–8.[21]

Despite their Schoenbergian pedigree, these "investigations" prove disappointing. Although he treats entire compositions—one chapter of forty pages is devoted to Beethoven's *Hammerklavier* Sonata, op. 106—Ratz never goes beyond general harmonic design and the disposition of individual phrases. A large structure thus appears as little more than the sum of its elements. Ratz fails to grasp the basic principle behind Schoenberg's analytical methods, the dynamic or generative powers of the motive. For Schoenberg, the external form is (or should be) not merely a succession of eight-bar phrases, but an outgrowth of motivic development. Had he lived to read the *Einführung*, Schoenberg might have commented that it adopts his general analytical "style" or procedure without understanding the fundamental "idea"—that is, the concept of developing variation.

[20]Erwin Ratz, *Einführung in die musikalische Formenlehre*, p. 11.

[21]Ratz, *Einführung*, p. 23.

In the third chapter of *Composition with Twelve Notes* (1952), Josef Rufer comes closer to communicating the significance of developing variation for large-scale composition. Much of this chapter reads like diluted Schoenberg; Rufer explains how the basis of composition is the repetition of a motive and how the motive must be continuously varied. He then seeks to show how music of the classical period established these principles, which also lie behind Schoenberg's twelve-tone works. Like Ratz, Rufer offers some of Schoenberg's favorite Beethoven examples, including the opening of the Fifth Symphony and of the Piano Sonatas, op. 2.[22] But then he attempts something we find in neither Schoenberg nor Ratz—an analysis of an entire Beethoven sonata from the viewpoint of developing variation.

Of the C-Minor Sonata, op. 10, no. 1, Rufer notes that "in order to ensure the thematic unification of a work and thus the unity of its musical content, all the musical events in it are developed, directly or indirectly, out of one basic shape [*Grundgestalt*]."[23] For Rufer (as for Schoenberg), the "basic shape" connotes more than simply an interval or rhythm; in this instance it includes the first four measures of the sonata, divided by Rufer into two motives, labeled a (bars 1–3, with ascending arpeggios in dotted rhythms) and b (bars 3–4, containing the feminine half cadence to V).

Rufer's verbal account extends only through the exposition and development of the first movement; the rest of his analysis consists of musical examples that superimpose the different themes of all the movements and connect certain pitches with dotted lines. (See his Tables I and II.) Unfortunately, many of his suggested associations and transformations are unconvincing. Rufer focuses almost exclusively on contour, disregarding tempo, rhythm, meter, and harmonic context. Any triadic portion of a theme (even if only a grace-note figure) is labeled a; any idea that descends by step across a bar line becomes b. With such methods, almost every piece of music could be shown to grow organically from a *Grundgestalt*. Although he seems to have understood Schoenberg's basic principle better than Ratz, Rufer's analyses nevertheless constitute a debasement and misapplication of the concept of developing variation.

This very problem afflicts a much more renowned—indeed, notorious—analytical study that appeared shortly before Rufer's, *The Thematic Process in Music* (1951) by Rudolf Réti. Although neither a pupil nor close associate, Réti had frequent contact with Schoenberg during the 1910s and 1920s. As a pianist and critic in Vienna, Réti became an ardent champion of the composer's atonal works. In 1911 he gave some of the earliest performances of the Piano Pieces, op. 11, and wrote an analytical commentary on the first piece for the periodical

[22]Josef Rufer, *Composition with Twelve Notes*, pp. 27–28, 32.

[23]Rufer, *Composition*, p. 38.

Der Merker.[24] In a letter of July 1911, Schoenberg thanked Réti for his support and remarked, "You are a person who stands very close to my sphere of thought."[25] Although Réti acknowledges no debt to Schoenberg (and eschews altogether a bibliography), his book bears out this observation; as Keller has noted, Réti's work "would be unthinkable" without Schoenberg.[26]

In scope, *The Thematic Process* extends well beyond any of the studies discussed so far. Réti offers dozens of analyses to prove that each great work of music, from Bach through Debussy, evolves organically from a single motive; or, more precisely, that a motivic kernel underlies and thus unifies all the ostensibly contrasting themes of a piece. "Thematic transformation" is Réti's equivalent for Schoenberg's developing variation—and an equally unfortunate term, too easily confused with specific romantic procedures of Schubert, Berlioz, Liszt, and the young Brahms. Réti devotes an entire chapter (Chapter 4) to detailing how the elements of a theme may be transformed. Among his classifications are not only the common devices of inversion and retrograde, of change of tempo and rhythm, but also such procedures as "thematic compression" and the "thinning" and "filling" of themes. Several of these last categories correspond closely to Schoenberg's developing variations of the broken chord motive in *Fundamentals* (see ex. 5).

Réti gives a fuller, although not much more sophisticated, historical or chronological account of "thematic transformation" than Schoenberg, Adorno, or Rufer. He sees its earliest manifestation in certain procedures of Dufay and Palestrina (Chapter 10), and its real emergence in the music of J. S. Bach, which (as in Schoenberg's view) makes the transition from the "contrapuntal" to the "thematic" era (Chapter 3). With Wagner and Strauss, techniques of thematic transformation and unification begin to be superseded by harmonic and coloristic effects.

Réti's most persuasive single analysis is that of Mozart's G-Minor Symphony, no. 40—especially of the first movement, which is seen to evolve from continuous reinterpretation of the basic motives of the first theme, the descending semitone E♭–D and the ascending sixth D–B♭ (Chapter 5). Réti makes a good case for a genuine *process* in the Mozart, whereby the initially unstable motives move gradually toward "fulfillment" or "resolution" in more rounded themes. Most of the other analyses in the book are disappointingly shallow,

---

[24]Rudolf Réti, "Formale Erläuterungen zu Arnold Schönbergs Klavierstücken." Réti also contributed a brief paragraph (p. 304) to the 1924 Festschrift for Schoenberg which was published as a special issue of *Musikblätter des Anbruch*.

[25]The letter is reproduced in facsimile and translated in Rudolf Réti's *Tonality, Atonality, Pantonality*, pp. 48–49. The Rudolf Réti Collection at the Library of Congress contains this and one other letter from Schoenberg to Réti, dated 7 June 1912. The Schoenberg Collection at the same location contains eleven communications (letters or cards) from Réti to Schoenberg. I am grateful to Mr. Wayne Shirley, reference librarian, for this information.

[26]Keller, "Chamber Music," p. 93.

however. Like Rufer, Réti superimposes the different themes of a work or movement, isolating pitches with little regard for rhythmic or harmonic context; he simply relegates to small print any notes that do not fit the shape he is trying to construe.

Brahms, untouched by Rufer's analyses (except for one brief example), now falls victim to this procedure. Réti grossly distorts the main themes of the two Rhapsodies for piano, op. 79, in order to reveal their supposed relationship; by further manipulation he manages to derive the second theme of each piece from the first.[27] He deals in a similar fashion with the themes of Brahms's Second Symphony. "If we single out certain notes of the new theme [bar 44], the first theme comes to the fore," he writes. "If we single out others, the second theme [bar 102] appears."[28] Close thematic relationships are not, in fact, unusual in the mature works of Brahms (as we shall see); David Epstein has recently demonstrated them in this very piece.[29] But the arbitrariness of Réti's pitch selection—his "singling out" of notes—ultimately, and fatally, discredits his analyses of Brahms. Although he claims to be uncovering a continuous, dynamic process (as he did in Mozart), his isolation and superimposition of themes actually treat the music from above rather than within.[30]

Réti's analyses have drawn fire from numerous commentators,[31] although others have been strongly attracted to his notion of a "thematic process." In 1956, Hans Keller presented a method of "functional" analysis which by his own admission draws on both Schoenberg and Réti. He makes the familiar claim that "a great work can be *demonstrated* to grow from an all-embracing basic idea."[32] In his earliest published analyses (of Mozart), Keller sought to be more sensitive than Réti to temporal and harmonic issues, especially to the relation of analysis and performance. Indeed, Keller's analyses soon became exclusively non-verbal "performances": in a series of radio broadcasts beginning in 1957, he presented the background structure of works by playing reductive analytical scores.[33]

---

[27]See Rudolf Réti, *The Thematic Process in Music*, pp. 70–72, 139–51.

[28]Réti, *Thematic Process*, p. 81.

[29]See Epstein, *Beyond Orpheus*, pp. 162–77.

[30]Réti's theories are the subject of a Ph.D. dissertation by Donald M. Schwejda, "An Investigation of the Analytical Techniques Used by Rudolf Réti in *The Thematic Process in Music.*" On Réti, see also Ian Bent's excellent article, "Analysis," in *The New Grove Dictionary of Music and Musicians*, 1: 365–66, 371–74.

[31]See Charles Rosen, *The Classical Style*, p. 41; Leonard Meyer, *Explaining Music*, pp. 59–67; and Epstein, *Beyond Orpheus*, p. 10.

[32]Hans Keller, "K. 503: The Unity of Contrasting Themes and Movements," p. 50.

[33]See Bent, "Analysis," 1: 366, 373–74.

The Schoenberg-Réti-Keller analytical legacy was perpetuated by Keller's student Alan Walker, whose *A Study in Musical Analysis* (1962) deals exclusively with issues of thematic continuity and unity in the standard masterworks. Walker attempts to support some of his analytical observations with data from experiments that tested music students' ability to perceive relationships among themes.[34]

In 1969, Karl Wörner attempted a more comprehensive study along Rétian lines, *Das Zeitalter der thematischen Prozesse*. Like Réti and Schoenberg, he sees an entire era dominated by thematic procedures—an era extending from about 1720 to 1950 and including figures as diverse as Vivaldi and Janáček. Wörner creates a typology of thematic processes, one of which, the *Abspaltungsprozess*, he finds particularly characteristic of Brahms. This process, which closely resembles certain procedures described by Schoenberg, consists of the splitting off and recombination of small motives. Using thematic charts like Rufer's, Wörner analyzes Brahms's Second Symphony, which he calls "without doubt, a masterpiece of the technique."[35] But this analysis, too, suffers from a tendency to view themes in isolation.

IV

Brahms's thematic and formal procedures have received more sensitive treatment in writings devoted solely or primarily to his music than in those that attempt to apply an analytical technique to a wide range of composers. One of the finest such studies is Arno Mitschka's *Inaugural-Dissertation* on Brahms's sonata forms.[36] Although his chapter headings ("Hauptthema," "Seitensatz," etc.) portend a rather schematic approach, one of Mitschka's chief concerns is to demonstrate thematic continuity across broad segments of the sonata structure. Mitschka was apparently unfamiliar with the writings of Schoenberg and his followers, for he actually reinvented the concept of developing variation with the inverted title *variierende Entwicklung*, or "varying development."

Mitschka suggests that Brahms's sonata forms cohere by a careful balance between "striving" and "restraining" forces. The result is a "static architecture" that maintains a tension between "the rush of development" and "the risk of

[34]Alan Walker, *A Study in Musical Analysis*, pp. 65–72, 142–43.

[35]Karl H. Wörner, *Das Zeitalter der thematischen Prozesse in der Geschichte der Musik*, p. 113.

[36]Arno Mitschka, *Der Sonatensatz in den Werken von Johannes Brahms*. For other valuable studies of Brahms's sonata forms, see Viktor Urbantschitsch, "Die Entwicklung der Sonatenform bei Brahms"; Edwin von der Nüll, "Strukturelle Grundbedingungen der Brahmsschen Sonaten-exposition im Vergleich zur Klassik"; Robert Pascall, "Some Special Uses of Sonata Form by Brahms"; and James Webster, "Schubert's Sonata Form and Brahms's First Maturity (II)."

disintegrating into small, lyrically rounded units." By the use of varying development, Brahms is able to avoid the closure that such rounded themes imply.[37]

Mitschka demonstrates how varying development shapes the sonata structures of three works by Brahms: the F-Minor Sonata, op. 5; the F-Minor Piano Quintet, op. 34; and the E-Minor Violoncello Sonata, op. 38. In the piano sonata, all the themes of the first movement are derived by "progressive transformation of the head motive." Similarly, all themes in the cello sonata are "expressive variants" of the head motive of the main theme. And in the piano quintet, Mitschka observes,

> the basic elements of the main theme appear continually in altered form and with different expressive content; they comprise the leap of a fourth followed by an upward second and a triadic figure. . . . All the motivic-thematic shapes are part of a developmental chain that leads first away from the head motive and then back again. This developmental process, however, condenses into individually molded thematic shapes, which contrast with each other in character and affective content.[38]

The processes of developing variation, then, generate the larger form, but they do not prevent the emergence of coherent and expressive thematic shapes.

Given Mitschka's evident sensitivity and articulateness, it seems odd that he intentionally restricts his comments on *variierende Entwicklung* to these three relatively early works, claiming that after them Brahms virtually abandoned the procedure. "Brahms never again used the variation principle as clearly," he observes. "The expositions of opp. 5, 34, and 38 must be viewed as shapes unfolding *sui generis* according to varying development."[39] Unique these pieces may be, but they constitute just three of many works that Brahms constructed by developing variation. Mitschka seems to apply the principle too narrowly; with Brahms it becomes a highly flexible tool that can operate on different levels (the theme, the phrase, the group, the exposition) and in different dimensions. Furthermore, it seems unlikely that a composer as scrupulous as Brahms would renounce such a powerful and sophisticated technique, once he had refined it to the high level of the piano quintet.

In a seminal 1965 monograph on Brahms's D-Minor Piano Concerto, op. 15, Carl Dahlhaus enhanced Mitschka's insights with a more specifically Schoenbergian viewpoint. This short analytical study was Dahlhaus's first publication on Brahms; he followed it three years later by a monograph in the same series on Schoenberg's Orchestral Variations, op. 31. The association of these two

---

[37]Mitschka, *Sonatensatz*, pp. 315–16, 321.

[38]Mitschka, *Sonatensatz*, pp. 31, 97–98. Throughout this book, unless otherwise noted, all translations from German sources are my own.

[39]Mitschka, *Sonatensatz*, pp. 99–100.

composers is no coincidence, for Dahlhaus has since emerged as the most articulate, provocative, and prolific spokesman for the Schoenberg-Brahms critical
tradition.

In his monograph on the concerto, Dahlhaus observes that Brahms arranged
the themes of the first movement in distinct clusters, the equivalent of Mitschka's "rounded units": six in the double exposition, one in the development
section, and four in the recapitulation and coda.[40] Reaching across these clusters
is a high-level process of developing variation, by which Brahms alters themes
as they reappear. This procedure tends to supersede, or at least overshadow, the
traditional functions and divisions of sonata form, for developing variation extends over the entire structure—exposition, development, recapitulation, and
coda:

> Brahms continually presents the main theme in different shapes, without ever
> going back to an earlier version where, according to the scheme of sonata form, we
> would expect him to—in the solo exposition or in the reprise. The "plastic" ele-
> ment of the grouping and the "logical" element of continuing [*fortschreitenden*]
> variation support each other mutually.[41]

Like Mitschka, Dahlhaus sees a tension or balance between developmental
(logical) and stabilizing (plastic) forces.

Dahlhaus demonstrates how Brahms refashions the main theme by isolating
and elaborating its individual elements [*Teilmomente*]. At the second statement
(bar 66), a canon exploits the element of imitation suggested in the opening
theme (bars 15–18). In the solo exposition (bar 110), Brahms highlights the
chromatically descending bass line first heard on a large scale in bars 1–25. The
recapitulation constitutes the most astonishing "development" of the theme:
it returns (bar 310) above the original D pedal but now outlines a different
harmony, an E rather than a B♭ dominant seventh.

The kind of "developing variation" that Dahlhaus describes here differs
from the procedures discussed by Schoenberg and the other writers. He is not
dealing with the continuous, moment-to-moment modification of motives, but
with the reinterpretation of a theme on the broader level of its reappearances in
the sonata form. This is indeed one of Brahms's most powerful strategies: we
can learn much by examining especially the different ways Brahms approaches
that most crucial moment of reinterpretation, the recapitulation. As adumbrated by Dahlhaus, however, this higher-level developmental process does not
differ greatly from that used by the Viennese classical composers, Haydn, Mozart, Beethoven, and Schubert, who also alter thematic returns with considerable imagination and variety.

[40]Carl Dahlhaus, *Johannes Brahms: Klavierkonzert nr. 1, d-moll, op. 15*, pp. 9–10.

[41]Dahlhaus, *Johannes Brahms*, p. 15.

In a more recent essay, "Issues in Composition" (1974), Dahlhaus has made a stronger claim for the uniqueness of Brahms's local methods of developing variation. Adopting Schoenberg's analytical techniques, Dahlhaus shows how the first group in the first movement of the G-Minor Piano Quartet, op. 25, is built from the continuous variation of two brief motives, the D–B♭–F♯–G figure of bar 1 and the descending second of bar 11 (see ex. 22, p. 67); these are developed by such procedures as inversion, augmentation, and diminution.[42]

Dahlhaus also suggests that this kind of developing variation affects the larger dimensions of Brahms's music—that it in fact becomes the primary "expositional" procedure. He does not, alas, support this claim, for his actual analyses remain, like Schoenberg's, on the level of the individual theme. But he does advance a cogent reason why Brahms would have chosen to build larger instrumental forms by developing variation. The technique, he says, emerged as one response to the central "problem" faced by composers in the later nineteenth century: how to create large forms from very concise thematic material.

Clearly echoing Adorno, Dahlhaus claims that in Beethoven the musical form and the musical idea maintained balanced structural roles, but that after Beethoven, form became dependent on the "idea"—that is, the initial motive or theme: "Musical form now presented itself primarily . . . as a consequence drawn from thematic ideas, not as a system of formal relations."[43] The thematic ideas tended to become very concise because composers felt a strong pressure to be "original," to do away with such conventional material or "filler" as we might find in music before Beethoven.

Building on the distinction Schoenberg makes in "Criteria for the Evaluation of Music," Dahlhaus suggests that composers of the later nineteenth century devised two different methods of generating large formal structures from such drastically reduced thematic material. Liszt and Wagner adopted the technique of real, or literal, sequence, whereby themes are not "developed"—not pulled apart and reshaped—but are repeated more or less exactly at different pitch levels. Real sequence is "a means of elaborating a musical idea which in itself—like the Yearning motive from *Tristan*—needs no continuation and would not tolerate conventional 'rounding-off' in a closed period."[44] The alternative technique was provided by Brahms's developing variation, in which the concise thematic material is continuously reinterpreted.

Dahlhaus's characteristic dialectics, whether between real sequence and developing variation, or between "logical" and "plastic" compositional forces (as in the Brahms concerto analysis), are always suggestive; they cannot be taken quite literally. Both Liszt and Wagner use thematic development, and not only

[42]Carl Dahlhaus, "Issues in Composition," p. 49.

[43]Dahlhaus, "Issues," p. 42.

[44]Dahlhaus, "Issues," p. 46.

sequential repetition, to build large structures. As Anthony Newcomb has recently shown, the first scene of Act III of *Siegfried* unfolds in part by the progressive transformation and modification of a brief motive.[45] Even the mature Brahms employs literal sequence on a large scale, as for example in the transition to the second subject in the first movement of the Third Symphony (bars 15–31). Yet there is no doubt that the kind of intense motivic processes that Dahlhaus finds in op. 25, Mitschka in opp. 5, 34, and 38, and Schoenberg in opp. 51 and 99 are more fundamental to Brahms's musical language than to Liszt's or Wagner's.

Contemporary German scholars continue to investigate these procedures in Brahms. Most of the discussion occurs in relatively brief articles,[46] but three extended studies have appeared, by Christian Schmidt, Klaus Velten, and Rainer Wilke. Schmidt's monograph (1971) is an extraordinarily detailed analysis of the F-Minor Clarinet Sonata, op. 120, no. 1. He claims that "three models [*Modelle*] govern the selection of all pitches, influencing the formation of motives and the shaping of themes."[47] Each model is a succession of ascending or descending intervals—seconds, thirds, and fourths respectively. These "models" are unfortunately so abstract that they could (and do) inform almost all pitch-based music. Indeed, much of Schmidt's analysis seems tautological or self-evident. Like Rufer and Réti, he ignores rhythmic values, concentrating only on note groupings. He also tends to distort the music, as when he reduces the main theme of the first movement to a chain of fifths on one level and thirds on another, by omitting certain important notes and changing the accidentals on others.[48]

Klaus Velten (1976) also restricts himself to a single Brahms work, the G-Minor Piano Quartet, op. 25. His analytical method more closely resembles those of Dahlhaus, Mitschka, and Schoenberg himself. In fact, his principal aim is to show how Schoenberg's orchestration (prepared in Los Angeles in 1937) of Brahms's op. 25 reveals or highlights the motivic structure of the music. Velten precedes that discussion with his own motivic analysis of the first-movement exposition. He parses the main theme differently from Dahlhaus (see above), finding only one basic motive, a minor second, which is presented in ascending form in bar 1 (F♯–G) and descending in bar 2 (E♭–D). Velten then charts an elaborate *Ableitungsreihe*, a chain of derivations in which each successive theme or transitional idea evolves from one of these two motive forms. He

[45]See Anthony Newcomb, "The Birth of Music Out of the Spirit of Drama," pp. 58–64.

[46]See, for example, Werner Czesla, "Motivische Mutationen im Schaffen von Johannes Brahms"; Rudolf Klein, "Die konstruktiven Grundlagen der Brahms-Symphonien"; and Victor Ravizza, "Konflikte in Brahms'scher Musik."

[47]Christian M. Schmidt, *Verfahren der motivisch-thematischen Vermittlung in der Musik von Johannes Brahms*, p. 18.

[48]Schmidt, *Verfahren*, p. 41.

suggests that the prevailing direction of the basic interval within a theme (up or down) gives the exposition its characteristic ebb and flow of tension, an alternation between "rising" and "falling powers."[49]

Velten seems more sensitive than Schmidt to the actual surface of the music and to the role of developing variation in articulating the sonata form. Like Réti in the Mozart analysis, he argues that "the transformational process of the basic motive and its derivations finds its goal" in the highly articulated, periodic succession of themes in the second group.[50] But, also like Réti, Velten is determined to find the *Grundgestalt* everywhere; his analysis therefore becomes a self-fulfilling prophecy, since (as Schoenberg's imagined skeptic might have said) minor seconds can be found in almost any theme.

Rainer Wilke's monograph on motivic processes in the quartets of Brahms, Reger, and Schoenberg (1980) is the most impressive of the three studies. Wilke elegantly traces a preoccupation with thematic-motivic issues in writers on Brahms since, and including, Max Kalbeck; he also discusses and documents Schoenberg's statements on developing variation.[51] Before presenting his own analyses, Wilke carefully delimits his terms—such as motive, theme, and variant—and provides a typology of variational processes. He admits that "in such a systematization . . . there is initially a certain remoteness from the actual relationships within a piece."[52] His analyses are in fact more flexible than his categories suggest. Yet too often he seems intent on pigeonholing rather than illuminating the musical processes. Like other writers in the Schoenberg tradition, he tends to select pitches somewhat arbitrarily. His methods can also bring about a *reductio ad absurdum*: a weighty account of the first movement of Brahms's C-Minor Quartet, op. 51, no. 1, concludes with the assertion that a tiny accompaniment figure of four notes, appearing in bar 24, is the unifying element of the whole work.[53]

V

It will surely have been remarked that all the writers examined in this chapter were born and educated in Europe, mostly in Germany and Austria. Although

[49]Klaus Velten, *Schönbergs Instrumentation Bachscher und Brahmsscher Werke als Dokumente seines Traditionsverständnisses*, pp. 66–74. See also Velten's analysis in his earlier article, "Das Prinzip der entwickelnden Variation bei Johannes Brahms und Arnold Schönberg," especially pp. 549–52.

[50]Velten, *Schönbergs Instrumentation*, p. 74.

[51]Wilke, *Brahms, Reger, Schönberg Streichquartette*, pp. 17–30.

[52]Wilke, *Brahms*, p. 17.

[53]Wilke, *Brahms*, p. 82.

there has been a considerable amount of activity in England since Keller,[54] the Schoenberg critical tradition has been slow to establish itself in the United States—and this despite the fact that Schoenberg lived and taught here for many years. One reason undoubtedly is the dominance of Schenkerian analysis and theory. Another is that, as I have suggested, Schoenberg was not himself a systematic thinker; his concepts cannot easily be shaped into the kind of unified, comprehensive theory of music favored by many American academics.

Yet Schoenberg's concepts have stimulated important analysis and criticism, especially about Brahms. My aim has been to show that an impressively large group of writers shares the belief that Brahms's music unfolds by a characteristic process of motivic-thematic development. Although they differ in approach and in merit, and although some fail to acknowledge their intellectual heritage (or are perhaps unaware of it), all these commentators present analytical viewpoints that have found their most powerful expression in Schoenberg's notion of developing variation. The limitations of each writer—whether a tendency to focus on too local a level of composition, to engage in dialectics that obscure the music, or to trace every theme of a piece back to a tiny motive—suggest the need for a more sensitive study of Brahms.

Before turning to the music we might do well to let speak one critic whose authority has not been invoked at all, the composer himself. Of course, the intentional fallacy may bid us beware of an artist's explanation of his own work: such testimony is not necessarily relevant or illuminating. With Brahms we need not worry too much, for he was notoriously unforthcoming about most personal subjects, including his own creative processes. As is well known, he destroyed almost all evidence of his working methods.[55]

Brahms's many letters and reported remarks are also generally unhelpful, but on several occasions he did let slip utterances that are directly relevant to our investigation. Once he responded firmly to a rather superficial, Rétian thematic analysis of the *German Requiem* by Adolf Schubring, a friend and music critic. In 1869, shortly after the score of the *Requiem* appeared, Schubring wrote a review-article in the *Allgemeine musikalische Zeitung* that demonstrated thematic unity in the third movement, "Herr, lehre doch mich":

---

[54]Of particular merit are Jonathan Dunsby, *Structural Ambiguity in Brahms*, especially Chapters 2–5; and the recent dissertation by Michael Musgrave, "Schoenberg and Brahms."

[55]For two good accounts in English of Brahms's inscrutable character and of his attitudes about the creative process, see Karl Geiringer, *Brahms: His Life and Work*, pp. 327–43; and Hans Gal, *Johannes Brahms: His Work and Personality*, especially "Secrets of the Workshop" (Chapter 7). See also Donald M. McCorkle, "Five Fundamental Obstacles in Brahms Source Research," especially pp. 256–58.

All the melodies . . . are derived by inversion, diminution, by the addition of pre-fixes and suffixes, from the following three main themes, which are themselves conceived in triple counterpoint:

Even the fugue theme

der Ge-rech- ten See-len

clearly originates in Theme III.[56]

Schubring's fragmentary examples are difficult to locate in the actual music. Theme I evidently refers to bars 3–4, and Theme II to bar 105, although in Brahms's score the ascending line appears above, not below, the descending line, in flutes and oboes. Theme III appears to be just a different representation of the same measure; it appears nowhere in the movement as Schubring quotes it. Schubring's example displays, of course, no "triple [*dreifach*] counterpoint," only combinations of two themes.

Brahms did not pick apart Schubring's analysis in this way. Rather he found fault with its basic premise, writing to his friend:

> I disagree that in the third movement the themes of the different sections have something in common. (Except for the small motive ♩· ♫♩.) If it is nevertheless so—I deliberately call back nothing from my memory—I want no praise for it, but do confess that when I am working, my thoughts do not fly far enough away, and thus unintentionally come back, often with the same idea.

Brahms thus admits that in spite of his conscious compositional process, the different thematic ideas might in the end be closely related. But, he goes on to add, if he *does* want a relationship to be heard, he will ensure it: "Yet if I want to retain the same idea, then it should be clearly recognized in each transfor-

---

[56]Adolf Schubring, "Schumanniana Nr. 12," p. 10.

mation, augmentation, inversion. The other way would be a trivial game and always a sign of the most impoverished invention."[57]

Neither Schubring's analysis nor Brahms's response has been commented on before, to my knowledge (although Brahms's subsequent remarks in the same letter on the art of writing variations have often been cited). But together they offer what is surely one of the most penetrating glimpses available into Brahms's workshop. Even so disciplined a composer as he acknowledges the role of the unconscious in the creative process. He grants, in effect, that the procedures of developing variation—the continuous reinterpretation of thematic material— can create valid relationships without the composer's awareness. Indeed, Schubring's analysis, though superficial, is fundamentally accurate: the various themes of Brahms's movement do seem to be closely related. At any rate, there are certainly more unifying elements to be found than the little rhythmic figure which Brahms cites as the only "intentional" common denominator.

Brahms's attitudes strikingly recall those of his greatest modern apologist, Schoenberg. Though much less grudgingly than Brahms, Schoenberg also admits that the unconscious—or subconscious, as he calls it—plays an important role in creating thematic relationships and coherence. On several occasions he points to a connection between two themes of his Chamber Symphony, op. 9, which he claims to have noticed only years after composing the work.[58] Like Brahms, too, Schoenberg seems to have resented anyone's making too much of the purely technical aspects of such relationships. When he was once sent a comprehensive twelve-tone analysis of the Third Quartet, he responded much as Brahms did to Schubring, gently but firmly expressing disapproval: "This isn't where the aesthetic qualities reveal themselves, or, if so, only incidentally. I can't utter too many warnings against overrating these analyses."[59] Neither Schoenberg nor Brahms denies the probable accuracy of the analysis presented to him; but both assert that the more important features of a piece—the "aesthetic qualities"—cannot be conveyed simply by associating themes or counting rows.

But let us return to Brahms, and to his most often-quoted statement on his creative process, which seems to suggest that both conscious and unconscious

---

[57]"Ich streite, dass in Nr. 3 die Themen der verschiedenen Sätze etwas miteinander gemein haben sollen. (Ausgenommen das kleine Motive . . .) Ist es nun doch so (ich rufe mir absichtlich nichts ins Gedächtnis zurück): So will ich kein Lob dafür, sondern bekennen, dass meine Gedanken beim Arbeiten nicht weit genug fliegen, also unabsichtlich öfter mit demselben zurückkommen.

"Will ich jedoch dieselbe Idee beibehalten, so soll man sie schon in jeder Verwandlung, Vergrösserung, Umkehrung deutlich erkennen. Das andere wäre schlimme Spielerei und immer ein Zeichen armseligster Erfindung." Johannes Brahms, *Johannes Brahms Briefe an Joseph Viktor Widmann, Ellen und Ferdinand Vetter, Adolf Schubring*, p. 216.

[58]See *Style and Idea*, pp. 85, 222.

[59]Schoenberg, *Letters*, p. 164.

forces can operate by a kind of developing variation to generate an entire work from a single thematic kernel. In a journal kept during his acquaintance with Brahms, George Henschel reports that the composer said to him one day:

> There is no real creating without hard work. That which you would call invention, that is to say, a thought, an idea, is simply an inspiration from above, for which I am not responsible, which is no merit of mine. Yea, it is a present, a gift, which I ought even to despise until I have made it my own by right of hard work. And there need be no hurry about that, either. It is as with the seed-corn; it germinates unconsciously and in spite of ourselves. When I, for instance, have found the first phrase of a song, say,

Wann der sil - ber-ne Mond

> I might shut the book there and then go for a walk, do some other work, and perhaps not think of it again for months. Nothing, however, is lost. If afterward I approach the subject again, it is sure to have taken shape: I can now begin to really work at it.[60]

For Brahms, composition begins with the "gift" of a musical idea, which grows and expands of its own accord. Then, in a separate and fully conscious process, the composer draws all the implications and possibilities from that initial idea: "nothing is lost." (This is also Schoenberg's view—that a composition is "foreseen" in, and then drawn step by step from, the theme.)

And what of the outward form that such a process creates? It is a pity that Brahms left behind no specific accounts of how he approached his beloved sonata form, which he employed throughout his creative life and which will be my principal concern in the chapters that follow. We do, however, have the valuable testimony of Gustav Jenner, who in 1888 became Brahms's only private student in composition. Brahms told Jenner to examine the sonata forms of Beethoven, paying particular attention to the influence of a theme on the design of a move-

---

[60]Cited by George Henschel, *Personal Recollections of Johannes Brahms*, pp. 22–23. (I return to this song, "Die Mainacht," in Chapter 4.) Three other reported statements by Brahms on his creative process closely resemble the Henschel quotation; they use either the seedcorn metaphor or the idea of going out for a walk, or both. See the comment to Simrock cited in Max Kalbeck, *Johannes Brahms*, 2: 182; the remark cited by Gustav Jenner, *Johannes Brahms als Mensch, Lehrer, und Künstler*, p. 42; and the conversation between Brahms and Arthur Abell given in Robert H. Schauffler, *The Unknown Brahms*, pp. 177–79. Though there is no reason to doubt the authenticity of these stories, they do bear a somewhat disturbing resemblance to the statements on the creative process once attributed to Mozart and Beethoven, but now shown to be fictitious. See Maynard Solomon, "On Beethoven's Creative Process: A Two-Part Invention."

ment.[61] Jenner was also encouraged to compare Beethoven with Schubert in this regard. From Brahms, Jenner learned that a sonata structure must grow logically from a theme, that "one has not written a sonata if one holds together a few ideas merely with the outward form of a sonata; on the contrary, the sonata form must of necessity result from the idea."[62] What mattered to Brahms, Jenner reports, was the spirit, not the schema, of sonata form.

As in the Henschel quotation, Brahms stresses that the basic "idea" is the progenitor of the larger form. With these statements he anticipates Schoenberg's more polemical formulation of developing variation as the basis of true composition, in which there "is nothing but the endless reshaping of a basic shape." We also see Brahms openly espousing as a principle what Dahlhaus claimed as the characteristic "problem" of the later nineteenth century: musical form becomes dependent on, and consequent to, the initial idea. As I hope to show, Brahms applied the principle—or solved the problem—with considerable success. In his best music, form becomes a luminous expression of the flexible, powerful procedures of developing variation.

[61]Jenner, *Johannes Brahms*, p. 60.

[62]Jenner, *Johannes Brahms*, p. 6.

2

Transformation and Development
in Early Brahms, 1852–1854

I

Implicit in "Brahms the Progressive" and *Fundamentals of Musical Composition* is Schoenberg's belief that Brahms evolved his characteristic techniques of thematic development from the Viennese classicists, especially Mozart and Beethoven. The claim is largely justified, as I have attempted to show by elaborating on the examples in *Fundamentals*. Neither Schoenberg nor any other writer examined in Chapter 1, however, adopts a sufficiently historical or comparative approach: we get little impression of how Brahms's works relate to one another or to important earlier and contemporary music. Most of these analyses focus on isolated mature pieces, or small portions thereof. Schoenberg treats opp. 51, 99, and 121; Réti opp. 73 and 79; Schmidt op. 120; and Wilke op. 51— all works composed after Brahms's fortieth year. Velten and Dahlhaus choose the somewhat earlier op. 25, but treat it as "paradigmatic" of a mature technique. And Mitschka groups opp. 5, 34, and 38 together as examples of a single principle.

While such commentary can illuminate individual works, it also lends tacit support to Schumann's famous overstatement: that Brahms emerged as a composer fully equipped, like Athena from the head of Zeus. But, of course, Brahms did not create all at once his armory of sophisticated methods for developing variation. His earliest surviving music presents an image very different from the intensely motivic and fluent examples adduced by most critics.

The sonata-type works of 1852–54, including the three Piano Sonatas, opp. 1, 2, and 5, and the original version of the Piano Trio, op. 8, exhibit a remarkable confluence of musical techniques and aesthetics. Specifically, Brahms attempts

EXAMPLE 12: Brahms, Piano Sonata, op. 5, I.

to reconcile the principles of thematic development and thematic transformation. As is well known, the latter technique is most characteristic of Liszt and
his school, although it is also found in Beethoven and Schubert. A transformed
theme retains its original melodic outline but may change its mode, harmony,
tempo, rhythm, or meter. This procedure differs fundamentally from "development," in which the smallest elements of a theme—its intervals and rhythms—
are continuously modified.

The clearest example of the young Brahms's efforts to combine these techniques is the ambitious first movement of his third and last Piano Sonata, op. 5
in F Minor, composed in October 1853. This piece can be profitably compared
with important (and possibly influential) sonatas by Beethoven, Schubert, and
Liszt.

As early as 1862 Adolf Schubring, our enthusiast of thematic unity, noted
that the first movement of op. 5 is virtually mono-motivic.[1] This time Schubring
was right, for (as others have observed since then) Brahms derives each theme
and each segment of the sonata structure from a terse head motive. The opening
theme, 1a, which we might tend to hear as only a progression of chordal splashes
in F minor, proves in fact to contain a genuinely polyphonic structure (ex. 12a).
The head motive appears in two principal forms, x and y, each of which Brahms
will exploit during the course of the movement. The ostensible upper line, x,
moves stepwise down a third from A♭ to F, then leaps up a minor sixth to D♭.
This figure is actually a composite of two voices: the high D♭ is shifted up from
the C of the alto, while the A♭–G–F figure circles back to G, creating a stepwise
motive form, y (ex. 12b). In the tenor, Brahms places a rhythmically identical
figure, which in bar 1 rises a fourth but in bars 2 and 3 becomes an inversion of
y (y').

---

[1]Schubring, "Schumanniana Nr. 8," p. 102. Schubring's remarkable series of articles discusses
all of Brahms's works published up to 1862 (through op. 18).

The y form of the motive, obscured by the continuous registral transference in the first few bars, becomes dramatically explicit in the broad F–E♮–D♮–E♮ figure that concludes the first phrase (bars 5–6). (See Appendix, ex. A, pp. 171–75, for the entire exposition and development of op. 5.) Brahms immediately transforms the climactic half cadence into a hushed minor-mode theme, 1b (bar 7)—an impressively precocious instance of the linkage technique examined in Chapter 1. Theme 1b forms the middle section of a tripartite opening period. When the initial idea returns at bar 17 as 1a′, the texture is inverted: x is now on the bottom (in the tenor), and a somewhat truncated y′ appears on top, displaced to the last beat of the bar.

After the next half cadence, in bar 22, we expect a formal transition that, as in most classical sonatas, will gather steam and prepare the modulation to a new key; but Brahms simply leaps into the new key (III) and continues unruffled his exploration of the head-motive complex (2a/transition, bar 23). Theme 2a has its ancestry in both themes 1a and 1b. Its rhythmic gesture and melodic contour—a downward stepwise motion followed by an upward leap—clearly recall motive x as heard in 1a. And, lest we fail to make that association, Brahms diligently places in the left hand a closer approximation of the original rhythm and pitches of x. Theme 2a is built as a sequence of ascending three-note figures, C–B♭–D♭, D♭–C–E♭, E♭–D♭–G♭. This design derives from theme 1b, where successive statements of y yield an interlocking chain with the same pitch relationships, E♭–D–(F), F–E♭–(G), etc.

Only in its last four bars (35–38) does 2a become genuinely "transitional," providing the secondary key, A♭, with the dominant preparation lacking in the sudden leap across bars 22–23. At bar 39, Brahms confirms the modulation with a new lyrical theme, 2b. This too, however, proves to be derived from the ubiquitous head motive, which Brahms now expands over four bars into a warm *cantabile*. The wash of harmonic color—a sensational, *Lohengrin*-like shift to C♭ (♭III of A♭) at bar 43—once again disguises a multi-voiced structure. The upper line displays the skeletal version of x much as we heard it in 2a/transition; the alto clearly suggests the stepwise y, which here acquires expressive appoggiaturas (A♭–G, B♭–A♭). For his codetta (bar 56), Brahms develops x into an animated *poco accelerando* by rapid sequential treatment of the disjunct fourth (G♭–C, F–B♭, etc.).

Despite its tight thematic logic, the exposition of op. 5 sounds stiff, even clumsy. Although there is some variety in phrase lengths, four of the themes display similar antecedent-consequent structures: 1b (5 + 5 bars), 2a (8 + 8), 2b (4 + 4, then an extension), and the codetta (8 + 8). Emphatic half cadences and pauses after each phrase tend to make the joints in the sonata form painfully obvious. As Joachim was later to say of the exposition in Brahms's G-Minor Piano Quartet, op. 25, the "cement" [*Kitt*] stands out.[2]

[2] Johannes Brahms, *Johannes Brahms im Briefwechsel mit Joseph Joachim*, I: 306.

On a lower level, each phrase is constructed by means of sequential repetition of the head motive (bars 1, 2, and 3 of 1a, for example). Furthermore, all the sequences rise except the last, in the codetta, which descends rapidly almost as if in embarrassed compensation. Each theme also has an analogous spot where, after a few bars of the sequence, Brahms ruffles the rhythmic pattern slightly with a hemiola (as at bars 4–5 and 49–50) or an acceleration (9–10, 20–21, 27–28). Between themes 1b and 2a, this analogy approaches identity: compare bars 9–10 (and their equivalent in the consequent phrase, 14–15) with 27–28 (and 35–36).

The shape of this exposition, then, almost suggests strict variation procedure. As Arno Mitschka has remarked, "If the segments were not of different lengths, and if the propelling forces did not constantly reassert themselves toward the end of each part to prevent closure, the shape of this movement would be created not only by the variation principle, but by variation form itself."[3] Mitschka does not specify the "forces," but I take it they would include the rhythmic animation we observed toward the end of each "variation."

The development section does little to dispel our impression of a strange *Mischform* combining features of both variation and sonata. First come slightly altered statements of themes 1a and 1b (bars 75–87), and then the grandest variation of all. Pulsating syncopations at bar 88 pave the way, providing generous dominant preparation for the key of D♭. The left hand enters, presenting underneath this chordal halo a broad, lyric melody derived from the y form of the head motive. As in all segments of the exposition, the first element, here a three-bar phrase, is repeated sequentially; the harmonic shift toward III of D♭ (F major) at bars 101–2 seems to echo the similar move in theme 2b (bar 43). This large, stable D♭ episode cadences langorously in bars 108–11 and then, with some reluctance, modulates to G♭, where Brahms provides a further variation—a *maestoso*, major-mode rendering of theme 1a (bar 119). This in turn leads to the retransition and to the recapitulation, which begins at bar 138.

As Mitschka notes, the development is constructed on the same principles as the exposition, with "measure groups all appearing as variants of the main theme."[4] In fact, the development takes up the material of the exposition in its original order. Its first part (bars 75–87) corresponds closely to 1a and 1b; the D♭ episode then "develops" the lyricism and the harmonic vocabulary of 2b.

In Chapter 1, we observed how Mitschka uses the term *variierende Entwicklung* to describe the process in op. 5 by which Brahms continuously refashions a brief motive into different thematic shapes. But the awkwardness of this sonata results precisely from a lack of genuine *Entwicklung*. The thematic shapes remain too closed, too immobile: in the terms of Mitschka's own dialectic, the "restraining" forces overwhelm, rather than balance, the "striving" ones. The

[3]Mitschka, *Sonatensatz*, p. 31.

[4]Mitschka, *Sonatensatz*, p. 32.

head motive appears in a succession of guises without ever undergoing the fluid, dynamic evolution that Schoenberg was to demonstrate. From Schoenberg's point of view the head motive of op. 5 is not actually "developed." He no doubt would have considered the different themes or segments to be mere "variants."[5]

Nevertheless, I believe the static discourse of the sonata is in fact an early manifestation of the same basic impulse of developing variation that is later to shape Brahms's more sophisticated works like the op. 51 Quartets and the op. 99 Cello Sonata. In op. 5, however, the "development" is expressive rather than abstract or absolute: Brahms is more concerned with exploring the different possible moods of his themes than with manipulating their metrical and phrase structure or their basic pitch relationships.

The distinction between these kinds of development becomes clear if we examine Brahms's treatment of the linkage technique. In two of the examples cited in Chapter 1, Schoenberg's "Brahmsian" sentence and the Allegretto theme from Brahms's Second Symphony (exx. 9 and 10), the multiple repetition of the linking motive deliberately obscures the juncture between phrases. The new phrase evolves as if by magic, without our knowing precisely when or how it commences. But in op. 5, Brahms does not attempt (or probably was not capable of) such prestidigitation. Indeed, the division between themes 1a and 1b (bars 6–7) is made dramatically conspicuous by the broad half cadence and the sudden shift in dynamics. The magic, or intended magic, is thus different from that of the symphony's Allegretto: Brahms clearly wants his listeners to be aware of the phrase juncture and to focus on the wondrous metamorphosis of the motive from a frenzied half cadence into a muted sigh.

Brahms's procedure in op. 5 is essentially that of thematic transformation (a topic to which I return), which here takes precedence over other techniques that Schoenberg saw as characteristic of Brahms. The first movement unfolds not as an essay in thematic development, but as a series of discrete character studies of a single motive. We encounter its *maestoso* temperament (1a); its potential for repressed agitation (1b); a strong and determined side, *"fest und bestimmt,"* as Brahms himself indicates (2a); a *cantabile* disposition (2b); and a still more meditative lyricism (the D♭ theme in the development).

The emphasis on sharply articulated "variation" also creates a lack of coordination between harmonic, thematic, and formal processes. Theme 2a in A♭ is approached abruptly from the half cadence on V (bars 22–23); the ostensible reason is that, as a variation of the head motive, 2a can begin on a firm (if unprepared) harmony. Yet since 2a is also to function as a sonata-type transition, Brahms must *reculer pour mieux sauter*: he retreats from A♭ only to work his way back via the bars of real dominant preparation, 35–38. The result is, to my ear, an unfortunate formal-harmonic ambiguity.

The ambiguity is compounded by the bizarre harmonic syntax within 2a/

[5]See Chapter 1, p. 10.

transition. The sequences of bars 23–26 move from A♭ to an unexpected *minor* dominant (in F minor, v of III), jarring because A♭ itself has not been established sufficiently to accommodate such a modal shift. The next phrase cadences on F major (bars 29–30), which is heard as V of ii (in A♭); but the chord of resolution, B♭, disrupts the diatonic progression again by arriving in the "wrong" mode— in major—ostensibly to correspond with the A♭ major that began 2a. These abrupt modal substitutions betray a lack of focus and purpose. Only in bar 34 does Brahms resume a progression moving functionally toward A♭: F minor becomes vi; D♭, IV; and E♭, V.

Still more remarkably, Brahms then relinquishes A♭, closing the exposition instead in the key of D♭. The harmonic flux of the second group and codetta is then followed by a harmonic stasis of about forty measures. For Brahms not only ends his exposition in D♭, but builds the larger part of his development around the same key. The impressive-sounding sequence of diminished-seventh chords in bars 72–74, constructed over F♯, D♯, and B♯, proves to be a lot of fuss about nothing, since at the cadence to C♯ minor in bar 75 we end up where we began. After 1a and 1b obediently appear in this key, Brahms at last manages a modulation to its dominant, G♯ (bars 84–88). But within a few moments the G♯, now respelled as A♭, yields to the inevitable magnetic force of D♭ major (alias C♯), which retains its power until bar 119. Even more than in the exposition, the parade of themes in a single key in this development section bears out Mitschka's claim for variation procedure.

In short, the thematic, formal, and harmonic procedures create a highly unusual sonata structure in op. 5—one that Mitschka has rightly labeled "unclassical." Just how unclassical it really is can be seen by comparing op. 5 with its most famous predecessor in F minor, Beethoven's *Appassionata*, op. 57, a sonata that Brahms surely knew well and that he may even have used as a rough model.

II

As Charles Rosen has demonstrated, the *Appassionata* is one of Beethoven's most rigorously classical works, especially in the concise and symmetrical structure of its first movement. All the segments (exposition, development, recapitulation, and coda) are clearly demarcated; all begin with the main theme and go on to present the principal material in the same order.[6] Such a lucid design may well have suggested to Brahms the extreme compactness and articulation of the first movement of his op. 5, as well as a development whose thematic plan closely parallels that of the exposition. Brahms's exposition progresses from a rather jagged, melodically unstable opening, across the sturdier *Bestimmtheit* or resoluteness of the transition, to a broad, lyrical second subject (2b). Beethoven's follows a similar course, from the volatile bare octaves of the

[6]Rosen, *The Classical Style*, p. 400.

opening bars to the expansive *dolce* theme in A♭ (bar 35). Like Brahms's, this second subject is clearly derived from the main theme, of which it forms a free inversion smoothing out the initially angular rhythm. Both expositions push past these lyrical episodes into more animated codettas.

More significant than these general similarities of form, however, are the radically different ways in which each composer achieves motivic economy. Like Brahms, Beethoven works with a basic motive, but he is concerned less with its continuous transformation than with its outward expansion. Rosen has observed how the laconic four-note D♭–C motive in bar 10 of the *Appassionata* encapsulates the Neapolitan relationship Beethoven has set up at the opening between the tonalities of F and G♭, and their respective dominants C and D♭.[7] In fact, the motive does much more than that: Beethoven molds most of the transition and codetta from the same half-step idea, which is transposed to E♮ (F♭)–E♭ but still represents the ♭6–5 scale degrees (now in the key of A♭). Brahms attempts no such dynamic expansion. His basic motive merely appears in a succession of different guises, thereby producing a form much more static than Beethoven's.

Despite its prominent chromaticism, Beethoven's exposition displays none of the harmonic awkwardness of Brahms's op. 5 because all harmonic gestures grow from the basic motive. Like Brahms, Beethoven is able to push past his lyrical A♭, here to a dark and turbulent A♭ minor. (Even this evocative change of color and mode can be said to derive from a half step, C♮–C♭.) Beethoven thus achieves contrast while still retaining a single key area throughout the second group. Then he demarcates the beginning of the development section by a striking move to E major (bars 66–67), produced by respelling and reversing the ♭6–5 half-step shift as D♯–E♮. Brahms, however, abandons his A♭ *during* the exposition to seek the greener pastures of D♭, the same key in which most of the development is to unfold. His harmonic design thus fails to reflect the sonata structure. Nor do his frequent and distracting modal alterations relate, like Beethoven's, to a basic motive.

A comparison of the two development sections reveals even more clearly the differences between the mature Beethoven and the young Brahms. Both developments, as has been noted, take up the material of their respective expositions in order. Furthermore, at the center of both lies a big D♭-major episode derived from the second theme. Like Brahms, Beethoven gives us advance notice of its arrival. As Tovey remarks, "Beethoven has taken the extraordinary risk of arresting his action not only by reproducing the whole passage of dominant preparation [i.e. bars 24–35] on the threshold of this D♭, but by actually adding four bars to it [105–8]."[8]

We expect, adds Tovey, that this "calm theme, having thus entered with

[7]Rosen, *The Classical Style*, p. 89. See also the more extended discussion of the *Appassionata* in Rosen's *Sonata Forms*, pp. 190–94.

[8]Donald F. Tovey, *Beethoven*, p. 44.

enhanced impressiveness in D♭, should after four bars begin to repeat itself in the upper octave," as it does in the exposition (bar 39). But, of course, Beethoven eschews such stability, which can be perilous indeed in a development section. Instead, the theme unfolds as a large and dramatic sequence over a bass line that rises inexorably through two full octaves (bars 109–23). A series of diminished-seventh arpeggios then sweeps downward to the original point of departure, D♭, at which Beethoven proceeds to hammer away furiously; it finally responds by sinking to C to initiate the recapitulation (bar 134). What has begun as a lyrical episode has thus evolved rapidly into a bold sequential drive and a highly charged retransition. When the first theme materializes over a C pedal, we suddenly become aware that Beethoven has built the whole passage over an enormous expansion of the D♭–C motive. The tiny figure has been projected onto the largest imaginable structural scale.

The analogous D♭ theme in the development of Brahms's op. 5 forms just one part of a massive and, it must be admitted, somewhat tedious prolongation of C♯/D♭. It remains only a tuneful "variation," a ravishing but fundamentally undramatic transformation of the head motive. The theme does not push forward like Beethoven's, but cadences squarely in the key where it began and then—almost as if unsure where to turn next—tumbles into another variation (bar 119). Brahms's D♭ tonality thus lacks the integral relationship to the movement's key centers that Beethoven establishes so carefully with his Neapolitan harmonies.

Despite certain similarities to the *Appassionata*, Brahms's F-Minor Sonata simply does not proceed, or succeed, according to Beethovenian classical principles. Only in a later F-minor work, the Piano Quintet, op. 34, does Brahms rediscover—in his own terms, to be sure—Beethoven's techniques of motivic expansion and display the ability to integrate detail and whole in a coherent sonata design. But in the first movement of op. 5, Brahms's emphasis on transformation at the expense of development creates a fundamentally different kind of sonata from Beethoven's.

III

Transformation, as has already been suggested, involves a radical change in mood or character, while the theme's basic shape, especially its pitch contour or configuration, is retained. Tempo, rhythm, meter, harmonization, dynamics, articulation—all these may be altered, but the theme still retains a recognizable *Gestalt*. To use a more concrete analogy: the various garments with which the theme is clothed do not affect its basic anatomical structure, its flesh and bones.

Transformation has, of course, been a basic impulse of Western composers at least since the cyclic masses of the Renaissance. Within the common-practice era (the principal context of this study), the early works of Beethoven provide

EXAMPLE 13: Beethoven, Piano Concerto, op. 37, III.

one of the first—and certainly one of the most striking—manifestations of transformation, as H. C. Colles suggested as long ago as 1934.[9]

Near the end of the development section in the finale of Beethoven's C-Minor Piano Concerto, op. 37, the earnest main theme appears as a light *scherzando* tune in E major (bar 264, exx. 13a, b). Like the analogously placed Db theme in Brahms's sonata, this transformation is provided with a substantial introduction in order to make its entrance as conspicuous as possible: eight bars (bars 257–64) raise the curtain slowly and dramatically. This transformation involves mode, dynamic, and register. In the Presto coda of the movement, an alteration of meter and tempo makes for a still more dazzling metamorphosis (bar 407, ex. 13c), of which even Liszt would have been proud.

[9]H. C. Colles, *Symphony and Drama, 1850–1900*, pp. 30–31.

Brahms probably knew Beethoven's concerto when he wrote his piano sonatas in 1852–54, since Beethoven had loomed large in his studies with Eduard
Marxsen.[10] As Tovey has suggested and Rosen has demonstrated, Beethoven's
finale furnished the direct model for the last movement of Brahms's D-Minor
Concerto, op. 15.[11] (In the passage analogous to Beethoven's E-major transformation, Brahms's theme—at bar 275—likewise appears in major, in a higher
register, and at a softer dynamic level. This moment, however, is not as magical
as Beethoven's; nor does Brahms provide any equivalent for Beethoven's Presto
coda.)

It is Schubert who still more closely adumbrates the procedures of the
Brahms F-Minor Sonata. Brahms's "three-key" exposition (F–A♭–D♭) might
bring Schubert to mind, although Brahms avoids the dominant, which is normally Schubert's third key area. But there is a deeper, more significant resemblance in the way that Schubert combines developmental and transformational
techniques in his mature sonatas.[12] The exposition of the first movement of the
last A-Minor Sonata, op. 42 (D.845), for example, is sharply articulated by numerous pauses and half cadences. Like Brahms's op. 5, it unfolds to some extent
as a series of discrete character studies of motivic elements of the main theme.
As often happens in Schubert (especially in the G-Major and C-Minor Sonatas,
D.894 and D.958), the second group becomes almost a set of variations, in which
phrase structure, harmony, and melodic outline are preserved (compare bars 40–
48 and 51–59).

Schubert also anticipates Brahms strikingly in his tendency to focus the
development section around a tuneful transformation of an initially non-melodic idea. Although the main theme of the A-Minor Sonata has a regular,
essentially symmetrical phrase structure of 4 + 4 (+2) bars, it lacks the texture
and feel of a melody, largely because it is presented in bare octaves and block
chords (see ex. 14a). Like Brahms, Schubert recalls his theme in something like
its original form at the beginning of the development—he has also brought it
back in the codetta—and then moves grandly toward a half cadence (bars 103–
4; see ex. 14b). We now await an important event: the left hand enters in bar 105
with a rocking accompanimental pattern derived from the syncopated passage
at bars 10–11; above this, *pianissimo*, appears a metamorphosis of the main
theme. The austere octave doubling in the first two bars of the original theme
has been replaced by harmonic support, and the chordal response of bars 3–4 is
now dissolved into a fluid arpeggio (107–8), which functions as a truly splendid

---

[10]The cadenza for this concerto, long attributed to Brahms (even in the *Sämtliche Werke*), is by
Moscheles. See George S. Bozarth, "A Brahms Cadenza by Moscheles."

[11]Donald F. Tovey, *Essays in Musical Analysis, 3: Concertos*, pp. 74, 118–19; Charles Rosen,
"Influence: Plagiarism and Inspiration," pp. 91–93.

[12]Colin Mason (in his "Brahms' Piano Sonatas") has suggested other points of similarity between the Schubert and Brahms sonatas, but they involve only such superficial (and widely
encountered) features as four-movement design, "great length," and octave doubling in chords.

EXAMPLE 14: Schubert, Piano Sonata, op. 42 (D.845), I.

transformation of the repeated E's in the original theme. By sustaining a single diminished-seventh chord over the two bars, Schubert retains the idea or gesture of repetition, but makes it *harmonic* instead of *thematic*.

Equally poetic transformations are encountered in the first movements of Schubert's other late sonatas: the development sections of the D-Major (D.850), A-Major (D.959), and Bb-Major (D.960) sonatas all begin with similar metamorphoses. Schubert's mature sonatas had been published by the time Brahms began serious musical studies—three of them in Schubert's lifetime, the other three in 1839. Some of these publications would surely have found their way to Hamburg. Might not the young Brahms have been familiar with them when writing his own piano sonatas?

As is well known, Brahms came to love Schubert's music deeply and devoted much time to praising, performing, and even editing it; but the date of his first acquaintance remains in doubt. On the basis of the published correspondence and Clara Schumann's diary, James Webster has recently suggested that Brahms came to know Schubert's music only at the Schumann household, where in the spring and summer of 1854 he was playing—and playing very beautifully, according to Clara—the A-Minor, D-Major, and Bb-Major Sonatas.[13] It is, of course,

[13]Webster, "Schubert's Sonata Form," pp. 56–57.

possible that Brahms began to study these works immediately after his arrival in Düsseldorf (30 September 1853), in time for them to have an impact on the first movement of his F-Minor Sonata, written in his first month there.[14] But it seems unlikely that he could have absorbed or internalized their characteristics so rapidly.

Brahms may well have encountered Schubert in his training under Marxsen, who had ties to Schubert's Viennese circle. In 1830, not long after Schubert's death, Marxsen studied piano in Vienna with Carl Maria von Bocklet, who had been a good friend of the composer, the dedicatee of his D-Major Sonata and the first performer of his E♭-Major Piano Trio. Although Marxsen's own (largely unpublished) compositions apparently betray little influence of Schubert, according to Kalbeck, Marxsen might well have owned copies of the piano sonatas and shown them to his precocious pupil.[15]

Schubert's sonatas do not appear to have been played publicly in Hamburg during Brahms's youth, but the music historian of that city, Josef Sittard, reports that much of the chamber music was performed by a prominent local string quartet in the 1830s, '40s, and '50s.[16] Sittard also documents that in 1841 and 1848 the Hamburg Philharmonic played a "C-Major Symphony" by Schubert.[17] This would almost certainly have been the "Great" (D.944), performed by Mendelssohn in 1839, published (in orchestral parts) in 1840, and acclaimed by Schumann in his famous article of the same year. (The "little" C-Major Symphony, D.589, was not published until 1885.) Whether or not Brahms attended any of these chamber music or symphony performances, it is clear that Schubert was "in the air" in Hamburg.[18] And if the young composer developed a curiosity about Schubert's instrumental music, Marxsen would probably have been able to satisfy it.

There is more solid evidence for assuming that Schubert's methods of thematic transformation directly inspired another important figure, Franz Liszt. Here the influence came not from the sonatas, but from the *Wanderer* Fantasy (published in 1823 and thus also possibly available to Brahms), in which all the

---

[14]The most authentic sources for the dating of Brahms's works (besides the inscriptions on some autographs) are his own handwritten catalogue and his pocket calendars (now in the Wiener Stadtbibliothek). Only the catalogue, which extends through op. 79, has been published to date; it is transcribed in Alfred Orel, "Ein eigenhändiges Werkverzeichnis von Johannes Brahms." For op. 5, Brahms wrote "Oktober 1853 Düsseldorf, Andante und Intermezzo früher."

[15]On Marxsen, see Kalbeck, *Johannes Brahms*, 1: 26–36.

[16]Josef Sittard, *Geschichte des Musik und Concertwesens in Hamburg*, p. 200.

[17]Sittard, *Geschichte*, pp. 315–16.

[18]The fact that Brahms became so enthusiastic upon hearing the "Great" C-Major Symphony in Leipzig in December 1853 (see Brahms, *Briefwechsel mit Joachim*, 1: 18) does not, of course, imply that he had never heard it before.

themes of the different movements are related by transformation. Liszt was so taken with the piece that in 1851 he transcribed it for piano and orchestra. One might assume that he was attracted more by its virtuostic writing than by its purely musical qualities, but a little over a year later he applied the principle of thematic transformation on a similarly bold scale in his Sonata in B Minor (completed in February 1853).

Liszt's Sonata merits our consideration here because Brahms heard Liszt play it at Weimar in June 1853, just a few months before the F-Minor Sonata was composed. In a legendary story, the American pianist William Mason, a pupil of Liszt's, reported that Brahms fell asleep during Liszt's performance. But Mason admits that, although present at the occasion, he did not himself see Brahms doze off; he heard of this only later from Eduard Reményi, Brahms's unsympathetic (and probably unreliable) traveling companion. And when Mason attempted to corroborate the story in later years, Karl Klindworth, another Liszt pupil who had been present, made no reference to Brahms's drowsiness.[19]

Brahms was not comfortable in the atmosphere of adulation and sycophancy that surrounded Liszt at the Altenburg; nor was he likely in sympathy with much of the music he may have seen or heard—perhaps scores by Raff, Cornelius, and other followers of Liszt. But common sense tells us (as it has told several Brahms biographers) it is improbable that Brahms would have dozed off during a private performance by the greatest pianist of the century, of whom Brahms himself later said, "He who has never heard Liszt can really say nothing. Liszt came first, and after him for a long while came no one. His piano playing was something unique, incomparable, and inimitable."[20] If Brahms's eyes were indeed closed, he was probably concentrating on Liszt's flamboyant yet structural use of thematic transformation; and something of Liszt's procedures may have remained in his mind's ear when he composed the first movement of the F-Minor Sonata.

The Liszt Sonata is, of course, a *locus romanticus* of the device of transformation.[21] It has two distinct principal themes, both introduced at the opening: the first is bold and angular, presented in octaves by both hands; the second, compact and nervous, grumbles deep in the bass register. When they reappear at the close of the exposition (ex. 15), both themes take on completely new char-

---

[19]William Mason, *Memories of a Musical Life*, pp. 127–32.

[20]Quoted in Kalbeck, *Johannes Brahms*, 1: 90. Kalbeck also attacks Mason's account on several points (1: 86), reporting that a letter shown him (Kalbeck) by Marie von Bülow contradicts certain statements in *Memories*.

[21]For comprehensive analyses of the sonata see William S. Newman, *The Sonata Since Beethoven*, pp. 373–78; Rey Longyear, *Nineteenth-Century Romanticism in Music*, pp. 162–65; and Sharon Winklhofer, *Liszt's Sonata in B Minor*, pp. 115–20, 127–68. In his article on "Thematic Transformation" in *The New Grove Dictionary of Music and Musicians* (19: 117–18), Hugh MacDonald specifically cites the Liszt sonata.

EXAMPLE 15: Liszt, Piano Sonata in B Minor.

acters. Liszt transforms the jagged one into a broad, regular melody of sixteen bars and the grumbly one into a grand *cantando espressivo* with a flowing triplet accompaniment. To ensure we will not miss the point, he precedes each transformation with the initial form of its theme (bars 121–25 and 142–53).

Much like Liszt's two themes, the concise opening idea of Brahms's op. 5 is transformed near the close of the sonata exposition into a *cantabile*. Brahms retains the original notes and even the original polyphonic texture, but he decks them out in luxuriant new costumes. Common to both sonatas is our impression of apotheosis, as though the melodic potential of the opening material has now been fulfilled.

There are, however, two important and revealing differences between the methods of Liszt and Brahms. First, Liszt tends to work with more extended themes, Brahms with the briefest of motives. Second, Liszt's transformations do not constitute a continuous, developmental process. Although there is a limited amount of motivic work during the exposition of the B-Minor Sonata, including such traditional techniques as fragmentation and contrapuntal combination, the actual transformations are unveiled with little preparation beyond a brief reference to their original shapes. Brahms makes his theme work harder for its riches. The head motive evolves step by step toward its lyrical fulfillment, and its grandest transformation, the D♭ theme in the development section, appears only after themes 1a and 1b are reviewed.

Brahms thus attempts to rationalize, to shape a logical musical discourse from, Liszt's attractive but (he may have thought) self-indulgent procedures. In this impulse he resembles Schubert, who likewise gives his transformations a sober continuity. From the more strictly classical side of his compositional pedigree, especially from Beethoven, Brahms derives the technique of using brief motives. The F-Minor Sonata therefore stands as a fascinating hybrid in which Brahms subjects elements of Beethovenian conciseness to extravagant Lisztian transformations, within a sonata structure that seems to owe its classical cogency to both Beethoven and Schubert.

IV

Transformation operates not only within the first movement of Brahms's op. 5, but also *between* the different movements. The second and fourth movements (Andante and Intermezzo), written earlier than the others, are intimately related in this way; the latter bears an appropriate subtitle, "Rückblick." The tranquil A♭-major theme of the Andante, accompanied by rippling broken thirds, becomes in the Intermezzo a somber funeral march in B♭ minor, punctuated by timpani strokes. Wilibald Nagel has suggested another plausible transformation: the anguished climax of the Intermezzo (bar 38) recalls and reshapes the once-radiant D♭ theme from the coda of the Andante.[22] Now beginning at a harsh half step above the bass (the tonic B♭), the theme attempts to escape upward but soon capitulates to the rhythmic and tonal insistence.

Frank E. Kirby points to still more intriguing transformations when he

---

[22]Wilibald Nagel, *Die Klaviersonaten von Johannes Brahms*, p. 115.

EXAMPLE 16: Brahms, Piano Sonata, op. 5.

observes "a general correspondence between the parts of the sonata which are in the key of D♭ major."[23] There is indeed more than a general correspondence, for the coda theme of the Andante is really just a full-bodied version of the theme that appears among the sixteenth notes in the *Poco più lento* earlier in the same movement (exx. 16b, c). Both these themes constitute transformations of the grand D♭ melody in the development section of the first movement (ex. 16a), which likewise rises to the fourth degree, G♭, then sinks to the tonic by means of a neighbor-note motion, F–E♭–F, and the skip of a third, from F to D♭.

These relationships have important implications, apparently never discussed before, about Brahms's creative process in the F-Minor Sonata. As noted earlier, the D♭ theme in the development of the first movement appears to grow logically and gradually from the continuous transformation of the head motive; but since the Andante movement from which it derives was written earlier, Brahms may well have had the D♭ theme in mind *before* composing the rest of the first movement. In other words, the ostensibly germinal head motive was conceived after the big melody toward which it appears to "evolve."

---

[23]Frank E. Kirby, "Brahms and the Piano Sonata," p. 175.

This probable chronology provides fascinating evidence for the frequently encountered observation (or implication) that sonata form in the romantic era is conceived thematically or melodically, whereas classical sonata form (especially in Haydn and Beethoven) is generated by small, dynamic motives. Brahms seems to have approached the first movement of the F-Minor Sonata "romantically"; he thought first of a big, lyrical melody. He then attempted to rationalize or "classicize" the movement by placing the melody in the development section and abstracting from it a tiny head motive that could then grow toward the melody by successive transformations.

The genesis of the separate movements of both the F-Minor and C-Major Sonatas suggests a broader analogy in Brahms's conception of the sonata as a whole: he had a predilection for melodic movements as well as melodic themes. As with op. 5, the Andante of the C-Major Sonata, op. 1 (April 1852), preceded the remainder of the work (spring 1853).[24] Brahms seems thus to have written whole sonatas, not only individual sonata-form movements, from the inside out.

Like op. 5, the other works of 1852–54 are characterized by transformation between movements. In the F♯-Minor Sonata, op. 2, the procedure involves the main themes of all four movements; in op. 1, the outer movements; and in the Trio, op. 8, the first two. These relationships have often been discussed in print and need not be reviewed here;[25] but no commentator has suggested persuasively just where, if anywhere, Brahms might have found a model for these inter-movement transformations. Kalbeck's claim for the influence of the New German School will not bear serious consideration—at least for the first two sonatas, which were composed before Brahms had any contact with Liszt and his followers.[26] Liszt's large symphonic poems, the banner works of this "school," were not performed and published until well into the 1850s, after the period of Brahms's opp. 1–8. Geiringer has also pointed toward Liszt, suggesting that "Brahms utilized the old principle of thematically relating the different movements, which he found employed in the nineteenth century by Liszt."[27]

Brahms would certainly have been familiar with the practice of *recalling* themes intact, as happens in Mendelssohn's Octet and in Beethoven's E♭ Sonata, op. 27, no. 1, and Fifth and Ninth Symphonies. But *transformation* was not especially "old" or widespread by 1850. We do, however, find it in Schubert's *Wanderer* Fantasy, Mendelssohn's Third (*Scottish*) Symphony, Berlioz's *Fantastic Symphony* and *Harold in Italy*, and Schumann's *Carnaval* and First, Second,

[24]See Orel, "Ein eigenhändiges Werkverzeichnis," p. 530.

[25]See, for example, Kirby, "Brahms and the Piano Sonata," pp. 170–77. Most of the relevant literature on the sonatas is cited in Newman, *Sonata*, pp. 327–35.

[26]Kalbeck, *Johannes Brahms*, 1: 85.

[27]Karl Geiringer, *Brahms*, p. 206.

and Fourth Symphonies. Brahms might have heard some of these works performed in Hamburg, which, though far from such centers as Paris and Vienna, was certainly not a "provincial" or "backward" musical environment, as one commentator has recently claimed.[28] Berlioz conducted *Harold in Italy* there in 1843 and praised both the local players and the audience.[29] The Hamburg Philharmonic played Schumann's First Symphony in 1842, only a year after its composition.[30] In 1850, Robert and Clara Schumann returned to the city on a concert tour—the occasion on which Brahms tried unsuccessfully to interest Schumann in his music.[31] Clara played the Schumann Concerto, which makes significant use of transformation within the first movement, and (in another concert) the Schumann Piano Quintet, in which the main theme of the first movement is recalled and transformed as the fugue subject in the coda of the finale.[32]

Any of these works might have influenced the young Brahms, but it is also possible that he arrived independently at the idea of thematic transformation between movements. A logical mind like his may have devised it in order to provide his ambitious, large-scale works with some additional structural coherence.

V

Transformation between the movements of a work is not my principal concern. Such effects are, after all, relatively easily achieved, and were in fact much abused by composers of the later nineteenth century. (Brahms himself never again employed the technique quite so blatantly.) Rather, I have sought to characterize Brahms's remarkable attempt to combine transformational and developmental procedures within a sonata form. Other, more articulated formal structures, such as rondo, variations, and A B A, will naturally not display such features as prominently. In op. 5, as we have seen, the result is a first movement that is indeed novel and without precedent. Although neither of the two earlier piano sonatas employs this style of proto-developing variation so obsessively, their first movements show Brahms exploring the same issues of thematic,

[28]See Webster, "Schubert's Sonata Form," p. 56.

[29]See Sittard, pp. 239–41; Hector Berlioz, *The Memoirs of Hector Berlioz*, pp. 314–16.

[30]See Sittard, *Geschichte*, p. 315.

[31]See Kalbeck, *Johannes Brahms*, 1: 55–56.

[32]That Brahms claimed to "come to know and admire" Schumann's music only just before arriving in Düsseldorf in the fall of 1853 (see his *Briefwechsel mit Joachim*, 1: 9) does not preclude the possibility that in earlier encounters with Schumann's music he admired the use of transformation.

formal, and harmonic construction, and thus merit some brief examination here.

The exposition of the F♯-Minor Sonata, op. 2 (composed November 1852), is arranged almost as schematically as that of the F-Minor Sonata. Brahms articulates each segment—first theme, transition, second group, codetta—with a fermata, pause, or *ritardando*. As in op. 5, all the themes develop progressively and logically from the opening gesture. To create the *pianissimo* transition figure at bar 16, Brahms merely takes the first four notes of the movement, inverts the F♯–A descending sixth into a rising third, and raises the B to B♯; the motive has changed radically in character but not in pitch content. This transition figure is then transposed to the dominant minor to initiate the second group at bar 40. This theme is built from the sequential repetition of an explosive three-bar unit. In the first two bars, unharmonized octave repetitions of the basic motive climb rapidly up to a high C♯, poise momentarily at the precipice, and—as if breaking free of the motive—plunge down to begin an impassioned theme in C♯ minor with chordal accompaniment (bar 42). But the theme is cut off in mid-flight as the pattern begins again on a ii⁷ harmony (bar 43). The potential melody is again thwarted: the motive returns to C♯ minor (46), then moves to its dominant major (49). At this fourth leg of the sequence, a jarring B♮ ruptures the G♯-major harmony and forces a modulation to E major. Here the frustrated theme at last breaks free of the motive and the constricting pattern to fulfill itself in a fervent melody with throbbing accompaniment. Unlike the earlier themes of the exposition, this one has an extended phrase structure of 2 + 2 + 3 bars (bars 51–57). As in op. 5, we have a sense of thematic apotheosis: the E major unveils the melodic potential of material that has hitherto been fragmentary. The transformation is intended, I think, to be at once breathtaking and logical. As in op. 5 (but not the Liszt Sonata), the composer has guided us step by step toward the apotheosis: we are made to understand the process but we still marvel at the revelation.

The first movement of Brahms's C-Major Sonata, op. 1, begins to suggest even more closely the continuous thematic procedures of the F-Minor Sonata. Its exposition may seem at first little more than a loosely organized succession of ideas, but Brahms's progressive exploration of the two-note tail from the main theme (A–G, bar 2) projects a larger design over the whole. After he dutifully develops this and other components of the main theme in the transition (bar 17), Brahms incorporates the figure (actually the larger F–G–A–G motive of the main theme) into a new A-minor melody (bar 39). The status of the two-note figure has been elevated, so to speak, for as a prominent appoggiatura (C–B, D–C) it now bears the entire expressive weight of the theme. Brahms uses the two-note motive to initiate a new theme over the E pedal at bar 51. The appoggiatura figure then reappears to form the tail to a new roulade-like theme (bar 63).

The procedures of op. 5 are prefigured not only by the imaginative reinterpretation of the two-note motive, but by the presence of a large lyrical transformation/episode in the development (see ex. 17). At bar 136, Brahms halts the

EXAMPLE 17: Brahms, Piano Sonata, op. 1, I.

busy counterpoint of the development to make way for a tranquil reappearance of the exposition's A-minor theme. It finally arrives at bar 153 in the major mode (G major), adorned by an additional voice that functions as a canonic echo.

Brahms places this metamorphosis in roughly the same part of the development as the D♭ episode of op. 5, but here the passage creates a somewhat clumsy formal ambiguity. In bars 136–52, it is given an enormous dominant preparation that our ears (though not our eyes, which see it as V/V) might easily mistake for a retransition—particularly after such a lengthy development section. But we soon realize that the G-major theme at bar 153 is *itself* being made to function as a retransition; it leads after a very brief crescendo to the recapitulation at bar 173. Furthermore, in these measures Brahms undercuts any possible dominant tension, which might at least have prepared us for the real recapitulation. For, rather than pressing home toward C, the harmonies actually regress along the circle of fifths, G moving to D (bar 161), and D to a diminished-seventh chord built on C♯ (bar 167, sounding like vii°^{7} of D). The C♯ then suddenly drops to C♮, and Brahms bursts into the recapitulation through V^7/IV, having bypassed the tonic altogether (see ex. 17).

The formal process and harmonic syntax of this passage reveal that, as in op. 5, Brahms is attempting (though not particularly succeeding at) an unusual kind of sonata structure—one that undermines the force of a recapitulation: (1) by preceding it directly with a stable thematic episode, (2) by withholding genuine dominant preparation, and (3) by then passing immediately through the tonic to the subdominant. Once again a comparison with Beethoven, here with the analogous measures in the first movement of the *Waldstein* Sonata, op. 53, can help to set Brahms's "unclassical" tendencies in clear relief.

Brahms knew the *Waldstein* well, of course, having played it in public at the age of 15.[33] Mitschka has suggested that the first page of Brahms's op. 1—compared by most critics to the opening of Beethoven's *Hammerklavier*, op. 106—was actually inspired by Beethoven's big C-Major Sonata. The themes of both works, he notes, are played first in C and then begun again down a whole step in B♭; both also return to the dominant via the tonic minor (Brahms, bars 13–14; Beethoven, 11–12).[34] The *Waldstein* may well have provided a rough model for Brahms; the first part of the op. 1 exposition can, at any rate, be said to proceed along Beethovenian lines.

The end of Brahms's development, however, breathes an entirely different atmosphere. Beethoven's retransition is famous for its tremendous tension and excitement, which build across a fourteen-bar dominant pedal from a low *pianissimo* rumble to the exhilarating contrary-motion scales that finally close in upon the tonic. This retransition has no thematic content to speak of: the material is completely neutral, serving only to keep the V^7 harmony sounding. At the comparable point in the development section of op. 1, Brahms is concerned more with melodies than with formal exigencies, more with transforming a secondary theme in a foreign key (G hardly sounds like a dominant here) than with preparing the return of his main theme in the tonic. Indeed, the return

[33]The concert program is given in Florence May, *The Life of Brahms*, 1: 86–87.

[34]Mitschka, *Sonatensatz*, pp. 9–10.

almost seems to catch Brahms unaware; he rushes embarrassedly past it into the more comfortable parts of the recapitulation.

Mitschka has aptly summarized the important differences between Brahms's early development sections and those of his classical predecessors. He notes that although Brahms makes ample use of the same devices as Haydn, Mozart, and Beethoven, such as thematic fragmentation or imitative counterpoint, "the emphasis lies not on the deployment of thematic-motivic powers, but on the expressive content of melodic shapes, which emerge as the goals or results of the developmental process."[35] I think we may extend this observation to include the entire sonata structure in the three piano sonatas. The first movements of the F♯-Minor and the C-Major Sonatas reveal how Brahms tends to sacrifice dramatic development for the sake of stable melodic *Gestalten*. At its most extreme, this practice generates a sonata form like that of op. 5—a continuous series of such shapes, all of which are transformations of a basic motive. As we have seen, that movement is rescued from utter stagnation by the progression of the shapes toward what I have called lyrical fulfillment or apotheosis.

VI

Brahms abandoned none of these principles in his next instrumental work, the Piano Trio in B Major, op. 8. Although its massive first movement seems to have little in common with the compact op. 5, both are in fact products of the very same musical instincts. Brahms himself gives January 1854 as the date of the trio's composition, but Kalbeck surmises this represents only the date it was completed, and that "sketches for the four movements were underway already in Mehlem and Düsseldorf."[36] (No sketches survive, however.) Thus, the first movement may have been conceived at the same time as the F-Minor Sonata, in the fall of 1853. The trio was published in November 1854 and, as is well known, was extensively revised by Brahms thirty-six years later, the new version being issued in 1891.

The principal subject area—surely the most tuneful among the early instrumental works—greatly expands the A B A structure of op. 5 into a scheme we might represent as $A_{12} B_8 A'_8 B'_7 A''_9$ (the numerical subscripts indicate bar lengths). As Tovey points out, "Either this melody must be a normal item in a scheme that is breaking away from sonata style, or it must be an exceptionally big item in a normal sonata scheme."[37] In the original version of op. 8 Brahms

[35]Mitschka, *Sonatensatz*, p. 145.

[36]Kalbeck, *Johannes Brahms*, 1: 149. A convenient comparison of suggested dates of composition for all Brahms's chamber music is given in Klaus Stahmer, *Musikalische Formung in soziologischem Bezug*, pp. 1–10.

[37]Donald F. Tovey, "Brahms's Chamber Music," p. 226.

EXAMPLE 18: Brahms, Piano Trio, op. 8 (original version), I.

moves in the first direction, since every other theme or section is as massive as the opening. There is a proportionate, extended transition (bars 45–83), a large second group (bars 84–147), and a generous codetta (147–61).

Behind its ravishing and apparently seamless veil of tunefulness, the main theme (ex. 18) proves to be constructed, like the first theme of op. 5, from continuous recycling of very concise thematic material. Carl Dahlhaus's detailed analysis reveals:

> The essential thematic idea is given in bars 1–2; bars 3–4 are instantly recognizable as being related by inversion to bars 1–2; bars 5–8 transpose the melody of bars 1–4 up a third with a modification in bar 8; and in bars 9–10 material derived from bars 6 and 7 is placed at the beginning of a phrase, so that what were originally the second and third bars in the metrical structure are transformed into the first and second—this is variation achieved by metrical means.[38]

Dahlhaus's interpretation of the theme as a kind of progressive variation on the two-bar motive accords well with our view of the F-Minor Sonata. But his postulation of the metrical shift in bars 9–10 obscures a crucial point. Bars 1–8 divide clearly into four-bar phrases of 2 + 2 construction; each two-bar unit is based on some form of the ♪♪♪ |♪♪ motive. But the four-bar phrase at 9–12 cannot be bisected in this way, for it forms a single unit pushing through to the cadence. Brahms eliminates the seam by spreading the two-bar rhythmic motive *across* the center of the phrase (bars 10–11). Brahms has not, as Dahlhaus would have it, shifted two bars (6–7) from the center to the beginning of a phrase (9–10). (Dahlhaus at any rate ignores the important syncopations in the melody at bar 9, which surely weaken any analogy between 6 and 9.) Rather the basic rhythmic motive, whose twofold presentation has previously divided every phrase in half, is now placed astride the expected mid-point of the last phrase.

Brahms shifts the motive's metrical position not only to create cadential

---

[38]Dahlhaus, "Issues," pp. 61–62.

EXAMPLE 19: Brahms, Piano Trio, op. 8 (original version), I.

momentum but also to reveal a new aspect of the theme, which has been hidden by the square 2 + 2 structure of earlier phrases—this is the descending three-note figure, F♯–E–D♯. This motive (actually an inversion of the ascending third of the first bar) has been displayed prominently across bars 2–3, but is there, of course, divided between the two halves of the phrase. Brahms's two-bar slurs in the revised op. 8 (bars 1–2, 3–4, etc.) make the natural articulation clear. It is only in the last phrase that these notes, F♯–E–D♯, congeal into a recognizable motive. The piano's syncopated figure in bar 9 paves the way—thus the syncopations *are* important—and is followed by a twofold presentation of the motive in bars 10–12.

Brahms continues to evolve the three-note motive across the remainder of the first group. In A' and A'' he decorates the second bar of the theme, expanding the original F♯–E to F♯–E–D♯ (bars 22 and 37). A new cadential figure, also outlining a descending third, is added at bar 27 (ex. 19). The three-note motive and the new cadential figure are repeated again and again (the first in augmentation and diminution) as A'' blends into the transition from bar 41. Such motivic concentration even surpasses the obsessive discourse of op. 5! At bar 63, the motive initiates a 5 + 5–bar sequence modulating from B major to the mediant, D♯ minor. Now beginning on an upbeat and thus stressing its *second* note, the motive prepares and, in augmented form, even initiates the second group at bars 83–84, when the D♯ harmony at last resolves to G♯ minor.

The second group of the original op. 8 Trio (see Appendix, ex. B, pp. 175–77) is one of the most remarkable in all of Brahms's sonata-form movements. Its breadth—it contains three separate themes—results chiefly from Brahms's attempt to keep it in scale with the "normal" first group. First comes a mournful, recitative-like subject (2a), played by the piano alone. This unusual theme begins a chain of associations with the main subject that will build up across the entire second group. The first, rather faint echo is the two-note appoggiatura, which seems to emerge from the three-note motive and is prominent in 2a (at bars 84, 86, 88, 91). The next link is added when the recitative gives way to a theme resembling a Baroque fugue subject (2b, bar 98). The stepwise ascent from the first scale degree (here D♯) and the rhythm of a half note followed by two quarter notes both recall—rather subliminally, to be sure—bar 2 of the movement's opening theme.

To our surprise, 2b cadences on D♯ without ever initiating an actual fugue (this comes in the recapitulation): instead the recitative returns, played in canon

EXAMPLE 20: Brahms, Piano Trio, op. 8 (original version), I.

by the strings. The fugue subject then reappears in the principal key of the second group, G♯ minor, but once again fails to elicit a proper contrapuntal answer. The next two bars modulate abruptly to E major, where Brahms introduces a pastorale accompanied by a drone bass of open fifths (2c). This extraordinary theme constitutes a genuinely Lisztian metamorphosis of the fugue subject. It retains the initial rhythm of 2b but transforms the rather grim stepwise ascent into a graceful and open theme outlining the notes of the E-major triad. The simple soul of the pastorale has no use for the chromaticism and pseudo-polyphony of the third, fourth, and fifth bars of 2b (100–2). Instead, it merely turns back on its own first two bars in a free inversion.

The pastorale thus functions much like the *cantabile* placed analogously toward the end of the op. 5 exposition—as a melodic fulfillment of the preceding material (2a and 2b). It also completes, or makes explicit, the relationship between the second group and the main theme. Theme 2c ingeniously recreates the octave ascent heard in the opening bars of the movement, from the fifth below the tonic to the fifth above. Theme 2c also moves back down to the lower fifth across its third and fourth measures. Example 20 should clarify these relationships between the main theme, the pastorale (2c), and the fugue subject (2b).

The roulades of the codetta, from bar 148, seem to unravel the material of the exposition; they hover between E major and G♯ minor, finally settling into the latter key at bar 157. Here Brahms recalls the three-note motive that led into the second group but that has not been a strong presence for some time. This isolated reference is not, however, gratuitous, because the repeat of the exposition will set the two versions of the three-note motive side by side: its fully evolved form in G♯ minor, and its original form as split up between the two halves of the first phrase (bars 2–3). Brahms thus encapsulates for the listener the whole transformational process.

Mitschka finds the original second group of op. 8 an inadequate complement to the first theme. "Above all, contrast is lacking," he complains, "because all three themes [of the exposition] are lyrical-cantabile [*lyrisch-kantabel*]: the main theme, the secondary theme (bar 84) and the closing theme (bar 126). . . .

The first movement of the trio is relatively without tension in the large span."[39] Mitschka's assessment is unjust, I think, for the original op. 8 does display genuine contrast. The main theme may be *lyrisch-kantabel*, but 2a is no such thing. As Tovey remarks, "its movement is, intentionally and effectively, slower than that of the opening theme, which will contrast with it as sunshine after gloom."[40] The fugue theme, 2b, shares the "gloom" of the recitative, but its more regular, measured tread contrasts sufficiently with the open-ended declamatory style. The pastorale, 2c, differs in mood completely from both of the other secondary themes and even from the main theme; the drone bass has little in common with the noble syncopations that underpin the main theme. *Lyrisch* the pastorale may be, but scarcely *kantabel*.

Brahms reduces the contrast somewhat in the recapitulation, substituting a full-fledged fugato for the entire second group (from bar 354). In the original scheme of op. 8 this large digression represents, as Tovey says, "no fault." The fugato is the most logical transformation or fulfillment of the exposition's frustrated fugue subject (2b): in the recapitulation it thus supersedes the pastorale. At bar 396 the fugato leads into a new episode, which exercises the three-note motive with vigorous triplets.

The extraordinary second group received—along with the development—an extensive face-lift when Brahms came to revise the trio in 1889–90. A comparison of the two versions offers a rare and rewarding opportunity to observe the compositional, or re-compositional, process of a composer who elsewhere destroyed virtually every trace of his workshop.[41] Here we need only to review some of the changes in light of the compositional issues raised in this chapter. Aside from a few alterations in scoring and phrasing, Brahms preserved the first group intact in the revised version, but decided—as Tovey says—to make it "the largest item, instead of a mere indication of the average flow."[42] He rewrote the transition and second group completely, eliminating most of the progressive transformation of the three-note motive and moving directly to the second subject at bar 75. Brahms retains the original submediant tonality (G♯ minor) but composes an entirely new theme (ex. 21). It is a very characteristic late-

---

[39]Mitschka, *Sonatensatz*, p. 103.

[40]Tovey, "Brahms's Chamber Music," p. 227.

[41]The most comprehensive comparison is provided by Ernst Herttrich, "Johannes Brahms—Klaviertrio H-Dur, Frühfassung und Spätfassung." Herttrich brings to light a copyist's manuscript, in score and parts, of the revised version, apparently used by Brahms for performances in early 1890. This manuscript, which has survived incomplete, differs in several details from the published revised version; none of the changes affects the analysis presented here. For more critically oriented comparisons of the original and revised op. 8, see Tovey, "Brahms's Chamber Music," pp. 226–30; Ivor Keys, *Brahms Chamber Music*, pp. 47–50; and Gal, *Johannes Brahms*, pp. 157–63.

[42]Tovey, "Brahms's Chamber Music," p. 227.

EXAMPLE 21: Brahms, Piano Trio, op. 8 (revised version), I.

Brahms creation, with a first part built from descending thirds, much like the main theme of the Fourth Symphony or of the B-Minor Intermezzo, op. 119, no. 1. In its phrase structure of 1 + 1 + 2 bars the theme is fundamentally as square as the opening subject, but its unstable metrical framework betrays the hand of late Brahms, suggesting the techniques of displacement we shall examine later in the piano quintet and the Third Symphony. Initially the listener has no doubt that all phrases and subphrases begin on the fourth beat of the bar; but by bar 83, the syncopations across the barline begin to take on the character of downbeats, and the metrical grid seems to shift, now aligning with the fourth and second beats.

The most significant difference between the original and revised second groups of op. 8 is that, in the latter, Brahms makes no attempt to transform his thematic shapes, to reattire them in strongly contrasting garments, or to guide them toward melodic apotheoses. As Mitschka astutely observes, the new secondary theme derives from the descending thirds in the upper part of the piano accompaniment at bars 55–56.[43] But this *sub rosa* relationship hardly constitutes the kind of thematic metamorphosis by which themes are generated in op. 5 and the original version of op. 8. Nor is there a strong sense of evolution across the revised second group. In the original op. 8, we observed a progression from the speaking recitative to the singing pastorale; the revised second group, however, consists only of two parallel statements of the new theme (bars 83–95 and

[43]Mitschka, *Sonatensatz*, p. 106.

95–109), followed directly by the codetta. This new codetta introduces a triplet figure which, at least initially, is a decorated form of the familiar three-note motive (now in half steps, E–D♯–C×). But the motive is less effective here than in the original codetta. There it had at least earned its position through extensive development during the exposition. In the revised version, where Brahms has eliminated most of this development, the motive's appearance at the close of the exposition seems arbitrary.

Brahms had mixed feelings about undertaking the revision of op. 8. During initial negotiations with his publisher, Simrock, he wrote, with characteristic wit, that a new version "will be shorter, hopefully better, and in any case more expensive."[44] Later, however, he referred sarcastically to the process of revision as "castration" and told Simrock that the first version of the trio "was indeed poor, but I don't mean that the new one is good!"[45] When Brahms sent a copy of the revised work to his friend Elisabeth von Herzogenberg, she too expressed some ambivalence: "I was strangely affected by the old-new trio. Something within me protested against the remodelling. I felt you had no right to intrude your master-touch on this lovable, if sometimes vague, production of your youth." She added that, especially in the first movement, "I cannot get rid of the impression of its being a collaboration between two masters who are no longer quite on a level."[46]

One is inclined to agree with her, and with Tovey, who claims that "the new work is not an unmixed gain upon the old."[47] The magnificent opening theme of Schubertian innocence and the revised second group of late Brahmsian *savoir-faire* do indeed make rather strange bedfellows. Mitschka, as might be expected, approves of the newly won contrast: "The theme draws its tensions from a melodic construction which, because of its unusual interval series (layered thirds) and chromatic steps with altered harmonies, is far removed from folk-song-like simplicity."[48] But to my ear the original second group forms a more appropriate sequel to the main theme, appropriate not only in scale (as Tovey notes), but in spirit: its tentative character follows more naturally and logically from the youthful bloom of the B-major *cantabile* than does the suave, revised G♯-minor theme. With Frau von Herzogenberg, then, we might "shed a tear for the dear departed E-major subject [the pastorale]."[49]

[44]Johannes Brahms, *Johannes Brahms Briefe an P. J. Simrock und Fritz Simrock*, 4: 7.

[45]Brahms, *Briefe an Simrock*, 4: 36, 38.

[46]Johannes Brahms, *Johannes Brahms: The Herzogenberg Correspondence*, p. 389. A similar sentiment is expressed by Florence May (*Life* 1: 169).

[47]Tovey, "Brahms's Chamber Music," p. 229.

[48]Mitschka, *Sonatensatz*, p. 105.

[49]Brahms, *Herzogenberg Correspondence*, p. 400.

Above all, we should view the original op. 8 not as a youthful transgression, as Brahms seemed to view it in 1890, but rather as a remarkable testimony of the young composer's skill in maintaining—on a larger scale than he had ever attempted before—a delicate balance between the principles of transformation and development. Judging by the sonata-form movements up to and including op. 8, we would not find it easy to predict which way the scale would tip in Brahms's later works (though a glance at the revised op. 8 provides the answer). As Ivor Keys has observed:

> We have . . . no instrumental works before this op. 8 (except perhaps the Scherzo, op. 4) by which we could be certain that Brahms was not to follow his own version of a path trodden by Liszt and others which after all produced valid masterpieces. The fact remains that the first movement of op. 8 is the last occasion on which Brahms in "sonata-form" movements treats his main subject as the hero of a drama the interest of which lies in his constantly changing circumstances and the guises in which he meets them. A turning point indeed, if so.[50]

The op. 8 Trio does represent a turning point, or more accurately an endpoint. In the next chapter we shall examine how Brahms moves toward a new synthesis of transformational and developmental techniques in the chamber works of what Tovey called his "first maturity."

[50]Keys, *Brahms Chamber Music*, p. 49.

3

Developing Variation
in Brahms's First Maturity, 1861–1862

I

The B-Major Trio of January 1854 was the culmination of two and one-half years of intense and virtually continuous creative activity on Brahms's part, extending back to the E♭-Minor Scherzo, op. 4, of August 1851. Then, it would seem, his compositional fountain ran dry—or at least much more slowly—for he failed to complete another large-scale work until the first Serenade, op. 11 in D, of 1858. In fact, during this period Brahms finished only three instrumental pieces, the Variations in F♯ Minor, op. 9, the Ballades, op. 10 (both works finished in summer 1854), and the two variation sets of op. 21 (1856), all for piano. Even his impressive production of songs was halted: disregarding simple folk settings, the next songs after op. 7 (1854) were the eight Lieder of op. 14, composed in 1858.

The immediate reason for this creative lull was Brahms's extreme turmoil, internal and external, caused by Schumann's leap into the Rhine on 27 February 1854. Complicating Brahms's feelings about his mentor's illness (and death, in July 1856) was his evident infatuation with Clara, which was undoubtedly difficult to reconcile with his devotion to Schumann. A further internal conflict that might well have made composition more difficult arose from the reputation foisted suddenly on Brahms by Schumann's "Neue Bahnen" accolade of October 1853. As the younger composer wrote to Schumann, "The public praise that you have deigned to bestow upon me will have so greatly increased the expectations of the musical world regarding my work that I do not know how I shall manage to do even approximate justice to it."[1] Brahms never fully overcame the tendency to self-consciousness and self-criticism generated by "Neue Bahnen."

Brahms's anxieties seem to have converged on one piece of music, the Piano Concerto in D Minor, op. 15. Its unusually long and tortured gestation, extending from 1854 to 1857, reflects the composer's agitated state of mind in this period. As has often been pointed out, op. 15 embodies Brahms's most powerful emotional and musical relationships—with the Schumanns and with Beethoven, especially Beethoven's own titanic statement in D minor, the Ninth Symphony.[2]

Both life and musical composition began to flow more easily for Brahms toward the end of 1857. He left Düsseldorf, accepted his first official position at the Court of Detmold, and soon began once again to conceive and complete large sonata-type works: the two serenades, opp. 11 and 16, composed in 1857–60, and the String Sextet in B♭, op. 18, composed in 1859–60. In technique and aesthetic, these works bear little resemblance to the B-Major Trio. As has often been noted, they are essentially throwbacks, representing (in Tovey's words) "a deliberate reaction toward classical sonata style and procedure."[3] Brahms abandons the strange fusion of Lisztian transformation and Beethovenian development for a purer idiom that recalls Haydn and early Beethoven (especially in the serenades) and, as James Webster has shown, Schubert (in the sextet).[4]

The creative rhythm of most composers might lead us to expect some perpetuation of this neo-classical style in the large chamber works Brahms completed in 1861–62—the Piano Quartets in G Minor and A Major, opp. 25 and 26, and the Piano Quintet in F Minor, op. 34 (first scored as a string quintet). But we find no such reassuring continuity. Although the sonata-form movements retain the large dimensions of the serenades and sextet, they turn back abruptly to confront the compositional issues Brahms had explored in his piano sonatas and trio of 1852–54. This aspect of the piano quartets lends some plausibility to Kalbeck's claim that they were begun (and even given trial performances) at Detmold in 1857–58, thus before opp. 11, 16, and 18.[5] Brahms may have found himself unable to complete the quartets—just as he had been unable earlier to finish the D-Minor Concerto and the C♯-Minor Piano Quartet—and decided to freshen his compositional palette with the simpler, primary colors of the serenades.

Even in its final form (the only one surviving), the G-Minor Piano Quartet seems to struggle for large-scale coherence. Although this is the one work of

[1]Johannes Brahms, *Letters of Clara Schumann and Johannes Brahms*, 1: 1.

[2]See the discussion in Gal, *Johannes Brahms*, pp. 111–17.

[3]Tovey, "Brahms's Chamber Music," p. 230.

[4]Webster, "Schubert's Sonata Form," pp. 61–62.

[5]See Kalbeck, *Johannes Brahms*, 1: 232 (note), 287, 312. Kalbeck reports that Joachim recalled having played the two piano quartets with Brahms at Detmold, and that Karl Bargheer remembered a performance of the G-Minor Quartet there. Geiringer (*Brahms*, pp. 227–28) adopts the 1857–58 dating for these works. Brahms himself, however, noted "Herbst 1861" for both opp. 25 and 26 in his catalogue (see Orel, "Eigenhändiges Werkverzeichnis," p. 534).

Brahms that Schoenberg chose to orchestrate, its musical processes do not yet constitute developing variation as Schoenberg understood the term (and as it has been defined in Chapter 1). Genuinely developing variation appears only with the A-Major Piano Quartet, op. 26, whose warmth and lyricism seem to melt away the troubles of its G-minor sibling. The magnificent F-Minor Quintet, op. 34, builds on the understated triumph of op. 26 and at the same time captures the Beethovenian energy and technique only hinted at in Brahms's earlier F-minor attempt, the op. 5 Sonata. In the quintet, Brahms for the first time employs meter as a tool of developing variation: the thematic-motivic processes actually bring about a displacement of the metrical framework.

II

In his review of Brahms's first concerts before the Viennese public in November 1862, Eduard Hanslick praised the talents of the young pianist and composer but could not warm to the G-Minor Piano Quartet. "For one thing, the themes are insignificant," he complained. "Brahms has a tendency to favor themes whose contrapuntal viability is far greater than the essential inner content. The themes of this quartet are dry and prosaic. In the course of events they are given a wealth of imaginative derivatives, but the effectiveness of a whole is impossible without significant themes."[6] A year earlier Joachim had written Brahms in much the same terms about the lack of genuine *Erfindung*, or invention, in the themes of the first movement, although like Hanslick he admitted that "what you make out of the themes is often truly superb."[7] From a more technical standpoint Carl Dahlhaus has recently echoed the views of Brahms's contemporaries, for in his analysis of op. 25 Dahlhaus too stresses that the themes of Brahms's first group are "in themselves of no great significance" and that our interest is held only by what Brahms builds from them.[8]

The opening themes of the works we examined in Chapter 2 display strong, "significant" profiles—in rhythm (as in the basic motives of opp. 1, 5, and 8), in melody (op. 8), and in harmony (the powerful descending bass line of op. 5 and the sweep of op. 8). The opening of op. 25, however, is utterly neutral: its theme unfolds inscrutably in even quarter notes and (at first) bare, unharmonized octaves (ex. 22). As Klaus Velten has perceptively remarked, this greyness seems to serve a specific purpose: "Brahms presents his motives without any rhythmic profile. The listener thus concentrates only on the interval content."[9]

---

[6]Eduard Hanslick, *Music Criticisms 1846–99*, p. 84.

[7]Brahms, *Briefwechsel mit Joseph Joachim*, 1: 303.

[8]Dahlhaus, "Issues in Composition," p. 49.

[9]Velten, *Schönbergs Instrumentation*, p. 67.

EXAMPLE 22: Brahms, Piano Quartet, op. 25, I.

EXAMPLE 23: Brahms, Piano Quartet, op. 25, I.

For Velten and Dahlhaus, we recall, the primary interval in the first theme of op. 25 (1a) is the second, which is heard ascending in bar 1 (F♯–G) and descending in bars 2, 3, and 4 (E♭–D, etc.). Theme 1b (bars 11–27), the central part of a large A B A′ first group, becomes even more obsessed with the descending second, which now assumes a rhythmic profile withheld in 1a, appearing in sequence and imitation. In 1a′ (bar 27), a counterstatement that blends into the transition, the strings isolate the half-step motive and drive it upward sequentially—presumably to balance the downward sequences of 1b. The ur-interval also appears in an important new sixteenth-note figure that the piano introduces underneath the counterstatement. This motive (x) seems to be a free, yet recognizable, diminution of the second bar of the theme (ex. 23). (The simultaneous presence of the original theme, of course, strengthens the association.) Motive x gradually comes to dominate the transition, exploding outward in bar 35, where its third expands to an octave.

The thematic process of Brahms's first fifty bars is thus fully as economical as in opp. 5 and 8, yet still fails to qualify as developing variation. Brahms does not, as in the earlier works, build his exposition as a series of transformations—the procedure of metamorphosis is reserved for the recapitulation, as we shall see—but neither does he treat his primary interval as flexibly as in the examples Schoenberg so admired. The interval and its related motive x are indeed ubiquitous; but the feeling is less of development than of repetition or reiteration, largely because the first group of op. 25 keeps returning stubbornly to theme 1a. The theme, or a portion of it, appears four separate times in only fifty measures: at the opening (bar 1), at the outburst that concludes 1b (bar 21), at the counterstatement (1a′, bar 27), and just before the second group (bar 41). This last return is truly surprising, since the preceding bars clearly prepare for a new theme and a new key (the dominant), both of which are then kept waiting by the odd thematic regression.

Although the thematic returns halt forward development, they seem to form part of a larger compositional strategy, a process somewhat like the proto-developing variation examined in the Trio, op. 8. Brahms keeps 1a continually in our ears during the first group so that across the second group he can build up a chain of associations with that theme; the chain links up with the literal return of 1a at the start of the development section (bar 161). The process unfolds on an even more ambitious scale than in op. 8. In the trio, as Tovey remarks, Brahms attempts at least to preserve the relative proportions, if not the customary dimensions, of classical sonata form: the first and second groups are about equal in length. But Brahms renounces any such symmetry in op. 25 by dwarfing his first group with a virtual parade of four large, rounded secondary themes, each of which is provided with an ample counterstatement.

Clara Schumann was nonplused by the second group of the quartet. She wrote Brahms that the exposition ["*der erste Teil*"] was "too little in G minor and too much in D major."[10] Joachim likewise confessed to the composer that "the long D-major [section] does not seem to me symmetrical with the concise first theme."[11] James Webster adopts a more charitable view (indeed, a generous one), calling the succession of themes "one of the largest coherent second groups in history." He also remarks that "the means whereby Brahms keeps this gigantic section from breaking down would make a fascinating study."[12] As I have suggested, the "breakdown" seems to be prevented—although it can scarcely be said that coherence is achieved—by the ongoing chain of associations with 1a. Let us trace this process in the second group.

The bold cello theme (2a) that begins at bar 50 at first sounds, and is surely intended to sound, new and refreshingly different from the much-reiterated 1a (despite Velten's claim that the rising chromatic motive F♮–G–G♯–A is built from the familiar seconds).[13] It presents itself as the first full-blooded melody of the movement, and yet soon abandons that role. The first, very subtle deviation is a metrical elision. The five-bar antecedent phrase (bars 50–54) ends on a normal half cadence, but the consequent begins prematurely in the same bar. At bar 56 the theme renounces melodic as well as metrical symmetry when, in the midst of the presumed consequent, motives from the first group suddenly appear over an unexpected, chromatically descending bass line. The violin and cello

[10]Brahms, *Letters of Clara Schumann and Johannes Brahms*, 1: 132.

[11]Brahms, *Briefwechsel mit Joachim*, 1: 306.

[12]Webster, "Schubert's Sonata Form," p. 64.

[13]Velten, *Schönbergs Instrumentation*, pp. 71, 178.

EXAMPLE 24: Brahms, Piano Quartet, op. 25, I.

present motive x in augmentation (bars 56–57) and then a cadential figure directly derived from the distinctive closing idea of theme 1b (bar 18; ex. 24).

After a counterstatement of the entire theme by the piano (bars 59–68) and a sequential modulatory extension of the cadential figure that provides a new preparation for D major (68–78), secondary thematic material ventures forth once again. 2b begins as a major-mode rendering of 2a: it shares the earlier theme's initial chromatic ascent, as well as the rhythm of its first two bars. Then 2b goes its own way, seeming to break free of the gravitational pull of the first group.

With theme 2c, however, the association begins to build again. This is a vigorous, rustic melody accompanied by a drone bass of open fifths. It seems to occupy the same innocent world as the E-major pastorale of op. 8; it also occupies a similar place in the sonata structure, serving as a resolution or fulfillment of previous material. The principal motive of 2c derives clearly from the neighbor-note figure of motive x—which Brahms had strategically kept in our consciousness by recalling it at the transition to 2b (bars 77–78) and employing it as accompaniment to 2b itself. Now Brahms elegantly shifts its metrical emphasis. Beginning on an upbeat, x pushes through to its third note and thus gives theme 2c an appropriate and attractive vigor. A deceptive cadence at the close of 2c's counterstatement (bar 113) leads into a sequential extension similar to that of 2a at bar 68. Also recalling that passage is the prominent descending second, which ultimately hearkens back to the first group. The association with 1b becomes explicit in bar 119, where the sighing, slurred seconds directly recall bar 16.

In the original op. 8 Trio, Brahms carefully deploys thematic allusions to the first group so as to prepare the pastorale transformation and then the repeat of the exposition. Here the reminiscences lead into what I call 2d/codetta (beginning at bar 130). In size and general structure, this segment functions much like the previous secondary themes: it is large, well-articulated, and has a full counterstatement (bars 141–53), which is then extended. At the same time the tranquil return to first-group material fulfills the role of a traditional sonata-form codetta (although the diminutive seems a misnomer here). Bar 130 brings back the opening of 1a, now in the major mode and appropriately modified to suit its new position in the sonata structure. At the opening of the movement, 1a had begun on the fifth scale degree, D, and, after its first bar, had glided sinuously away from the tonic. In 2d, however, the same thematic idea begins on the first scale degree (now D), settles peacefully on the fifth, and then immediately ushers in the sighing seconds of 1b to reaffirm the dominant.

Theme 2d thus alters the mood and the mode of 1a, while retaining its important interval structure. We have seen this kind of motivic reinterpretation before, in the transformations of opp. 5 and 8. Yet here the thematic process sheds its former extravagances and assumes a much more sober cast. Although the large, rounded themes (2a–2d) that constitute the second group indeed serve (as Velten observes) to "fulfill" the less stable, non-melodic first theme, they are not apotheoses like their counterparts in the sonata and trio. Brahms no longer dazzles us with the metamorphosis of an individual motive or theme. Instead he employs small motives that are in themselves "insignificant" (the second and its close relative, motive x), to build larger themes. The procedure begins to suggest, however faintly, the methods of genuinely developing variation, although the exposition is still clumsily articulated.

The bloated thematic process of op. 25 puts considerable strain on the correlation between harmony and form. In opp. 1, 5, and 8 Brahms seemed unable— or perhaps unwilling—to make harmonic progression and sonata superstructure coincide persuasively: the expositions of both the F-Minor Sonata and the trio lose their tonal direction by wandering deep into the subdominant area (D♭ in op. 5, E in op. 8). In the piano quartet, Brahms retains a single tonal area for the entire second group but still fails to create any prolonged harmonic tension. The problem arises largely because of the sharply articulated thematic design. With a garrulity that borders on the comic, Brahms prepares the dominant no less than four separate times in the exposition: in the first transition (bars 35–41), in the extension of the counterstatement of 2a (especially in 75–78), before 2c (98–100), and again before 2d (120–30). He has not yet discovered how to achieve variety and coherence over a harmonic root without resorting to naive tonal regression.

Joachim put his finger on one of the most awkward spots in the exposition, the abrupt return to 1a in G minor at bar 42 in the first transition. He wrote to Brahms:

Among other things, the transition to the second group [*Mittelsatz*] from p. 4 to p. 5 [of the autograph ms.] almost caused me pain. The G minor . . . sounds too illogical, since it arrives just when, after many (indeed, frequent!) short G-minor cadences, we have at last swung round to another important key. And all of this only for the sake, it seems to me, of an unfortunate sequence, from which you must then wind your way back to the main idea by means of a harmonized scale.[14]

---

[14]Brahms, *Briefwechsel mit Joachim*, 1: 306.

Tovey, who could find no passage in op. 25 that fitted Joachim's description, assumed that Brahms had amended the offending spot;[15] but in fact the published work still contains the source of Joachim's pain. The "many short G-minor cadences" are those in bars 33–37, which precede the preparation of the "important key," D major. The "unfortunate sequence" is, of course, the three-fold antiphonal exchange between strings and piano in bars 41–46; the "harmonized scale" ascends through bars 47–48.

Joachim's ear told him true, for the intrusion of G minor upon the dominant of its dominant in bar 41 is indeed harsh. Why, when he has at last succeeded in getting free of the oppressive tonic and first theme, should Brahms suddenly regress and repeat the whole operation? He could, in fact, have proceeded from bar 40 directly to bar 49—and apparently considered doing so. The autograph of op. 25, now in the Gesellschaft der Musikfreunde in Vienna, reveals that Brahms attempted two alternative revisions, whereby he removed the "painful" segment and spliced as in examples 25a and b.[16] In the first attempt, the first beat of bar 41 links up neatly with the second beat of 49. In the second, Brahms gives the piano a brief transition based on the opening theme. Brahms rejected both possibilities, however, and (against Joachim's advice) let the passage remain in its original form.

The recapitulation of op. 25 contains a harmonic-formal-thematic miscalculation on an even larger scale. Several commentators have observed and admired how Brahms takes advantage of the double-theme structure of his first group to begin the reprise not with 1a, but with 1b in the tonic major (bar 237).[17] The conception of this recapitulation is indeed remarkable, but to my ear its execution falls short of Brahms's apparent intentions, for G major simply does not *sound* like a tonic here.

The end of the development section (see Appendix, ex. C, p. 178) moves to D major, which Brahms confirms with strong Neapolitan and dominant chords (bars 226–31). Instead of then pushing through to the tonic, however, the retransition lingers on D and soon vanishes into silence (bar 235). Because D major has made itself so comfortable—it has effectively been tonicized—the subsequent G major sounds not like the resolution of a V–I progression, but like a subdominant episode. We recall that at the analogous spot in the first movement of op. 1, Brahms's dominant stubbornly refuses to act like a dominant: instead of pressing toward resolution, the harmonies actually regress along the circle of fifths. The awkwardness of the op. 25 retransition is less blatant—its harmonic

---

[15]Tovey, "Brahms's Chamber Music," p. 241.

[16]I am grateful to Flynn Warmington of Brandeis University for sharing with me her reconstruction of Brahms's attempted revisions of this passage.

[17]See, for example, Tovey, "Brahms's Chamber Music," p. 241; Keys, *Brahms Chamber Music*, p. 14; and Webster, "Schubert's Sonata Form," p. 64.

EXAMPLE 25: Brahms's alternative revisions for Piano Quartet, op. 25, I.

progressions do not grate on the ear as in op. 1 or the "painful" transition of the exposition—but we still sense Brahms's difficulty in proceeding persuasively across the important joints in the sonata structure.

Webster has observed that Brahms's retransition and modal surprise at the recapitulation are strongly indebted to the analogous moments in the first movement of Schubert's String Quartet in G major (op. 161, D.887). Both retransitions, he notes, "die away to a *pianissimo* dominant" articulated by *pizzicato* strings.[18] Schubert's first theme then enters in minor, instead of the expected major; Brahms reverses this procedure.

Webster is certainly right about the borrowing, but he has missed its most revealing feature: the precise way in which the two passages "die away" to their dominants. Like Brahms, Schubert employs a strong secondary dominant and a prominent ♭VI (bars 252–63); but he organizes his harmonies over an ascending bass line of almost Beethovenian power and cogency (cf. my discussion of the *Appassionata* retransition in Chapter 2). The C♯ of bar 252 rises inexorably step by step up to the G of 261, and then sinks more rapidly back down to D across 263–67; the individual chords are carried aloft by this exciting bass ascent and thus never stop to affirm D. (The A[7] and E♭ chords do not appear in root position.) Even at the arrival in bar 267 we do not mistake D for a tonic: Schubert includes the seventh, C♮, which—despite the *diminuendo* and thinning of texture—yearns for tonic resolution. Brahms was surely not unaware of the stability of his own D-major triad; like any first-year harmony student he knew that a flatted seventh would have propelled the chord toward tonic resolution. But I think he miscalculated the effect of G major which, in order to make his retransition work, must sound like the tonic. As it stands, the chord is sweet and radiant, but its power is vitiated by harmonic and formal ambiguities.

Since 1b has usurped the opening position in the first group, the place it originally occupied must be recomposed (1b'; see ex. C). Hence, Brahms embellishes the descending second, preceding it with a new upward-striving motive (cello, bar 249); he then inverts and extends the original cadence figure (cf. bars 19–20 and 255–58). The new 1b' preserves the original modal contrast of the first group by beginning in D minor, but the recomposition is uninspired. The preceding major-mode 1b has said about all that need be said with the interval of the second, whose ornamentation in bar 249 now seems contrived. Furthermore, Brahms gives 1b' a new, equivocal role that the original 1b never had and that it seems unsuited to fulfill, for it behaves as a kind of retransition, pushing toward the tonic cadence of bar 265 almost as if to compensate for the weakness of the earlier "retransition" in bars 225–36. In short, 1b' is neither fish nor fowl, neither a convincing substitute for 1b nor a persuasive retransition. Once again, Brahms's formal, thematic, and harmonic procedures appear unsynchronized.[19]

The remainder of the recapitulation need not occupy us much further. Its most striking moment is the transformation of 2c in the tonic minor (bar 303).

---

[18]Webster, "Schubert's Sonata Form," p. 64.

[19]Flynn Warmington (see fn. 16) reports that Brahms considered eliminating bars 259–64—that is, the last segment of 1b', which reintroduces the opening thematic material and prepares the cadence to G minor. The excision would have made good sense. In its initial appearance (bars 21–26), this passage served to modulate from B♭ back to G minor; but now the modulation is no longer necessary, since throughout 1b' (bars 247–58), we are already on the dominant of G minor. Thus, as Brahms realized, bar 258 could lead directly to 265. As he had done in the exposition, however, Brahms changed his mind and retained bars 259–64, which are harmonically redundant.

As in the Lisztian metamorphoses of opp. 5 and 8, Brahms radically alters the mood while retaining pitches and harmonic structure. The once exuberant 2c (*"bacchantisch,"* Kalbeck calls it)[20] becomes a *tranquillo* feathery whisper shared only by the string instruments. But more significant than the transformational technique itself is its deployment in the sonata structure. The new 2c does not emerge from a continuous process, as in the earlier works, but stands as an isolated metamorphosis. Brahms has, in a sense, the best of both worlds, for by its position the new 2c fulfills both the demands of the sonata principle and Brahms's apparent impulse for such dazzling thematic reclothings.

The new 2c perhaps epitomizes Brahms's formal and thematic procedures in op. 25. Safely contained within the recapitulation, the transformation does not dominate the sonata structure, as it tended to in opp. 1, 5, and 8. Indeed, the sonata design of the piano quartet is fundamentally more conservative than those of the sonatas and trio. Brahms has abandoned the extravagant devices of the earlier works in favor of a thematic-formal process that is more sober and outwardly "insignificant." This process—in which brief motives undergo a limited development across highly articulated themes—stands midway between the continuous transformation of the op. 5 Sonata and the fluid developing variation of both the second Piano Quartet, op. 26 in A Major, and the Piano Quintet, op. 34.

III

In "Neue Bahnen," Schumann dubbed Brahms's piano sonatas "veiled symphonies," observing how they seem to strive beyond their medium.[21] Schoenberg apparently felt the same about the G-Minor Piano Quartet, and actually set about unveiling its symphonic possibilities by orchestrating the work in 1937.[22] He justified this extraordinary endeavor with characteristically laconic and direct remarks:

> My reasons:
> 1. I like this piece.
> 2. It is seldom played.
> 3. It is always very badly played, because the better the pianist, the louder he plays and you hear nothing from the strings. I wanted once to hear everything, and this I achieved.[23]

[20]Kalbeck, *Johannes Brahms*, 1: 449.

[21]Included in Robert Schumann, *On Music and Musicians*, p. 253.

[22]Arnold Schoenberg, *Johannes Brahms: Klavierquartett*. The score has been published as vol. 26 of Schoenberg's *Sämtliche Werke*.

[23]Schoenberg, *Letters*, p. 207.

As might be expected from a musician who thought and wrote about Brahms as profoundly as Schoenberg did, the orchestral score represents more than just an eccentric gesture of homage. In fact, it is a document of critical analysis. Much like the examples from his textbook, *Fundamentals of Musical Composition*, the orchestration becomes a purely musical explanation of Brahms's motivic procedures.

Klaus Velten has shown that Schoenberg's score sets in relief some of the continuous development that reaches across the relatively closed segments of the second group.[24] Schoenberg isolates the seconds of theme 2d in a pointillistic manner reminiscent of Webern's orchestrations of Bach. Expanding Brahms's original concept of antiphony between piano and strings, Schoenberg divides the theme among strongly contrasting groups of instruments. In the first phrase (bars 130–31), the horns take over the piano statement while oboe, bass clarinet, and cello play the strings' response. Schoenberg changes the instrumentation for the second phrase (132–33), where trumpet and trombone converse with flute, viola, and double bass. Schoenberg continues to vary the scoring with great imaginativeness, especially when Brahms's minor seconds are exchanged between the parts at shorter time intervals (136–38; see Appendix, ex. D, p. 181).

In theme 2d, then, Schoenberg spotlights motivic details already prominent in Brahms's original score. But in 2a Schoenberg performs an act of genuine analysis by actually extracting an important motive, motive x, from Brahms's piano accompaniment. This motive first appears as an accompanimental figure in 1a'/transition (bar 27) and then steps forth more boldly (at 56) to disrupt the symmetry of 2a. Few listeners notice, however, that x is also present subliminally among the flowing eighth notes of the piano in bars 50–51 (F♮–E–F♮–A, on the first and third beats of each bar). Schoenberg's sharp ear—which does indeed seem to "hear everything"—picks it up. In his orchestration, x appears in half notes in the first flute and bass clarinet; it is also played in inversion by the second flute and first bassoon (see Appendix, ex. E, p. 182). Schoenberg's ingenious scoring thus makes the development of x more logical and continuous and—if we have listened carefully—prepares the more obvious appearance of the motive in bar 56. Unlike Rudolf Réti's note extractions, Schoenberg's do not distort the music but illuminate it by revealing significant features or processes we might otherwise fail to notice.

Besides Schoenberg's brief remarks, cited above, and the orchestration itself, there is one further document that reveals something of his response to Brahms's piano quartet—really to Brahms's music in general. This is a single manuscript page, essentially a "doodle," preserved in the archives of the Arnold Schoenberg Institute and never before reproduced or discussed (see fig. 1). It must date from 1937 or later.

---

[24]See Velten, *Schönbergs Instrumentation*, pp. 82–86. See also Peter Gülke, "Über Schönbergs Brahms-Bearbeitung."

FIGURE 1: Manuscript page written by Arnold Schoenberg. Reproduced, by permission, from the archives of the Arnold Schoenberg Institute, Los Angeles.

Schoenberg had read or heard about (or perhaps had seen a facsimile of) Brahms's witty inscription on the autograph-fan of Johann Strauss's step-daughter. A great admirer of Strauss, Brahms had notated the first few bars of the *Blue Danube*, a work "unfortunately not by [*leider nicht von*] Johannes Brahms." After several attempts to imitate Brahms's handwriting, Schoenberg reproduced the entire inscription.[25] Beneath it, in what is now distinctly his own hand, Schoenberg wrote out the opening bars of Brahms's op. 25, and the phrase of regret analogous to Brahms's: "Unfortunately by [*leider von*] Johannes Brahms

[25]A photograph of Fräulein Strauss's fan appears in Karl Geiringer's Brahms biography, in the first German edition (Rohrer, 1935, facing p. 73); in the first American edition (Houghton Mifflin, 1936, facing p. 150); and in the first and second English editions (Allen & Unwin, 1936 and 1947, facing pp. 150 and 225 respectively). Schoenberg may have seen it here, or he may have seen the actual fan in Vienna. However, his imitation is not very accurate; he follows the spirit rather than the letter of Brahms's inscription. Brahms notated the waltz polyphonically (and thus more faithfully): the A of the rising triadic figure is sustained through bars 2–4, while an upper part (of which Brahms gives only the rhythm, not the proper pitches) plays the descending response. Furthermore, Brahms signed his first name in full, not in the abbreviated version ("Johs") given by Schoenberg.

. . . only orchestrated by Arnold Schoenberg." There could scarcely be a stronger, or more touching, demonstration of Schoenberg's identification with Brahms.

IV

It has often been observed that Brahms's first works in a medium tended to appear in pairs. The First and Second Symphonies emerged in 1876 and 1877 respectively; the two String Quartets, op. 51, were published in 1873; and the two Clarinet Sonatas, op. 120, in 1895. So too with the G-Minor and A-Major Piano Quartets, opp. 25 and 26, which were completed in 1861 and published in 1863. Like the other paired works, these quartets seem to stand in a special relationship: the first is turbulent and intense, the second more relaxed and expansive. Brahms himself was evidently more comfortable with op. 26, to judge from Clara Schumann's comments in a letter: "I must admit that you are right after all and that it [op. 26] is more beautiful than the G-minor, more important from the musical standpoint, and the first movement is much more finished."[26] From the musical standpoint I have taken in this study, the A-Major Quartet is indeed more important and more finished, for the sonata structure of its first movement engages with the principle of developing variation in a way that the G-Minor Quartet does not. We encounter for the first time in Brahms the flexible kind of developing variation that Schoenberg so admired in the Andante of op. 51, no. 2.

To summarize: the first movement comprises a more fluid, continuous process—or as Ivor Keys expresses it, "transition"—than any previous work of Brahms: "The linked procession of the exposition, whereby a foreground feature of one theme evolves from an unobtrusive background feature of a former one, is a beautiful example of the art of transition, though indeed 'transition,' with its implication of a period spent getting from somewhere to somewhere else, seems a misnomer."[27] Occasionally the motivic development triggers a metrical displacement, in which the theme moves outside its notated metrical framework. The procedures of developing variation also begin to obscure the conventional boundaries of the sonata form, especially the juncture between the exposition and development sections and between the development and the recapitulation. Yet with all this fluency and continuity, Brahms still manages to indulge his instinct for thematic transformation: a wonderfully tuneful apotheosis of the fragmentary main theme occupies the still center of the development section.

The first group (see ex. 26) retains the double-theme design of earlier works, but avoids the articulated closure that makes the openings of opp. 5 and 25

---

[26]Brahms, *Letters of Clara Schumann and Brahms*, 1: 157.

[27]Keys, *Brahms Chamber Music*, p. 17.

EXAMPLE 26: Brahms, Piano Quartet, op. 26, I.

stodgy. As Tovey points out, Brahms constructs "a complete binary organization in miniature," a scale-model sonata structure.[28] Theme 1a yields at bar 5 to 1b, a related idea, which prolongs the dominant and then leads back to a counter-statement (or recapitulation) of the original idea at bar 9. After four measures, 1b returns a fifth below its original pitch, thus behaving much like a second subject in a recapitulation; it expands into a small "development" (somewhat displaced, if we are to be strict about the sonata-form analogy). The tonic and theme 1a return at bar 27. This quasi-sonata plan of the first group keeps the two principal thematic ideas continually before our ears in a manner more cogent (and more appropriate to sonata style) than, for example, the luxurious A B A B A opening of the B-Major Trio, op. 8.

The analogous 1b themes of earlier works derive their content from 1a by either a stunning transformation (op. 5) or a sober interval extraction (op. 25). Especially when exaggerated by strong full or half cadences, both procedures seem somewhat stiff. In op. 26, however, the two themes unfold by a process so fluent and flexible that it almost defies verbal description. The diffident 1a seems literally answered—rather than simply followed—by the assured and measured tread of 1b. Theme 1a drifts immediately away from the tonic into tenuous subdominant regions, at first vi, then IV, then V/ii and ii; each chord appears in root position, as though unable to establish a firm harmonic syntax and smooth voice leading. But 1b leads confidently back to the dominant, on which it retains a solid footing for four bars.

Listeners no doubt sense a motivic relationship between 1a and 1b, but no analysis has, to my knowledge, ever pinpointed Brahms's remarkable motivic process, especially his subtle manipulation of duple and triple rhythms. Theme 1a presents two basic motives: x, a triplet figure composed of neighbor-note alternation and a descending third; and y, in duple rhythm, which rises a fourth and descends a whole step. Both motives begin on weak beats and move to a

---

[28]Donald F. Tovey, *Essays in Musical Analysis: Chamber Music*, p. 194.

downbeat; these rhythmic aspects, as well as the alternation between duple and triple division of the quarter note, give 1a its halting, hesitant quality. In 1b, motive x acquires the more secure duple rhythm and now sits serenely *on* the downbeat (x', bar 5). It changes its position yet again in the next bar, now straddling the second and third beats (its interval of a third has expanded to a fourth). When bar 7 repeats and ornaments bar 6, the first two notes (G♯–A) are elaborated into a triplet version of motive y (y'), which then dovetails with the duple x.

As in the Andante from the A-Minor String Quartet, all this fluid motivic development unfolds within outwardly regular phrases of two and four bars. Four-bar phrases are also characteristic of the large second group, where, as Tovey observes, they help to balance the "exceptional richness" of the thematic process.[29] In the second group of the G-Minor Quartet, Brahms had generally avoided such regular phrase structure—for example in the overlapping five-bar segments of theme 2a. One suspects the asymmetry was intended in part to compensate for his lack of a developmental thematic style. In op. 26, Brahms needs no such camouflage: he wants to display his newly won fluency in the clearest light.

The second group takes shape as a series of lyrical fragments in which, as in the first theme, motivic particles develop, split apart, and recombine quite freely. These fragments continually refer back to the first group (as in opp. 8 and 25) and also undergo a remarkable process of reduction, down to the two-note figure of bars 86ff., and then reconstruction into the broad melody that closes the exposition.

After the elaborate and energetic transition (bars 27–53), the laconic second subject (2a, bar 53) surprises us by returning unabashedly to the introspective mood and concise thematic material of the first group. The rising eighth-note figure moving toward a downbeat distinctly recalls motive y. Indeed, the exact pitch relationships of y appear in the last four notes of bar 53 (G♯–A–C♯–B). To ensure that we do not miss the allusion to theme 1a, Brahms places in the cello a freely inverted triplet version of the other principal motive, x.

The third statement of the y-derived figure (bar 55) is abruptly halted at the third note, G♯, and Brahms introduces a new idea, 2b (57–59), characterized by dotted rhythms and syncopation across the barline. This in turn gives way to 2c (bar 61), which revives the smooth, stepwise eighth-note motion of 1b, as well as motive x in both its two-note and triplet forms (B–A♯–B, in bars 61 and 65).

The thematic complex of 2a–2b–2c is now repeated in varied form (thus 2a'–2b'–2c'), moving toward the dominant minor. But a new development diverts 2c', which no longer falls into two parallel four-bar phrases (as in 61–68). Instead of providing the expected half cadence, the fourth bar (80) becomes a sequential repetition of the third bar and leads by a crescendo to a new thematic idea at bar

---

[29]Tovey, *Essays: Chamber Music*, p. 195.

81 (2d). Brahms creates this "new" theme by a splendid application of the linkage technique examined in Chapter 1: theme 2d evolves directly from the descending eighth-note pattern of the preceding bar (and from the rhythmic pattern of 2c as a whole).

The first melodic figure of 2a now reappears as the second bar of 2d. This represents a further striking development, for the figure is placed not on the first, strong bar of the phrase, as it was in bar 53, but on the second, weaker one. The metrical shift represents the first stage in a process of "liquidation" (as Schoenberg would call it), whereby the 2a figure is reduced to a mere two-note fragment (bars 86–94). Then, by another elegant use of the linkage technique, the fragment is reconstructed into a full four-bar phrase (2e, bar 95): F♯–E (bar 94) becomes F♯–E–D♯, etc.

The reconstruction culminates in a return to E major at bar 106 and the entrance of the first extended melodic gesture of the movement, a splendid fulfillment of the originally laconic 2b. In its earlier appearances (2b, bars 57–60, and 2b′, 73–75), the theme had given way to another idea after only four bars; now (as 2b″) it attains genuine melodic status. The first few bars retain the original rhythm and contour, but 2b″ is utterly relaxed and open in demeanor: it no longer pushes impatiently upward, but is content to circle around G♯ in its first three bars. Brahms manifests here the same impulse by which he brought about melodic fulfillment in the expositions of opp. 5 and 8. The apotheosis is now achieved less by a stunning thematic transformation—the basic mood of 2b is not changed—than by subtle modifications in the theme's pitch and phrase structure. (It is of interest that, like the similarly placed pastorale of op. 8 and the *bacchantisch* dance of op. 25, this theme has a repeating pedal point.)

Despite its greater melodic breadth, 2b″ has a less regular phrase structure than the preceding themes in op. 26. Its nine-bar expanse cannot be easily divided into symmetrical segments, largely because of the great metrical freedom within. We recall how in both the Andante of the A-Minor String Quartet and in the F-Major Violoncello Sonata, Schoenberg demonstrated that liquid motivic development tends to override the notated meter. Here too, the theme seems to obey only the rules of its own internal motivic expansion and, as a result, dislocates or obscures the written bar line (ex. 27).

Although the first beat of bar 106 provides a clear downbeat and a cadence to E, the new thematic idea begins only with the second and third beats. Our ears reorient themselves metrically to hear B–E, the motive with a dotted rhythm, as an upbeat to the G♯, which takes on the character of a downbeat; because it is tied over the bar line, this G♯ conceals the notated downbeat of bar 107. For two bars the theme thus seems to move in a displaced triple meter (as suggested in example 27). But Brahms's material is too volatile even for this irregular regularity, for in bars 108–10 a duple pattern emerges, which we tend to hear in $\frac{2}{4}$ (or $\frac{4}{4}$). On a higher level, the six beats extending from the tied B suggest a $\frac{3}{2}$ grouping. On the last beat of the notated bar 110, Brahms reintroduces the dotted rhythm; it seems at first to be an "extra" beat in the duple pattern,

EXAMPLE 27: Brahms, Piano Quartet, op. 26, I.

but proves in fact to be an upbeat, which now aligns properly with the bar line
and guides us at last into the notated triple meter. In my hypothetical rebarring
of the theme in example 27, I adopt the same principles that Schoenberg did in
his metrical analysis of the quartet theme (ex. 4): analogous notes or figures are
placed in the same part of a bar. The dotted rhythm appears as an upbeat;
rhythmic or melodic accents appear as downbeats or strong beats.

As with Schoenberg's example, however, this rebarring does not adequately
convey the metrical structure of the passage, for it includes only the melody in
the violin. Although the viola's rhythm follows the violin's, the accompaniment
in the cello adheres to the written meter, arpeggiating on every downbeat. There
is thus a tension between theme and accompaniment, which together seem to
resist any firm metrical framework.

These deliberate ambiguities, and the refusal of the counterstatement to
cadence (bars 120ff.), prevent 2b″ from settling into traditional closing-group
complacency. The final themes of Brahms's earlier expositions (especially opp.
2, 5, 8, and 25), as well as those of many classical composers, virtually close up
shop before giving way to a clearly demarcated development section. In op. 26,
however, the volatile 2b″ will not be so contained; it propels us forcefully back
to the repeat of the exposition or forward into the development—toward the
magnificent transformation that serves as the real fulfillment of the exposition's
lyrical fragments.

The transformation of theme 1a into a full eight-bar melody in C minor
occupies the center of the development (bar 144; see Appendix, ex. F, p. 183). As
in the original theme, motives x and y alternate for four measures; but now the
uneasy tension between duple and triple rhythms has vanished, and the blunt
quarter-note downbeats have been softened into slurred eighth notes. Rather
than developing into 1b after four bars, 1a now generates a purely melodic
continuation—one that still, however, uses the y motive—and then rounds itself
off with a half cadence to the dominant.

Tovey was impressed by this moment and characterized it in terms much
like those I have used to describe Brahms's earlier, Lisztian metamorphoses:

Such lines of thematic treatment were first invented by Brahms. Their peculiarity is that, while they utterly change the whole tone and mood of the theme, they differ so slightly from their original note by note that no intermediate steps are possible; whereas before Brahms's work all notable thematic transformations were gradual, and by the time a radical difference was attained, there were many steps to remember in tracing the new version to its original.[30]

Tovey has pinpointed the nature of the transformation—it modifies tone and mood while retaining pitches and contour—but we must alter the latter part of his statement in light of what we have discovered about Brahms's methods. However striking and sudden the transformation may appear, it is nevertheless the result of a gradual process. The analogous transformation in the development section of op. 5, the big D♭ melody, is every bit as stunning; yet Brahms carefully prepares it, not only by reiterating its motivic elements throughout the exposition, but by reviewing the whole process at the beginning of the development. In op. 26, the motivic treatment is perhaps less obsessive, but it is nevertheless continuous and logical. The elements of 1a appear throughout the exposition; as in op. 5 (and Liszt's sonata), the theme's original form is recalled just before the transformation (bars 140–43). *Pace* Tovey, then, it is precisely our awareness and comprehension of the process that make this moment so beautiful, so convincing. The breathtaking metamorphosis culminates the developmental process in a single, striking *coup de théâtre.*

Just as Brahms pushes past the end of the exposition in order to prepare the C-minor transformation, so does he blur the formal outlines at the other end of the development section. This juncture in the sonata form had proven a difficult spot for Brahms to negotiate successfully. In the sonatas, opp. 1 and 5, he is caught out transforming his themes and fails to prepare a harmonically persuasive return to the tonic and the main theme. In op. 25 the recapitulation is also undermined, though for different reasons. In the A-Major Piano Quartet, Brahms once again de-emphasizes the harmonic return, but his procedure no longer strikes us as awkward or incompetent. As he is to do in several later works—most notably in the Third Symphony—Brahms anticipates the tonic root just *before* the return of the main theme; the harmonic and thematic recapitulations do not coincide.

Energetic development of the transition motive (bar 176) and theme 2c (bar 184) leads at bar 193 to a thunderous cadence in A minor, where an *appassionato* 2b" bursts forth. As Tovey observes, "Over the close of this [bars 200ff.] the strings and pianoforte have some discussion whether it should be major or minor. The pianoforte will have it minor, but the strings insist on major—rightly, since it is suddenly discovered that we have for some time been back in our original tonic, as is shown by the calm appearance of the first subject [1a] at

[30]Tovey, *Essays: Chamber Music,* p. 196.

the outset, an octave lower [bar 209]; thus beginning the recapitulation."[31] Tovey's account is, as always, elegant, but does not quite communicate the extraordinary aesthetic effect and formal implications of this passage; for the powerful A-minor cadence usurps the tonic key area and actually diverts our attention from the modest, quiet return of 1a. (Of course, as Tovey notes, it is only at the reappearance of 1a that we realize we have been in the tonic.)

The recapitulation here, unlike that in op. 25, presents no real formal ambiguity: when the first theme enters, we know precisely where we are in the sonata structure. Thus, for the first time in the sonata forms of Brahms we have been examining, an apparently intended lack of synchronization between harmonic and thematic processes generates no unintended formal confusion.

The first movement of op. 26 genuinely displays what Dahlhaus claimed for (but did not persuasively demonstrate in) the First Piano Concerto, op. 15: that the conventional divisions of sonata form begin to be superseded (I should prefer to say supplemented, or reinterpreted) by a procedure in which "development" extends beyond the confines of a development section. The sonata framework of op. 26 evolves by an impressively fluent application of the procedures of developing variation—by the continuous modification and recombination of brief motives (x, y) within larger themes (1a, 1b, etc.). From this viewpoint the first movement of the A-Major Piano Quartet is a landmark work, and Brahms's finest achievement up to 1861; for it succeeds, where opp. 1, 5, 8, and 25 do not, in integrating motivic development, harmonic syntax, and formal design. The sonata structure no longer dissolves into a series of undramatic transformations (as in op. 5) or into a sharply articulated parade of large themes (op. 25), but takes shape as a logical and compelling discourse in musical prose.

Op. 26 is the most lyrical of Brahms's sonata-form movements before the G-Major Violin Sonata, op. 78 (which will be examined in the next chapter). If anything, it is perhaps too consistently songful, too opulent. We recall that Arno Mitschka complains of a lack of contrast among the themes of the original op. 8 Trio; he finds them all monotonously *"lyrisch-kantabel."* Such a charge, unjust in the case of op. 8, might less unjustly be leveled at op. 26: although they vary in length and in melodic stability, the themes certainly tend to be similar in character. In his next chamber work, Brahms strikes a better balance—many would say an ideal one—between the lyrical and the dynamic. And this he achieves without giving up any thematic flexibility.

V

In its initial form as a string quintet, op. 34 was completed just a year after op. 26, in the fall of 1862. Although Brahms anguished for two years over the proper medium—the work became a two-piano sonata and then a piano quintet—the

---

[31] Tovey, *Essays: Chamber Music*, pp. 196–97.

musical substance remained virtually unchanged throughout.[32] The composition and original scoring of op. 34 seem to have been stimulated most directly by Schubert's own String Quintet, op. 163 (D.956), which is likewise written for string quartet plus an extra cello, and which Brahms came to know well during the summer of 1862.[33] Tovey claims—and James Webster has recently tried to make good on this claim—that the quintet is the most profoundly Schubertian work of Brahms's first maturity.[34] Indeed, many features recall Schubert either indirectly or directly, especially the theme of the slow movement, shifting delicately between major and minor, and the abrupt *coup de théâtre* by which Brahms moves into a remote secondary key (vi, C♯ minor) in the exposition of the first movement. Furthermore, as Tovey remarks, "The savage flat supertonic acciaccatura (D♭–C) at the end of the scherzo comes straight from the end of Schubert's Quintet, and from nowhere else in the whole history of final chords."[35]

However much the spirit of Schubert haunts the F-Minor Quintet, it is principally Beethoven's ghost that Brahms summons and attempts to come to terms with. We see Brahms adapting the techniques of developing variation in two new ways that reflect the influence of Beethoven. First, like the Beethoven of the *Appassionata*—to which Brahms seems to return again for a model—he treats a two-note motivic kernel, D♭–C (representing ♭6–5, like Beethoven's), more as an abstract pitch relationship than as a figure to be "varied." That is, D♭–C appears not only on a local thematic level, but also on the higher level of harmonic and formal structure. Brahms thereby achieves the truly Beethovenian structural integrity that had eluded him (or that he had avoided) in his earlier F-minor endeavor, the Piano Sonata, op. 5. The treatment of the D♭–C idea is also infinitely more sophisticated than that accorded to the seconds in the G-Minor Piano Quartet, op. 25. The other new element in Brahms's style is an extensive use of meter as a tool of developing variation. In theme 2b″ of op. 26, we have already observed how motivic-rhythmic development can temporarily override the notated meter. In op. 34 such procedures become even more prominent and, like the manipulation of the two-note motive, suggest the influence of middle-period Beethoven, as well as of Schumann.

---

[32]A detailed account of the genesis of opp. 34 and 34 *bis* is given by Elizabeth Jean Lamberton, "Brahms's Piano Quintet, Op. 34, and Duo-Piano Sonata, Op. 34 *bis*: A Critical Study." See especially Chapter 2. Since this thesis, another source for op. 34 *bis* has appeared, a partly autograph manuscript in the possession of the descendants of Princess Anna von Hesse, to whom the work was dedicated; it is held in the Bibliothek der Kurhessischen Hausstiftung in Adolfseck bei Fulda.

[33]See the letter from Clara Schumann to Joachim relating that she and Brahms played through Schubert's D-Minor Quartet, C-Major Quintet, and Octet, in Joseph Joachim, *Letters from and to Joseph Joachim*, p. 254.

[34]Tovey, "Brahms's Chamber Music," p. 244; Webster, "Schubert's Sonata Form," pp. 65–68.

[35]Tovey, "Brahms's Chamber Music," p. 244.

Let us first examine how Brahms handles the D♭–C basic shape. The two pitches alternate portentously at the lower edge of the first theme, which unfolds in stark octaves, as in Beethoven's *Appassionata*. Like the mysterious Neapolitan triad in bar 4 of the Beethoven, the pitch D♭ and the attendant D♭ triad arpeggiated in the first two bars seem to demand further explanation. The fermata and half cadence at bar 4 (corresponding to the fermata in Beethoven's bar 16) give us a moment to ponder the possible consequences; then, like Beethoven's, the movement plunges forward to demonstrate them.

The D♭–C motive assumes melodic prominence at the half cadence of bar 22, then by means of the linkage technique is carried over into the next bar to initiate the transition to the second group. The motive continues to function as ♭6–5 when it is transposed to A♮–G♯ in order to effect the actual modulation to C♯ minor. An A♮ is prolonged throughout bars 30–32 (always present in an inner voice, even when the bass begins to rise chromatically) and in bar 33 resolves emphatically to G♯, the dominant of the new key area.

Tovey claims that in op. 34 Brahms abandons the double-theme structure characteristic of the piano quartets, but in fact both the first and second groups of the quintet show strong traces of such a plan. The minor-mode portion of the second group (bars 33–73) comprises a pair of alternating themes, which lead at bar 74 to the closing group in D♭ major:

theme:	2a	2b	2a′	2b′	2c
bar:	33	39	47	57	74

The ubiquitous ♭6–5 motive dominates both the theme and accompaniment of 2a (in the neighbor-note figure G♯–A♮–G♯) and also forms part of the circling melodic idea of 2b (A♮–G♯–F♯). It is no exaggeration to say that the first 73 measures of this movement are saturated with the basic motive and that the intensity and concentration of the process far surpass anything found in Brahms's earlier works.

The ♭6–5 motive finds its ultimate expression and fulfillment in the recapitulation of the movement. At bars 195 and 200, themes 2a and 2b return in the Neapolitan, F♯ minor, an appropriate fifth below their original position (see Appendix, ex. G, p. 184). But at bar 207 Brahms alters the ending of 2b: instead of repeating the previous bar at the same pitch level (as in the analogous spot in the exposition, bars 45–46), bar 207 drops a semitone, its bass moving from D♮ to C♯. Then at the entry of 2a′, where we *do* expect the half-step shift (as at bar 47), the bass drops once again, to C♮, over which a transformed 2a′ enters in the tonic, F minor.

Several commentators have discussed this wonderful moment. Keys writes of the "*pianissimo* F♯-minor . . . second subject, which slips magically back down the semitone to F minor."[36] Webster comments that Brahms "moves down

---

[36]Keys, *Brahms Chamber Music*, p. 11.

to the prevailing tonic F♯ minor one measure 'too soon'[207], so that the continuation may descend one half-step further . . . to the true tonic F minor!"[37] By
concentrating only on the general harmonic motion, both writers miss the full
significance of the C♯–C♮ bass resolution. In the exposition, the analogous A♮–
G♯ bass movement across bars 46–47 is obscured—actually undercut—by the
entry of the low C♯ tonic root in 47. In the recapitulation, however, Brahms
specifically avoids the tonic root at this moment. No F appears underneath the
C♮, which pulsates as a bass note for almost three full bars at the return of 2a'.

In Webster's quasi-Schenkerian graph of this passage, the crucial C♮ appears
only in parentheses. Like so many linear reductions, this one virtually obscures
the music's most essential structural details. The C♯–C♮ bass motion here
constitutes an apotheosis and a resolution of the D♭–C semitone motive heard
throughout the movement. The motive now effects the return to the tonic key
area, always one of the most important events in the sonata form.[38]

Brahms signals the significance of this moment by one of his most poetic
transformations: 2a', which in the exposition (bar 47) was a simple restatement
of 2a, here becomes a hushed *legato* utterance for the strings alone. This metamorphosis recalls the reclothing of 2c in the recapitulation of op. 25 (bar 303),
where the strings similarly explore the lyrical potential of a once robust theme.
The transformation in op. 34 serves a more specifically structural function,
however: it marks the moment of thematic and harmonic resolution, the final
descent of D♭ to C and the return of the tonic. (Both these resolutions are
withheld at the beginning of the recapitulation, where the dominant pedal, C,
pushes upward to D♭ at bar 166. The recapitulation opens unstably, avoiding a
firm tonic and omitting the first four measures of the first group.) For the first
time in Brahms's works, then, thematic transformation has become an integral
part of the sonata procedure. Or we might say that thematic transformation,
motivic development, harmonic process, and formal design are at last all beautifully and powerfully coordinated.[39]

[37]Webster, "Schubert's Sonata Form," p. 68.

[38]Schoenberg seems to have missed both the bass motion and harmonic shift in op. 34. In
Structural Functions of Harmony (p. 73) and *Fundamentals of Musical Composition* (p. 204), he
observes only that the second theme is recapitulated in F♯ minor, making no mention of the
return to F minor.

[39]Mention should be made of one other transformation in this movement, less specifically
structural but equally splendid. In the development section at bar 22, the first theme reappears
in B♭ minor. The actual pitches are the same in cello and piano, but the theme is no longer a
broad cantilena; instead it is split up into two-note fragments, which are treated in imitation. In
Tovey's appropriate words, the theme here assumes "the lilt of an ancient ballad" ("Brahms's
Chamber Music," p. 240). The function and position of this transformation are analogous to
those of the C-minor melody in op. 26: both are lyrical episodes built from the first theme and
lying at the heart of the development section.

VI

In our account of the quintet we have not yet examined the closing segment of the exposition, 2c (beginning at bar 74), which is less remarkable for its pitch structure than for its rhythmic and metrical aspects. And these are remarkable indeed. The theme begins conventionally, with two parallel four-bar phrases (74–77 and 78–81), but the symmetry breaks down rapidly. Brahms first reduces the theme to one of its component motives, a descending stepwise third in dotted rhythm (bars 81–82; see Appendix, ex. H, p. 185). The motive then assumes the shape of three equal eighth notes; the first note begins to lose its upbeat character and to sound stressed or accented. This development disrupts the original rhythmic groupings and the notated meter: in bar 83 the piano almost seems to create its own $\frac{9}{8}$ meter. As the three-note groups continue to pour forth, overlapping in piano and strings, even the most astute listener becomes utterly disoriented. (The disorientation is even more extreme in the two-piano version, written before the quintet although published only later. There is an "extra" bar of the three-note groups in both exposition [bar 86] and recapitulation [bar 248].)[40]

The listener awaits the re-establishment of a firm downbeat and a regular rhythmic-metrical pattern. These arrive on the second beat of bar 86, where the preceding motive D♭–A♭–G is broadened to three quarter notes, followed by a quarter rest in all parts. The successive repetitions of this figure seem to restore a $\frac{4}{4}$ meter, but one which does not correspond with the notated bar line! Because the notated first beat of each bar is empty in bars 87–95 (in both first and second endings) and the third beat in 90–95, they tend to *sound* like weak fourth and second beats respectively. The perceived meter has thus been displaced or dislocated from the notated one. This metrical procedure brings to mind theme 2b″ in op. 26 (examined above). But now there is no conflicting accompaniment; nor are the notated second and fourth beats heard as syncopated against any rhythmic-metrical background. In short, there is no element that aurally contradicts the "displaced" $\frac{4}{4}$ meter.

This remarkable phenomenon has another psychological or perceptual dimension. After the confusion of bars 83–85, the listener without a score before him (and without previous knowledge of the music) may not realize that the meter has been displaced; unless he has been keeping track of every eighth note, he may not know that the *forte* chord of bar 86 falls on the notated second beat. His awareness of the displacement will occur only at the double bar (if the exposition is repeated) or at the violin's entrance at the beginning of the devel-

---

[40]When writing out the autograph of the piano quintet (now in the Library of Congress), Brahms at first apparently retained the "extra" bar. But at some point after writing out the entire first movement he pasted over the passage, in both the exposition and recapitulation, reducing it by one bar. The first movement of the quintet is thus two bars shorter than the two-piano sonata.

opment section (bar 96), where bar 95 will seem to be (or to have been) one beat too short.

Surely all performers have noticed and have had to come to terms with such metrical displacements in Brahms's scores—indeed, much of the effect of these passages depends on rhythmic-metrical nuances provided by the performers— but few commentators have paid attention to them. Though Schoenberg deftly rebarred two Brahms themes (from opp. 51 and 99) to accommodate their inner metrical freedom, he never addressed the kind of larger-scale dislocation we find in op. 34. Recently, however, David Epstein has faced the matter head-on, ac- knowledging "the apparent metrical and rhythmic confusion that is so often encountered in his [Brahms's] scores, where attacks that seem qualitatively strong . . . are placed on metrically weak beats."[41] Epstein focuses on these procedures in the first movement of the Second Symphony, treating one passage that behaves much like the displaced theme 2c in the quintet. This is the canonic episode that appears rather suddenly in the middle of the second group (bars 136–52). To a pulsating, ostinato accompaniment of clarinets, horns, and violas, a chilling dialogue ensues between bassoons-cellos-basses and the violins. Brahms upsets our orientation, Epstein explains, "by displacing the melody metrically, beginning it on the second beat of the measure. Brahms removes the usual metric referents by which downbeat or upbeat orientation might be judged by destroying the metric background at this point. . . . Thus the passage floats, rhythmically and metrically ambiguous, its referents and normative properties all but destroyed."[42]

Epstein here says something that has needed to be said about Brahms: metri- cal and rhythmic ambiguities constitute a fundamental and fully intentional aspect of his compositional technique. I have suggested further that the metrical displacement can establish itself so solidly that, for the listener, ambiguity temporarily disappears, as in the last ten bars of the op. 34 exposition. Still, I think two more questions must be asked, one historical, the other critical: Where might Brahms have learned or studied such techniques? And—perhaps more significantly for our discussion here—just what purpose do they serve in his musical discourse; how do they affect the thematic, harmonic, and formal issues that have been treated in this study?

One possible answer to the first question is suggested by Brahms himself, in the annotations he made in his library of early music. It is well known that he was a serious collector and student (and, for a time, conductor) of Renaissance and Baroque vocal music. His personal collection, preserved today in the Ge- sellschaft der Musikfreunde, contained not only many printed editions—he was among the first subscribers to the *Gesamtausgaben* of Bach, Handel, and Schütz—but also many works that he copied out by hand. As early as 1853,

[41]Epstein, *Beyond Orpheus*, p. 169.

[42]Epstein, pp. 166–67.

Brahms began copying works by such Italian and German composers as Palestrina, Lotti, Isaac, and Senfl. Virginia Hancock has revealed that he frequently marked interesting rhythmic and metrical phenomena—for example, hemiola figures in Bach. More significantly, he would also correct or modify editorial bar lines. In his own handwritten copy of Isaac's famous "Insbruck, ich muss dich lassen," probably made in 1857–60, Brahms bracketed in red pencil an implied triple meter that had been obscured by the original editor's duple notation.[43]

Hancock has claimed that Brahms's own choral music reflects the same kind of metrical freedom he evidently admired in earlier music. She points to passages in the *Requiem*, op. 45, *Schicksalslied*, op. 54, and *Triumphlied*, op. 55, where metrical groupings temporarily override the notated bar line.[44] The F-Minor Piano Quintet, which antedates these works, is the first Brahms piece to display such procedures on a large scale. Although any specific connection between op. 34 and a Lied by Isaac seems unlikely, Brahms's characteristic metrical techniques may well have been stimulated by his own early, ardent study of Renaissance music.

For another, more immediate source we should turn to middle-period Beethoven, where we have already discovered important structural models for Brahms. In the rhythmically and metrically extravagant first movement of the Third Symphony, Beethoven frequently disrupts—and eventually displaces—the notated triple meter with strong accents and syncopations. The process begins with the strong second-beat *sforzandos* of bars 23–25 (ex. 28a), which are at first perceived only as athletic syncopations. From bar 27 on, however, the second beat begins to assert itself more forcefully, and for a longer period (up to bar 34).

At some point in this series of accents, a duple meter actually displaces in our ear the notated triple meter, for as I suggested in my account of the Brahms quintet, we cannot hear accents as syncopations if the written meter is not reinforced in some way. Or, as Moritz Hauptmann wrote in 1853, if "a series [of notes] is to appear syncopated, then the unsyncopated series must at the same time be present with it; for without the normal series, of which the syncopated forms the metrical contradiction, the syncopated would itself be shown normally accented."[45] That is, the metrical framework becomes displaced onto the "syncopated" series. Beethoven's dislocation is real but temporary, for the "third" beat reappears in bar 33. The triple meter still fails to coincide with the bar line, however: the displaced duple has simply added a beat. Complete metri-

[43]See Virginia Hancock, "Brahms and His Library of Early Music," pp. 294–95. For the dating of Brahms's copy, see pp. 99–100. The editor of the Isaac was Carl von Winterfeld.

[44]Hancock, "Brahms and His Library," pp. 295–98.

[45]Moritz Hauptmann, *The Nature of Harmony and Metre*, p. 342. Hauptmann appears to be the only nineteenth-century theorist to acknowledge the possibility of such displacement.

EXAMPLE 28: Beethoven, Symphony No. 3, op. 55, I.

cal regularity is restored only with the firm downbeat and the return to the main theme at bar 37.[46]

The rhythmic and metrical aspects of this passage resonate through the entire first movement of the *Eroica*. The transition to the second group, beginning at bar 45, emerges almost as excess run-off from the preceding accents and displacements. The new oboe motive and its numerous echoes enter on strongly accented second beats; the motive culminates in, and is at last grounded by, the *fortissimo* scale of bars 55–56, which descends emphatically to the downbeat and to the dominant, B♭. The "sore" second beat will not be so easily daunted, however: it returns to infiltrate the triumphant B♭ triadic theme of bars 109–17 and then audaciously triggers another chain of displaced duple measures at bars 128–31.

Metrical disputes come to a head in the development section, where the insistent second beat of the fugato theme (bar 236) generates a massive dislocation. By bar 248, the metrical framework has slipped off its grid and onto the second beat. Here Beethoven alternates six beats (two bars) of "normal" $\frac{3}{4}$ and twelve beats grouped in twos. I suggest that we hear these duple groupings no longer as six individual measures of $\frac{2}{4}$ (as in the exposition), but as a hemiola within the displaced $\frac{3}{4}$ meter, thus as two bars of $\frac{3}{2}$ (ex. 28b).

However an individual's ear chooses to organize the series of accents in these passages, all listeners sense that Beethoven is exploiting the tension—and

---

[46]For a similar analysis of this passage and of metrical procedures in this movement, see Philip Downs, "Beethoven's 'New Way' and the *Eroica*," especially p. 88.

EXAMPLE 29: Schumann, *Davidsbündlertänze*, op. 6, no. 16.

exploring the threshold—between strong syncopation, or hemiola, and genuine metrical displacement. The first composer after Beethoven to take up metrical experimentation of this kind was Schumann.[47] There are more than a few passages in Schumann's works that wreak havoc with the written meter, either by groupings that change constantly, or by a more consistent and uniform displacement. The former procedure resembles that used in theme 2b″ of Brahms's op. 26; the latter, in the last ten bars of the op. 34 exposition.

The sixteenth piece of Schumann's *Davidsbündlertänze*, op. 6, provides a good example of the first type (ex. 29). Because it comes at the very beginning of the piece, the strong G-major root-position chord is heard as a downbeat, not as an upbeat to the weaker E-minor triad. The first three beats group themselves as a $\frac{3}{4}$ measure, which is then followed by another built on the same rhythmic pattern. The next repetition of the pattern, however, is extended by one beat (the last of bar 3) to land on the written downbeat of bar 4 with an emphatic A-minor cadence. But Schumann has no sooner restored the notated framework than he displaces it again by adding four *forte* eighth-note chords, thereby creating an additional $\frac{2}{4}$ measure and an absurd reinforcement of a cadence that is already strong. The loud chords seem to represent Schumann's musical guffaw at his little deception. The second (notated) four measures repeat the scheme of the first four, except that Schumann provides a feminine cadence to the dominant on the downbeat just before the double bar. There are now no *forte* chords to

[47]We also find extraordinary metrical ambiguities in Berlioz—for example, in the last movement of *Harold in Italy*. Such devices are not as common as in Schumann, however, nor are they as likely to have influenced Brahms.

disorient us. How, then, do we interpret the G-major chord at the return: as an upbeat, or as a downbeat, preceded as before by a bar of $\frac{2}{4}$ (now in the form of a feminine cadence)? There is probably no single "correct" perception, only an awareness of disorientation and ambiguity. We might observe, however, that Schumann's metrical legerdemain is neatly contained within two symmetrical four-bar phrases. As so often in Brahms, the inner metrical freedom is balanced by an outwardly regular structure.

Schumann's other principal metrical procedure avoids such mercurial shifting in favor of a more sustained displacement, where perceived and notated meters fail to coincide for long stretches of time. Perhaps the best-known of such passages occurs in the second theme of the last movement of the Piano Concerto, op. 54 (bars 461ff.). For about forty measures the theme floats blithely in $\frac{3}{2}$, disregarding the written $\frac{3}{4}$ meter. Unlike in the *Davidsbündler* example or the *Eroica*, we are probably not aware of any conflict or discrepancy until the solo entry at bar 503. Indeed, I suspect that many listeners who (like myself) first come to know this piece from a performance or recording are startled to see the actual notation.

The opening six measures of Schumann's Third Symphony provide another, briefer example of what we might call an unperceived hemiola, whereby a $\frac{3}{2}$ meter is superimposed over a notated $\frac{3}{4}$ before the latter has been established. As Epstein has demonstrated, this symphony is a virtual compendium of Schumann's sophisticated rhythmic and metrical techniques. He also suggests that "Schumann appears very much the progenitor of these musical characteristics that have been widely associated with Brahms. There is more yet to be understood of this relationship and of the influence of the older man."[48]

I would propose for Brahms's metrical procedures a dual heritage, in both Beethoven and Schumann, although in fact Brahms sounds like neither composer. He rarely attains the extraordinary visceral excitement of the *Eroica*; he seldom exploits meter and rhythm for witty effects, as in the *Davidsbündler* (or in Haydn); nor do his metrical displacements last as long as those in the Schumann concerto. Even in his "light" music, the waltzes and Hungarian dances, Brahms's treatment of rhythm and meter is generally more sober and restrained.[49]

This characteristic brings us to consider the second question asked at the

[48]Epstein, *Beyond Orpheus*, p. 157.

[49]I have not considered here metrical procedures in Haydn and Mozart, with which Brahms would no doubt have been familiar. There are remarkable ambiguities and displacements in, for example, the trio of Haydn's "Oxford" Symphony; in the slow movement of Mozart's "Jupiter" Symphony (see bars 23–25, 51–55); and in the first movement of Mozart's G-Minor Piano Quartet, K. 478 (admired and analyzed by Schoenberg in "Brahms the Progressive," in *Style and Idea*, pp. 436–37). But these effects are not pursued as extensively by Haydn and Mozart as by middle-period Beethoven, Schumann, and Brahms; they do not constitute a fundamental element of the classical musical language.

beginning of this section: just what function do these techniques serve in Brahms's music? The answer, I believe, is that they become tools of developing variation, means for modifying and transforming thematic-motivic material. Brahms employs these procedures not at isolated moments, but throughout a composition or movement. In this way they can also serve to articulate the formal structure, as can be seen if we now return to the exposition of the Piano Quintet, op. 34.

Metrical-rhythmic development shapes not only the final measures, but also the first group, which unfolds by a compelling process of compression, expansion, and stabilization. The mysterious opening bars seem to contract or shrink the notated $\frac{4}{4}$ meter, without actually dislocating it. The C that appears as an upbeat to bar 1 becomes, as it were, squeezed within the next bar as a downbeat. Thus the initial melodic figure, consisting of a quarter-note upbeat plus a bar, is condensed into a single bar. This bar is then further reduced to only its triadic arpeggio figure (bar 3). The piano's C-major chord at bar 4 represents the ultimate compression: the arpeggio has congealed into a simultaneity. (Of course, the strings continue to play the arpeggiated figure.) After the fermata comes an expansion (or explosion) that is both expressive and metrical, for bars 5–8 stretch the notated meter into two large bars of $\frac{3}{2}$. The accents in these bars are widely spaced, coming six beats apart. Then follows a metrical compression, in which the stresses fall closer together. In bars 8–9 every other beat is marked *forzando*; in bar 10 all beats are *forte*, thus bearing equal weight. In themselves metrically and rhythmically disorienting, bars 8–11 serve to lead us back to the original $\frac{4}{4}$ pulse, which is now reinforced by the counterstatement of bars 12–22. As if to disperse the preceding chaos, Brahms explicitly restores the natural accents on the first and third beats of the piano part in bars 12–13, and the whole passage proceeds in regular two- and four-bar phrases. By its metrical stability and its duration (11 bars), this counterstatement serves to balance the highly charged eleven bars that open the movement.

Brahms's second group takes on a different kind of metrical activity: through a progressively greater emphasis on the second beat it prepares the metrical displacement of bars 86ff. The device of highlighting a beat recalls Beethoven's practice, of course; but Brahms's procedure is more moderate. Rather than periodically rattling the metrical framework, as Beethoven does, Brahms builds gradually toward a complete displacement. Both the bar of dominant introduction to 2a and 2a itself place unusual emphasis on the second beat: the principal motive cuts off abruptly and conspicuously on that beat as well as on the fourth beat. In bars 37–38, the stress on beat 2 becomes strong enough to obscure momentarily the notated meter. At the analogous spot in 2a' (bars 51–52), Brahms's additional dynamic markings, the crescendos and decrescendos, draw still more attention to the second and fourth beats. Genuine syncopation at the climax of 2b' in bars 69–73 carries the process a step further and leads directly to the *fortepiano* on the second beat of 2c at bar 74.

As we saw above, the continuation of 2c culminates the entire operation, first by utterly confounding the meter, then by displacing it onto the sore second beat, which has at last been granted its wish to become a downbeat. But what is the purpose of the dislocation, especially since by bar 86 the listener may not even be aware of it? As in the Schumann concerto, the perceived meter is less in conflict with the notated one than oblivious of it.

In Brahms, however, both the aesthetic effect and technical role of the process soon become apparent. In the last bars of the exposition, the piano meditates quietly upon a fragment of the opening theme (F–G–A♭). The motive climbs slowly in a rising sequence, when suddenly the double bar thrusts us back to the beginning of the exposition. This is a shocking moment, for as the D♭ of bar 95 (first ending) moves to the F of bar 1, and the theme begins its hollow course, we comprehend the deception: the metrical framework has abruptly been straightened. The repeat of the exposition is, of course, essential, for it juxtaposes the two versions of the opening theme's motive, or rather that motive's two metrical universes. We understand too that the displacement is, for Brahms, a means of developing variation—one way of modifying themes. The displaced motive of bars 91–93 reflects or embodies the metrical-rhythmic process that has in part shaped the exposition. The repeated exposition now takes on a new dimension as we, metrically wiser, listen for the evolution that culminates in the displacement of the F–G–A♭ head motive.

In the development section, Brahms actually superimposes the two metrical grids. At bar 96 the main theme returns in its proper position, beginning on the notated downbeat, but the displaced pattern continues underneath in the piano part. Although we can perceive the superimposition, we do not, I think, experience any real metrical conflict, for when the violin enters in the notated framework, we immediately perceive the displaced pattern once again as syncopation. In other words, it is probably impossible to hear or experience two identical but out-of-phase meters at the same time.

The analogous situation in the visual arts has been discussed by E. H. Gombrich, who suggests that the eye cannot actually perceive ambiguity. When viewing an optical tease like an Escher print or the well-known duck/rabbit drawing, we must choose *one* image—the stairway coming toward us, the rabbit—for we "cannot experience alternative readings at the same time."[50] Similarly, when the first violin enters in bar 96 of Brahms's development, we cannot really experience two meters at once: our ears select the most comfortable metrical "reading," that provided by the notated bar line.

The sophisticated metrical and rhythmic procedures of the piano quintet add a significant dimension to Brahms's art of developing variation. In the early piano sonatas, where motivic-thematic "development" is confined within metrically square "variations," Brahms relies on the device of transformation to

[50]E. H. Gombrich, *Art and Illusion*, p. 5. For an extended discussion of this issue, see especially Gombrich's Chapters 7 and 8.

achieve variety and color. Continuous development is also thwarted in the G-Minor Piano Quartet, op. 25, by the sharply articulated sonata exposition, which breaks down into a series of large separate themes. The A-Major Piano Quartet, op. 26, seems in one sense to regress: it has small-scale, almost schematic, two- and four-bar structures. But within and between the phrases, the motivic language becomes remarkably fluid and (in the case of theme 2b″) metrically more flexible.

Brahms's real achievement in the quintet, op. 34, is to combine that fluency with a still freer metrical process—or, we might say, to extend that fluency to the larger metrical framework of the music. Just as the opening theme of op. 26 unveils at once Brahms's new powers of motivic development, so does the process of compression and expansion in the first group of op. 34 reveal his metrical prowess. And in the rest of the exposition (and the movement) that prowess continues to enhance, and be enhanced by, the procedures of developing variation.

4

Song and Chamber Music, 1864–1879

I

During the years between the inception and the publication of the op. 34 Piano Quintet, from 1862 to 1865, Brahms completed three other multi-movement instrumental works: the E-Minor Violoncello Sonata, op. 38; the G-Major Sextet, op. 36; and the E♭-Major Horn Trio, op. 40. These chamber pieces do not quite attain the cogent fluency of op. 34; in some respects they actually seem to retreat. Although Schoenberg and Arno Mitschka both claim that the first movement of the cello sonata (1862) unfolds by means of developing variation, the thematic process proves less compelling than in the quintet, partly because it does not involve the metrical-rhythmic framework. The sonata-form movements of the sextet and the trio manifest a neo-classical reaction somewhat like that of the serenades and the B♭ Sextet. Indeed, the broad, square-cut themes and the harmonic coloring of the G-Major Sextet (1864–65) look back past the piano quartets and quintet to the earlier sextet. In the first movement of the horn trio (1865), Brahms takes the surprising step of avoiding sonata form altogether—the only such case in his entire oeuvre. (The movement is a leisurely, articulated rondo.) The scherzo of op. 40 is a full-fledged sonata form, and one of the finest of this period. But even here Brahms is more retrospective than progressive, looking back to the scherzo of (once again!) Beethoven's *Eroica*.

The horn trio marked the end of Brahms's remarkably productive "first maturity" of chamber music composition. Then, as in 1854–58, came a period in which he completed no large-scale instrumental works at all. Two C-minor works, a symphony and a string quartet, were gestating slowly; but the instrumental silence was broken only in 1873 when the latter appeared, along with the A-Minor Quartet, as op. 51. Brahms withheld the quartets well after their opus number had been assigned by Simrock: opp. 52–55, 57, and 58 all were published before op. 51.[1]

As these circumstances might suggest, the op. 51 Quartets—especially the C-Minor—represent a breakthrough for Brahms. He achieves a new style of extraordinary compression and intensity that is to dominate many sonata-form works of his later years. Also emerging in the mid 1870s is a more relaxed, lyrical idiom, best exemplified by the G-Major Violin Sonata, op. 78 (1878–79). Both these styles draw upon and refine the procedures of developing variation discussed in the preceding chapters.

A glance at just the titles of the pieces published in the eight-year instrumental hiatus tells us that Brahms may have developed new techniques and refinements not in sonata-form works, but in vocal music, for everything he issued between 1865 and 1873 contains the human voice. The centerpiece is, of course, the *German Requiem*, op. 45, whose composition spans principally the years 1865–68. Also dating from this period are another large vocal work, *Rinaldo*, op. 50 (1863–68); two pieces on a slightly smaller scale, the *Schicksalslied*, op. 54 (1868–71) and the *Alto Rhapsody*, op. 53 (1869); and the *Liebeslieder* waltzes, op. 52 (1869). During the years 1864–73, Brahms also composed an impressive number of solo songs, about fifty-six in all, comprising almost a quarter of his total output. These include all of opp. 32 and 57–59, and most of opp. 33, 43, and 46–49.[2] I believe that the thematic, formal, and harmonic procedures characteristic of the C-Minor Quartet and the G-Major Violin Sonata were explored less in the large choral pieces than in several important songs of this period.[3]

Gerald Abraham has pointed to the "stanza-like construction" of many of Brahms's instrumental themes and to the fact that Brahms on several occasions prefixed a movement or piece with a poetic fragment that fits the opening melody perfectly.[4] Brahms's instrumental music, Abraham implies, often aspires to the condition of song. Recently Eric Sams suggested precisely the opposite about Brahms's actual songs. They "inhabit that hinterland of the Lied

[1]For the dates of publication of Brahms's works, see Kurt Hofmann, *Die Erstdrucke der Werke von Johannes Brahms*. For a comparison of conflicting publication dates given by different sources, see Donald McCorkle's Supplement A, pp. xxxiii–xxxvi, in *The N. Simrock Thematic Catalogue of the Works of Johannes Brahms*. McCorkle's list was prepared before, and is to some extent superseded by, Hofmann.

[2]The most reliable and thorough dating now available of the individual songs in these collections is given by George S. Bozarth, "The *Lieder* of Johannes Brahms," especially pp. 24–68. Professor Bozarth has revised some of these datings in his paper, "The *Liederjahr* of 1868."

[3]For important discussions of motivic and thematic processes in the *German Requiem*, see William S. Newman, "A 'Basic Motive' in Brahms's *German Requiem*" and Walter Westafer, "Overall Unity and Contrast in Brahms's *German Requiem*," especially pp. 65–68.

[4]Gerald Abraham, *A Hundred Years of Music*, p. 166.

where song borders on absolute music," he observes; a Brahms song seems "always ready to turn into instrumental music."[5]

Sams elegantly articulates what most commentators have said in one fashion or another—that Brahms's songs are best appreciated as musical statements about a poem, rather than as poems set to music. Hugo Wolf represents the obvious, and the most frequently cited, antithesis. His songs become poetic recitations, the music wedded intimately to every nuance and gesture of the text. Brahms, on the other hand, rarely sacrifices a clear, easily comprehensible design—whether of melody, harmony, or large-scale structure—for the details of a poem. Brahms's song forms are fundamentally as conservative as his sonata forms: the great majority have either a modified strophic or ternary (A B A') design. As with his instrumental music, little insight into Brahms's songs can be gained from higher-level formal analysis alone.[6] The artistry lies within the framework, in the interaction of thematic, harmonic, and formal procedures.

As might be expected, these procedures are closely dependent on the type and the structure of the text being set. For most of his early songs, from 1851 to about 1860, Brahms chose simple *volkstümlich* poems. The verses tend to have clear, stanzaic forms that employ rhyme and fall into conventional, regular meters. For such poems, Brahms drew either on the work of early Romantic poets such as Eichendorff and Uhland, or on anthologies of folk poetry—in particular Herder's *Volkslieder*.[7] The musical dress for such poems is correspondingly plain. Most songs in this first period are strophic; the melodic style is often folk-like and uncomplicated. We find little in the way of adventurous motivic or thematic development, at least nothing to compare with the techniques Brahms was working out boldly in his instrumental sonata forms at the time.

There are, however, two notable exceptions, "Der Kuss" and "An eine Äolsharfe," op. 19, nos. 1 and 5 (1858). Here Brahms chose texts that do not rhyme, scan, or fall into the regular patterns of folk verse. The first poem is a typical product of the late eighteenth-century neoclassic poet Ludwig Hölty, who (with a number of his contemporaries) sought to abandon the restrictive accentual-syllabic meters of German verse and to recreate the more fluid quantitative meters of ancient poetry. The second poem is Eduard Mörike's free, rhapsodic apostrophe to the legendary Aeolian harp. Brahms's settings of these texts are musically more flexible and fluent, both in overall design and in phrase and

---

[5]Eric Sams, *Brahms Songs*, p. 5.

[6]For a summary and discussion of Brahms's song forms, see Rudolf Gerber, "Formprobleme in Brahmsschen Lied."

[7]The most comprehensive account of the poetic and musical sources for Brahms's songs remains Max Friedlaender's *Brahms's Lieder*. Supplementary information and some rectifications of Friedlaender are provided by Sams, *Brahms Songs*; Bozarth, "The *Lieder* of Johannes Brahms," especially pp. 161–233; and Konrad Giebeler, *Die Lieder von Johannes Brahms*.

melodic structure. However, these songs also tend to ramble, to become too discursive: Brahms does not yet know how to handle such poems persuasively.

In the years 1864–73, the period in which his output of instrumental music dwindled, Brahms turned more and more to this kind of text (although he never stopped setting folk-like poems). For several he returned to Hölty; many others were the translations and adaptations of foreign verse he found in Georg Friedrich Daumer's collections *Polydora* (1855) and *Hafis* (1846, 1852). Unlike the early songs (even the op. 19 Hölty and Mörike settings), these now benefit from some of the most powerful and characteristic techniques of Brahms's instrumental music.

For example, "Die Kränze," op. 46, no. 1 (probably from early 1864), contains one of Brahms's most splendid "recapitulations." Brahms took the poem, originally a Greek lyric, from Daumer's *Polydora* and added the title himself:[8]

Die Kränze

Hier ob dem Eingang seid befestiget,
Ihr Kränze, so beregnet und benetzt
Von meines Auges schmerzlichem Erguss!
Denn reich zu tränen pflegt das Aug' der Liebe.
Dies zarte Nass, ich bitte,
Nicht allzu frühe träufet es herab.
Spart es, bis ihr vernehmet, dass sie sich
Der Schwelle naht mit ihrem Grazienschritte,
Die Teurere, die mir so ungelind.
Mit einem Male dann hernieder sei es
Auf ihres Hauptes gold'ne Pracht ergossen,
Und sie empfinde, dass es Tränen sind;
Dass es die Tränen sind, die meinem Aug'
In dieser kummervollen Nacht entflossen.

The Wreaths

Here above the doorway be fastened,
You wreaths, showered upon and moistened
By the painful outpourings of my eye!
For the eye of love is wont to weep copiously.
This tender flow, I beg of you,
Let it not drip away too soon.
Save it, until you hear that she herself
Approaches the threshold with her step like the Graces,
The dear one, who is so unkind to me.

---

[8]I cite the text of this poem, as well as those below, from the standard source: Gustav Ophüls, *Brahms Texte.* I have, however, brought the spelling (of words such as "*Thränen*") into conformity with more modern usage, as found in Brahms's *Sämtliche Werke.* The translations are mine, but draw freely on the excellent prose renderings by Stanley Appelbaum in the Dover reprint series of the songs (vol. 2, New York, 1979).

Then all at once let it be poured down
Onto the golden splendor of her head,
And let her realize that these are tears;
That these are the tears, which from my eye
Flow in this sorrowful night.

The fourteen-line poem is divided neither into stanzas nor into sonnet-style segments. There is a prevailing meter of iambic pentameter, but no regular rhyme scheme. Brahms attempts to convey the poem's discursive quality—German critics have called it *prosaähnlich*[9]—but his structural instincts demand some kind of "poetic" return or rounding off. He thus constructs a song whose thematic-harmonic-formal design might best be represented as Ax B Cx'. Here x represents the cadential phrase and piano postlude of the A section (bars 14–22). Ax is in the key of D♭ major, B in C♯ minor, and C in A major. The final x' brings back the tonality, and the cadential phrase and postlude, of the A section.

To some extent, Brahms's spacious setting diffuses the poem's concentrated imagery and sentiment. Sams faults the song's "rhythmic restlessness," remarking that "despite its melodic charm ['Die Kränze'] is afflicted by the piano's curious inability to settle down into any one figure."[10] It must be admitted that the B and C segments seem to drift aimlessly away from the fine opening. (The cadence of B, however, clearly recalls x and thus provides some welcome coherence.) But at the return to x' from the thematically and harmonically remote C section, in bars 44–48, we immediately recognize Brahms the master (see Appendix, ex. I, p. 186).

Taking his cue from Daumer's slightly altered repetition of the phrase *"dass es Tränen sind"* in lines 12–13, Brahms ushers in x' by a wonderfully poignant use of the familiar linkage technique. Underneath the first *"dass es Tränen,"* at bar 44, Brahms reintroduces the piano figuration—stepwise ascending seconds exchanged between left and right hands—which appears originally at x (bars 14–19) but which has not been heard since the B section (bars 23–30). The harmony now floats above a dominant pedal of A, shifting delicately between minor and major; the piano prolongs the tonal suspense by echoing the last two bars of the vocal phrase, *"empfinde dass es Tränen sind,"* ending on the same melodic note, A. Now (bar 47) Brahms respells the E♮ bass as F♭, and the voice re-enters a semitone lower, on A♭. The chord thus formed, a first-inversion D♭ minor, is for the moment still heard as functioning in the key of A (as iii or C♯). But on the downbeat of the next measure, the bass drops another half step to E♭, bringing us back (as V⁷/V) into the orbit of the song's proper tonic, D♭.

Above this exquisite harmonic transformation the voice repeats the preceding melodic phrase, to which, however, the words are now fitted differently. In

[9]See Gerber, p. 40; Giebeler, p. 46.

[10]Sams, *Brahms Songs*, p. 33.

bar 44 the conjunction *"dass"* appeared on the high note (D♮); at the repetition Brahms shifts the weight toward the first syllable of the central image, *"Tränen."* And the musical phrase does not linger on the dominant, as it did in bars 45–47, but pushes through into x', the original cadential section of A (slightly modified but easily recognizable: cf. bars 14–19 and 50–55), and then into the large piano postlude.

Brahms's musical instincts may have been aroused by the syntactical construction of Daumer's text. The first of the phrases, *"dass es Tränen sind,"* is a free-standing direct object of the verb *"empfinde"* (and is followed by a semicolon), and as such suggests at least partial musical closure. In the repetition Daumer has placed the article *"die"* before *"Tränen,"* which is now qualified (or more precisely, modified) by the clause *"die meinem Aug' . . . entflossen."* Brahms captures this verbal syntax admirably by reiterating the musical idea but leading it forward toward the climax of x'.

Precisely as in the examples of the linkage technique already discussed in the context of instrumental music, Brahms employs a single idea both to conclude and to initiate musical phrases. Even more remarkable is Brahms's fusing of that technique with the sonata-derived procedure of recapitulation, for the *"dass es Tränen"* music concludes the central—and to some extent developmental—B and C sections and then ushers in the partial return of the opening. In Brahms's chamber music we have seen the linkage technique used to join two phrases or to generate a new theme from the tail of another. In this song, Brahms has actually raised the procedure to a higher structural level: the end of the "development" generates the beginning of the "recapitulation." In its way, then, "Die Kränze" represents a small-scale triumph for Brahms. From the intimate domain of the Lied, it points ahead to the massive symphonic statements to be examined in Chapter 5, works in which Brahms projects the principles of developing variation onto the broadest dimensions of structure.

Two other songs of this period, both settings of Hölty texts, look forward in a slightly different way, adumbrating what are to become the principal stylistic poles in Brahms's instrumental music after about 1870. "Die Schale der Vergessenheit" (op. 46, no. 3, composed in 1864) explores the intensely motivic, harmonically explosive idiom that is to reappear in such works as the C-Minor String Quartet, op. 51, no. 1, and the C-Minor Symphony. By contrast, one of Brahms's most popular songs, "Die Mainacht" (op. 43, no. 2, composed in April 1866), unfolds in a style that is continuously lyrical and fluid, yet no less concentrated than that of "Die Schale." The techniques of "Die Mainacht" inform the gentler works of Brahms's later years, perhaps especially the piece directly inspired by song, the G-Major Violin Sonata, op. 78.

II

Brahms was reportedly displeased with his own setting of Hölty's "Die Schale der Vergessenheit," which records a feverish attempt to drown love's sorrows in a "goblet of oblivion." He called the song *"wüst"* (waste) and had decided not to publish it; he changed his mind only when persuaded of its merits by his friend, the baritone Julius Stockhausen, who sang through the song with him one day.[11] As Brahms was undoubtedly aware, "Die Schale" is not one of his most polished creations. Yet it can intrigue us with its raw, unbuttoned (and perhaps naive) vigor. Like some of Brahms's boldest songs ("Von ewiger Liebe," for example), this one seems to aspire beyond the medium of the Lied. Sams has remarked, "Its look on the page is that of a piano or violin sonata."[12]

Although Hölty did not divide his twelve-line poem into stanzas, it falls naturally into two halves, and each half falls into equal three-line segments:[13]

Die Schale der Vergessenheit

Eine Schale des Stroms, welcher Vergessenheit
  Durch Elysiums Blumen rollt,
Bring', o Genius, bring' deinem Verschmachtenden!
  Dort, wo' Phaon die Sängerin,
Dort, wo Orpheus vergass seiner Euridice,
  Schöpf' den silbernen Schlummerquell!
Ha! Dann tauch' ich dein Bild, spröde Gebieterin,
  Und die lächelnde Lippe voll
Lautenklanges, des Haar's schattige Wallungen,
  Und das Beben der weissen Brust,
Und den siegenden Blick, der mir im Marke zuckt,
  Tauch' ich tief in den Schlummerquell.

The Goblet of Oblivion

A goblet from the stream, which
  Through the flowers of Elysium spreads oblivion,
Bring, O guardian spirit, bring to your thirsting one!
  There, where Phaon [forgot] the poetess [Sappho],
There, where Orpheus forgot his Eurydice,
  Draw the silvery source of slumber!
Ha! Then shall I plunge your image, obstinate mistress,
  And your laughing lips full
Of lute tones, the shadowy convulsions of your hair,
  And the heaving of your white breast,
And your conquering gaze, which darts through me sharply,
  I shall plunge them deep into the source of slumber.

[11]Kalbeck, *Johannes Brahms*, 2: 299–300, fn. 3.

[12]Sams, *Brahms Songs*, p. 33.

[13]Brahms set a version of the poem altered by Johann Heinrich Voss. For the original, see Friedlaender, p. 65. The basic structure, twelve lines in alternating meters, remains the same in both versions.

Some asymmetry is generated by the metrical plan of Hölty's poem, in which four-foot asclepiadic lines (with the quantitative pattern $-\smile \mid -\smile\smile- \mid -\smile\smile- \mid \smile-$) alternate with three-foot glyconic ones ($-\smile \mid -\smile\smile- \mid \smile-$). Thus each tercet inverts the scheme of the preceding one: x y x become y x y, etc.

Brahms's setting (see Appendix, ex. J, pp. 187–88) is expansive, but its overall structure less opaque than that of "Die Kränze." Robert Pascall suggests a large binary form corresponding to the two halves of the poem: two sections of 40 and 44 bars, respectively, the first moving to the mediant major (actually concluding in the dominant of the mediant), the second returning to the tonic.[14] Although it is possible to hear such a sonata-like structure, there is an equally obvious A B A' design. In the B section, which comprises Hölty's second tercet (lines 4–6), the key and mode are changed and the mood becomes lyrical. A' equals AB in length and incorporates the entire last half of the poem. Each segment of this A B A' structure concludes with a substantial (indeed, rather long-winded) cadential passage and a brief piano postlude. These cadence sections are closely related: the one in A' (bars 68–74) recalls the one in B (bars 33–39) especially clearly—a musical device no doubt suggested to Brahms by the symmetrical placement of "*Schlummerquell*" at the end of each half of the poem.[15] The structure of the song is thus a kind of binary-ternary hybrid, in which the contrasting B section and the placement of the cadential passages suggest the latter, and the relative length of the segments (and the treatment of "*Schlummerquell*") suggest the former:

40 bars	44 bars
$A_{cad}B_{cad'}$	$A'_{cad'}$

Within this well-articulated structure Brahms's thematic and harmonic language surges forcefully in an earnest attempt to project the poet's quest for *Vergessenheit*. The tonic E is continually side-stepped, arriving in root position only four measures from the end of the song. Most of the first line pours forth over a highly unstable and ambiguous seventh chord. This sonority is soon understood to function as a subdominant or secondary dominant; but its precise nature is at first made deliberately unclear by the E–D♯ appoggiatura in the bass. In bar 5 the bass descends to B and the dominant emerges clearly; but Brahms harmonizes the ostensible melodic resolution—the E in the voice in bar 6—with a startling C-major chord. This soon sprouts an A♯ to justify itself as an augmented-sixth chord, which moves logically to the dominant at bar 9. The tonic at last arrives two bars later, but only in first inversion. And, as becomes clear by bar 15, that chord's bass, G♯, will establish itself as a new key area

[14]See Robert J. Pascall, "Formal Principles in the Music of Brahms," pp. 75–76.

[15]In the original version of the poem (see n. 13), "*Schlummerquell*" is placed not at the halfway point, line 6, but at line 8.

(although not before a substantial extension of its own dominant, D♯, in bars 15–20).

The thematic process of the A section fully reflects this harmonic turbulence. Indeed, the vocal line seems perpetually kept aloft by the avoidance of cadence or closure. The themes grow by a highly charged, if somewhat inelegant, process of developing variation—by the continuous reinterpretation of brief motives. A stepwise descending third (x; see ex. J) shapes the first seven measures, appearing first in bar 2 (C♯–B–A), then across bars 3–4 in the broad hemiola rhythm that is to be so prominent in this song. At *"durch Elysiums"* the third appears in both ascending and descending forms (E–F♯–G♮). The neighbor-note figure on *"Blumen rollt"* (y) will reappear later in the song. The principal motive from bar 11 on is the bold leap of a descending sixth (z), which—like x—is repeated in the hemiola rhythm (bars 13–14) and then further modified during the prolonged cadence to G♯ minor. The descending scales for *"Verschmachtenden"* in bars 14–16 and 18–21 clearly recall and expand motive x.

The B section of "Die Schale" presents all the same motives in their original order, but in the tranquil sphere of A♭ major, alter ego of the agitated G♯ minor. The first four bars (23–26) employ x and y. In the next phrase, x appears both in shorter values and in the hemiola extension. As in the A section, the disjunct sixth and descending scale lead to the cadence, here on V of A♭.

Brahms intensifies the return to A′ by carrying over the final harmony of the B section. The vocal part in the first eight bars of A′ is the same as at the beginning of the song, but its initial C♯ has become, astonishingly, the seventh of a D♯ (E♭) chord. In bar 51 Brahms does not sustain the tonic and introduce motive z (as he had done at the parallel spot in bar 11); instead, he moves back to the augmented-sixth harmony and places the x motive in the piano (in the inverted and regular forms, as it appeared in bars 6–7). The motive pushes boldly upward in a sequence that at last attains V^7/V in bar 61. Over this harmony the opening theme materializes once again, its C♯ now reinterpreted as the fifth of F♯. Only at bar 68 does motive z appear, in broad augmentation, guiding the anguished vocal line toward a *Schlummerquell* in the final, prolonged cadence to E major.

In "Die Schale," Brahms clearly strives to project some of the thematic-harmonic dynamism onto the larger form. Although the three segments of the song are well demarcated, Brahms spreads the seams beyond the double bar lines. The harmonic continuities have already been mentioned: the G♯ minor of the A section becomes A♭ in B, and the concluding E♭ of B is transformed into a D♯-seventh chord to initiate A′. There are thematic or motivic blendings as well. The piano closes the A section with the same E♭–D♯ appoggiatura that was heard in the bass at the opening; this continues to throb, now as F♭–E♭, under the vocal entrance of the B section, changing to F♮–E♭ as the mode becomes major. The B section also concludes with this appoggiatura figure, now appearing as A♭–G. A moment later the motive—still at the same pitches—becomes once again the bass appoggiatura that began the song: A♭–G♮ is respelled as G♯–F𝕩. The motive now permeates even the upper edge of the accompaniment, appearing in the right-hand triplets as E–D♯.

It is indeed possible to feel that the tumultuous thematic-harmonic process of this song overwhelms rather than enhances Hölty's text. For example, the hemiola on motive x in bars 3–4 distends the unimportant pronoun *"welcher"*; and the ordinarily weak last syllable of *"Vergessenheit"* falls on the strong downbeat of bar 6, then is further accented by the *sforzando* and the sudden harmonic shift to ♭VI. But despite its careless declamation and frantic style, we can be grateful that Brahms decided not to consign the song to oblivion.

We can be still more grateful that two years after writing "Die Schale," he approached another Hölty lyric with greater sensitivity and skill. Of all Brahms's middle-period songs, "Die Mainacht," op. 43, no. 2 (composed April 1866), makes perhaps the most effective use of the techniques of developing variation explored in the big chamber works of the early 1860s. As Brahms implied in his famous remark to George Henschel (cited in Chapter 1), the song does indeed grow logically outward from the opening motivic seedcorn—and it does so more lyrically and more cogently than "Die Schale."

Brahms set only three of Hölty's four stanzas, shaping the song as a ternary structure in which (as in "Die Schale") the conclusion of the middle section returns at the close of the song. The structure is thus A Bx A'x'. Each of the stanzas in the poem has four lines (indicated below as a, b, c, d), the first two identical in meter (asclepiads), the third and fourth similar to each other (pherecratic and glyconic respectively) but shorter than the opening lines:

Die Mainacht

1a	Wann der silberne Mond durch die Gesträuche blinkt,
b	Und sein schlummerndes Licht über den Rasen streut,
c	Und die Nachtigall flötet,
d	Wand'l ich traurig von Busch zu Busch.

[second stanza not set by Brahms][16]

2a	Überhüllet vom Laub girret ein Taubenpaar
b	Sein Entzücken mir vor; aber ich wende mich,
c	Suche dunklere Schatten,
d	Und die einsame Träne rinnt.

3a	Wann, o lächelndes Bild, welches wie Morgenrot
b	Durch die Seele mir strahlt, find' ich auf Erden dich?
c	Und die einsame Träne
d	Bebt mir heisser die Wang' herab.

---

[16]For the text of this stanza, see Ophüls, *Brahms Texte*, p. 34, or Friedlaender, *Brahms's Lieder*, p. 60.

The May Night

When the silvery moon gleams through the shrubbery,
And spreads its drowsy light over the lawn,
And the nightingale sings,
I wander sadly from bush to bush.

Covered over by foliage, a pair of doves coo
Their delight before me; but I turn away
To seek deeper shadows,
And the solitary tear flows.

When, O smiling image, which like dawn
Streams through my soul, will I find you on earth?
And the solitary tear
Trembles hotter down my cheek.

In Brahms's setting, the two halves of the first musical phrase (bars 3–5)
become almost perfect melodic and rhythmic mirror images of each other, con-
veying both the quantitative values and the symmetrical arrangement of feet
(an x y y x pattern) in Hölty's line 1a (ex. 30).[17] The phrase rises from the low Bb
to G (emphasizing the rising stepwise third Eb–G), then sinks in the same
rhythm from the high Bb back to the tonic. Line 1b is set as a sequential reiteration of 1a, slightly varied: it ascends through the third F–Ab, then returns from
C to the supertonic. Lines 1c and 1d together comprise an expansion or development of the pattern established by each of the first two phrases. As in the first
half of lines 1a and 1b, line 1c rises through a third (Bb–Db) with the "seedcorn"
rhythm, but contains an additional descent back to the Bb on the last syllable of
"*flötet.*" Line 1d retains the initial rhythm but only the general melodic contour
of the descent heard in the second half of lines 1a and 1b. At "*Busch zu Busch*"
Brahms distends the final descending third, Gb–Eb, emphatically reversing the
initial major-mode ascent from Eb to G in bars 3–4.

In drawing out this cadence, Brahms also departs deliberately from his scrupulous observance of the poem's quantitative values. "*Busch*" is, of course, an
unromantic word, especially when juxtaposed with other natural images like
silvery moons and fluting nightingales. Brahms's rhythmic augmentation highlights Hölty's intentionally dull repetition of this plain word, thus effectively
communicating the oppressive sameness the poet finds in his surroundings.
Brahms has also conveyed the syntactic design of the first stanza. The conjunction "*Wann*" introduces a series of three verb phrases comprising "*blinkt,*"
"*streut,*" and "*flötet.*" Brahms begins each of these with the "seedcorn" rhythm
and an emphasis on the rising third. At line 1d Hölty provides the main clause
of the stanza, and its principal idea, the poet's *Traurigkeit.* Here, then, is where
Brahms presents the greatest "development" or expansion.

---

[17]See the discussion in Jack Stein, *Poem and Music in the German Lied from Gluck to Hugo
Wolf,* pp. 142–44.

EXAMPLE 30: Brahms, "Die Mainacht," op. 43, no. 2.

The motivic and rhythmic development in the A section of the song is complemented by a process of metrical expansion that shows how skillfully Brahms adapts the dynamic procedures of the piano quintet to a more lyrical context. The piano introduction forms a two-bar unit, which is then broadened to three bars in each of the first two vocal phrases (bars 3–5 and 6–8; see ex. 30). (The three-bar units divide clearly into 1½-bar segments, thus implying a broad $\frac{3}{2}$ meter that overrides the notated $\frac{4}{4}$ in bars 3–8.) The last two lines of the stanza are then perceived as comprising a still larger 4½-bar unit. The metrical expansion can also be felt on a lower level, from the entrance of the voice on. The four 1½-bar (or six-beat) segments of bars 3–8 become augmented to a two-bar (eight-beat) segment in 9–10, then to a 2½-bar (ten-beat) unit in 11–13.[18]

Harmonic "development" is perfectly coordinated with the other developmental processes. The first 5½ bars remain entirely diatonic. Then Brahms gently and discreetly intensifies the subdominant and dominant, respectively, with the chromatic notes D♭ (bar 6) and A♮ (bar 8). The final six-bar segment (9–14) moves off into the non-diatonic regions of ♭III and i.

The next stanza of the poem (as used by Brahms) repeats the general plan of the first, beginning with a natural image—here a pair of cooing doves—then turning inward again to the poet's despair. Brahms at first preserves the "seed-corn" motive with only minimal variation; in B major (the lower fifth analogue of the G♭ employed for the birds in the first stanza), the line rises from the fifth below the root to the third above. But now both poetic and musical processes develop more rapidly. The poet reacts in the middle of line 2b, at *"aber ich wende mich,"* and the force of his response to the love birds is conveyed by the unexpected intrusion of the piano in bar 19. After this outburst, the vocal line descends slowly into the gloom of E♭ minor, emphasizing the G♭–E♭ third much as it did at the end of the A section.

Brahms has now posed himself a kind of poetico-musical problem, for at the

[18]Besides Schoenberg's brief examples of metrical or phrase extensions in Brahms's songs ("Brahms the Progressive," in *Style and Idea*, pp. 418–22, 440), there has been only one study (also brief) of metrical fluidity in the Lieder; see Hugo Riemann, "Die Taktfreiheiten in Brahms' Liedern." I return to metrical issues in discussing "O Tod" in Chapter 6.

end of line 2c he has already reached the tonal and emotional goal not attained until the *last* line, 1d, of the previous stanza. There is thus one line of text still remaining. Rather than prolonging the dark tonic minor, Brahms sets this line as a wonderful apotheosis, sustaining the dominant as the vocal line climbs slowly and chromatically from B♭ to E♭. Brahms seems to read Hölty's line *"Und die einsame Träne rinnt"* as a kind of emotional breakthrough for the poet: this stirring, spacious ascent reverses the pessimistic descent from E♭ to B♭ on the preceding *"Schatten."* To our great surprise, however, this grand climax is left unresolved here. A fermata at bar 32 brings everything to a halt, and the A section returns tranquilly—as if taking no account of the massive build-up that has preceded. But as so often happens in Brahms, the apparent slackening of tension serves really to *reculer pour mieux sauter*; it is a lull that prepares a still grander climax.

Brahms sets the first two lines of stanza 3 like lines 1a and 1b (with, however, a new and richer triplet accompaniment). But at line 3c he departs from the original pattern, taking his cue from Hölty's reintroduction of the *"einsame Träne"* image from the end of stanza 2. By a stroke of genius at once logical and breathtaking, Brahms sets 3c as he did 2d, thus importing music (x') from the B section into A'. Of course, the original music will not fit, since line c is shorter than line d. But Brahms cleverly takes advantage of the enjambement between lines 3c and 3d, borrowing the verb *"bebt"* to fill out the musical phrase.

This transference effectively points up the parallel between the verbs *"bebt"* and *"rinnt,"* a correspondence less obvious in Hölty's arrangement. The new verb greatly intensifies the earlier one: while in the second stanza the teardrop had "flowed," now, strikingly, it "trembles." Brahms responds to the stronger verb, and to its still stronger modifier *"heisser,"* with a bold move to the Neapolitan, E major (F♭) in bars 44–45. (The repetition of *"heisser"* is, of course, Brahms's, not Hölty's.) He thus has returned to and expanded the dominant left unresolved before the fermata; he extends the melodic range of the vocal part by pushing the high E♭ of *"Träne"* up a half step to the climactic F♭ of bar 45. The F♭ arpeggio in this bar likewise seems to expand upon the downward arpeggiation of the ii⁷ chord that had followed the E♭ in bar 30. Only now does the aching dominant find its tonic resolution, in the first unequivocal root-position tonic chord of the song (bar 48).

The appearance of x' is especially effective because its melody resembles at first the music we are expecting to hear—something analogous to *"und die Nachtigall flötet"* in bars 9–10. As in the earlier passage, the voice moves up chromatically from B♭ to B♮ (C♭); even the opening words, *"und die,"* are the same as in line 1c. By the last beat of bar 39—or certainly by the *"ein-"* on the downbeat of bar 40—we realize that we are hearing not the original music for line 1c, but a return of the music (x) used for line 2d. The association with line 1c, however, has served to reveal the motivic derivation of x and x': we now clearly understand the ascending chromatic fourth B♭–E♭ as an expansion, both rhythmic and melodic, of the basic motive of the "seedcorn," an ascending third, which appeared as B♭–C♭–D♭ at line 1c.

As in "Die Schale der Vergessenheit," Brahms has brought back part of the central B section to conclude A', but in "Die Mainacht" that formal-thematic technique assumes a power never approached in the earlier song. In "Die Schale," a rather unassuming cadential passage from B simply reappears to wind down the song's frenzied climax. Since the basic motive of the cadence (z) has been heard numerous times in both A and B, its return comes as no great surprise. In A' of "Die Mainacht," however, Brahms returns quite unexpectedly to a climax (x) left hanging at the end of B, and, before providing resolution, expands it into an even greater climax (x').

The fluidity and lyricism of the musical language in "Die Mainacht" represent the opposite extreme from the intense, headlong style of "Die Schale." "Die Mainacht" is undoubtedly a more effective song: Brahms seems to have felt more at home in the melancholy moonlight than in the churning waters of Lethe. But both songs, along with "Die Kränze," show Brahms in the mid 1860s employing certain "instrumental" techniques of thematic, harmonic, and formal development on the smaller scale of the Lied. We will now see how these styles and procedures shape the larger canvases of Brahms's chamber music of the 1870s.

III

In 1873 Brahms broke his eight-year instrumental silence with the publication of the two String Quartets, op. 51, works that were apparently the results of prolonged labor. In his *Werkverzeichnis*, Brahms noted that they had been "angefangenen früher"—he did not say how much earlier—and then "zum 2. mal geschrieben . . . Sommer 1873."[19] On stylistic grounds alone Kalbeck suggested that the first two movements of the A-Minor Quartet (no. 2) originated during Brahms's Detmold-Hamburg years, 1859–62.[20] Even in its published form, the first movement could possibly antedate the more innovative sonata forms of opp. 26 and 34. But the thematic process of the Andante—which, we recall, Schoenberg held up as a prime example of Brahms's sophisticated art of developing variation—far outstrips any slow movements of Brahms's first maturity. The Andante is thus unlikely to have been written near them in time.

Only the C-Minor Quartet (or at least *a* C-minor quartet) has a documented existence before 1873. As early as 1865 Joachim asked Brahms, "Is your String Quartet in C Minor ready?" Apparently it was not, for Joachim inquired about the work again in 1867 and 1869. Clara Schumann noted in her diary in 1866 that Brahms had played her part of a C-minor string quartet. Brahms himself

[19]See Orel, "Eigenhändiges Werkverzeichnis," p. 538. Brahms reportedly claimed to have written over twenty string quartets before venturing to publish any; see his remark cited in Kalbeck, *Johannes Brahms*, 2: 440. Brahms considered including a B-minor quartet (not surviving) among his first published works; see Brahms, *Briefwechsel mit Joseph Joachim*, 1: 11–12.

[20]See Kalbeck, *Johannes Brahms*, 2: 451.

hints at the phantom work in a letter to his publisher of 1869, but Simrock was not to receive it until the fall of 1873.[21]

Of course, no substantial account of the work's genesis can be constructed from these isolated references. We can probably believe Brahms when he says that the C-Minor and A-Minor Quartets were "written for the second time" in 1873. But from the fleeting evidence we also learn that the first quartet originated and grew slowly, perhaps fitfully, during the entire eight-year instrumental hiatus and that it held unusual significance for Brahms. In fact, the C-Minor Quartet is a milestone, the nature of which is communicated well in this admittedly grandiose assessment by Karl Geiringer: "[Brahms] had not only conquered a new form of ensemble, but at the same time his style developed to its full maturity. He had now achieved an economy which refused to tolerate a single superfluous note, but at the same time he had perfected a method of integration that would give an entire work the appearance of having been cast from one mold."[22]

This impression of economy, and of a single "mold," arises most immediately, perhaps, from the thematic relationships among the four movements. Op. 51, no. 1, is the first instrumental work since the early piano sonatas to display such connections so prominently. As has often been observed, the rising stepwise third that opens the first movement reappears in both its original and in a descending form to shape the main theme of the Romanze. Both the main theme and countersubject of the Allegretto also clearly derive from the basic motive. And the finale bursts in with a theme that directly recalls the main idea of the first movement, and then goes on to include several other reminiscences of the earlier movements.

In his impressively detailed analysis, Rainer Wilke has suggested that the C-Minor Quartet displays more than thematic unity or consistency—that there is a real *process* spanning the whole work. He points to the extreme brevity of the finale and to its lack (unusual in Brahms's last movements) of a separate development section. Because the basic motivic material of the quartet has already been developed so extensively in three movements, he argues, Brahms may have felt there was no need for a lengthy, complete sonata form.[23] This is indeed a striking and attractive notion, from which we may extrapolate another about this quartet: it is the first work in which Brahms shows a concern for such

---

[21]See Brahms, *Briefwechsel mit Joachim*, 2: 38, 40, and 57; Berthold Litzmann, *Clara Schumann*, 3: 194; and Brahms, *Briefe an P. J. und Fritz Simrock*, 1: 74–75.

[22]Geiringer, *Brahms: His Life and Work*, pp. 231–32.

[23]Wilke, *Brahms, Reger, Schönberg Streichquartette*, pp. 79–80, 82–84. On motivic relationships in op. 51, see also William G. Hill, "Brahms' Op. 51—A Diptych." The finale of op. 51, no. 1, is classified by Arno Mitschka as a *kontrahierten* (contracted) sonata form; see his *Sonatensatz*, pp. 277–79.

higher-level thematic processes, rather than mere thematic recall or transformation.

The relatively brief total time span of the quartet—it lasts just over thirty minutes—helps point up these processes. The C-Minor Quartet is one of Brahms's most concise four-movement instrumental works; beside it, the fifty-minute long piano quintet appears gargantuan. Regardless of its absolute duration, however, the quartet *seems* short because its musical discourse is so compressed and intense. In op. 51, Brahms seems to have stripped down to their bare essentials the procedures developed in his earlier works. The luxuriance of opp. 25, 26, and 34 and the spaciousness of their thematic-harmonic-formal processes become reduced to a style of extreme concentration. In this op. 51 style, as I shall call it, Brahms imports into the sonata form some of the techniques explored primitively in "Die Schale der Vergessenheit." Harmonies, especially in the first and last movements, churn continuously, carrying aloft very small thematic or motivic fragments: the music rarely settles down into harmonically stable, melodically rounded episodes.

Schoenberg on two occasions expressed his admiration for the remarkable harmonic language of the C-Minor Quartet; as might be expected, his brief remarks about the first and third movements can help light the way to a better understanding of the op. 51 style. In his chapter on the construction of "periods" from *Fundamentals of Musical Composition*, Schoenberg quotes the opening of the Allegretto to show how Brahms can enrich a symmetrical, 4 + 4–bar structure from within by "prolific exploration of the multiple meaning of harmonies."[24] (See Appendix, ex. K, pp. 189–90.) Although the key signature announces F minor, the first six bars contain few harmonies related diatonically to that key, Schoenberg observes. The opening F-minor chord (supporting a striking ♭6–5 appoggiatura in the melody) moves directly to a G[7]: this progression strongly implies not F minor, but iv–V[7] (colored by a Neapolitan) in C minor. But the resolution to C minor is sidestepped as the theme moves in its third measure toward A♭, nominally "the mediant region of F minor," as Schoenberg says. Again, however, Brahms remains on the dominant (E♭) of the key area, refusing to provide the implied tonic. The second half of the period returns to the opening bars (5–6 repeat 1–2), then reaches a cadence on the real dominant, C.

This taut but fluid harmonic structure supports a highly economical motivic process. Joachim and Hanslick would surely have claimed a lack of *Erfindung* in this theme, which Brahms builds entirely from chains of descending seconds to which is added an agitated counterpoint of rising thirds in the viola. Such streamlining goes even beyond the economy of opp. 25 and 34, where semitones are likewise ubiquitous but the themes are longer-breathed. In op. 51 Brahms continually, obsessively reiterates his short motives, such as the descending second, and prevents them from expanding into broader themes or

[24]Schoenberg, *Fundmentals*, p. 30. The musical example is on p. 54.

melodies. This process is complemented by—and actually seems to float on the surface of—the flexible kind of harmonic language Schoenberg discusses.

These thematic-harmonic procedures profoundly affect the sonata structure as a whole, as we see if we look past the theme Schoenberg quotes, at the rest of the movement (see ex. K for the exposition and development). Unlike many of the allegretto or intermezzo movements that Brahms often substitutes for the traditional scherzo, this Allegretto is a fully formed sonata structure.[25] After the first theme (1), seven bars (2a/transition) serve to confirm the dominant. At bar 15, over a pulsating C pedal, comes the promise of a sweet, lyrical melody (2b). In its second measure, however, this theme suddenly curtails itself and begins to repeat small fragments. The sixteenth-note figure, A♮–B♮–G–C, that concludes the slur across bars 15–16 is repeated in sequence, beginning on G. The tail of this idea, the fourth F–B♭, is then restated a step lower to generate a new, triadic sixteenth-note figure, E♭–A♭–C–A♭, which in turn is echoed by the second violin.

Where we expect lyricism, then, Brahms has given us thematic fragmentation: a potential melody has doubled back on itself, has reined itself in. As in the D♭-major theme of op. 34 (2c), the thematic fragmentation triggers a metrical displacement. At the end of bar 16, the $\frac{4}{8}$ meter becomes dislocated onto the fourth beat; that is, it yields to the slurring of the theme (see ex. K). As in the earlier examples we have discussed, all parts support the new meter. The framework fluctuates when the theme begins again in bar 19 (now in the second violin and viola) but is firmly displaced anew in bar 20. The conclusion becomes wonderfully disorienting. In bar 23 the upper three instruments begin to readjust to the notated meter (see my brackets), then land on a firm downbeat at bar 24. But the solitary cello (also bracketed) continues for a moment in the dislocated pattern, refusing to align with the others.

As in op. 34, the metrical displacement has been foreshadowed or anticipated throughout theme 1 by the strong accentuation of the normally weak fourth beat. Thus in this small-scale exposition, Brahms has drawn liberally on the techniques of earlier works (especially opp. 26 and 34) but has compressed them most remarkably. The displacement of 2b arises and subsides within the brief span of ten bars. And it seems to have the specific function of circumventing melodic fulfillment: the melodic potential of 2b is nipped in the bud.

Fulfillment is also withheld at the place where Brahms customarily provides his most expansive apotheoses, the development section. In the developments of opp. 5, 26, and 34, we recall, Brahms plants a striking lyrical transformation of one of his principal themes. In the Allegretto of op. 51 he seems to build toward just such a moment, but the tune never materializes. The first part of the development explores the viola's syncopated counterpoint to theme 1, which is traded between the outer parts as the harmony drifts downward from

---

[25]On these movements see Mitschka, *Sonatensatz*, pp. 236–43.

C minor into the regions of B minor and B♭ minor. In bars 35–37 the instruments pause on a diminished-seventh chord built over D♮ and ascend in unison and octaves to the seventh, C♭. Then, in one of the most delicately conceived and scored passages in all of Brahms's chamber music, the bass moves to D♭ and the diminished chord melts into a dominant seventh of G♭. Simultaneously, the once disquieted viola motive is transmuted into a poignant, lyrical triplet figure, now exchanged between first violin and viola to the *pizzicato* accompaniment of cello and second violin. But instead of burgeoning into a melody, the little motive is repeated (and inverted) for six bars. The technique is essentially that of lyrical transformation and represents the same kind of gesture we have seen in earlier Brahms developments. But instead of spinning out a big tune here, Brahms focuses almost obsessively on a single motive. This passage, and this type of transformation, epitomize the op. 51 style, which restrains both lyrical effusion and metamorphosis.

In the explosive first movement of the C-Minor Quartet all these thematic, harmonic, and formal characteristics are magnified. Schoenberg was impressed enough with the harmonic aspects of this movement to cite part of the first group, at the very beginning of his "Brahms the Progressive," as an example of "how great an innovator Brahms was in respect to harmony."[26] The first group (see Appendix, ex. L, p. 191) has an A B A' structure, much like others we have examined: 1a moves to a strong half cadence on V, and the conclusion of 1b leads through the dominant back to 1a' in the tonic. As in the Allegretto theme, Brahms enriches this conventional design from within: instead of leading directly to 1b, the dominant half cadence of bars 7–8 is repeated a whole step lower, thus ushering in the subdominant minor at bar 11. 1b remains in this key until at bar 18 a bass F♯, supporting a diminished-seventh chord, prods it back toward the dominant of C minor. The dominant dutifully arrives, but in the astonishing two bars that follow, the harmony returns to and, as it were, gets stuck on the same F♯. In a wrenching shift of perspective the F♯, played in unison by viola and cello in bar 21, suddenly comes to sound like the dominant of an utterly remote B minor! In the next bar Brahms returns just as suddenly to the true dominant, G, and descends hastily to the tonic.

As is so often the case in Brahms, these harmonic procedures are closely bound up with motivic ones; indeed, tonal ambiguity here seems a result of the subtle motivic process. In its initial appearances the principal three-note figure of 1b always traverses scale degrees $\hat{8}$–♭$\hat{6}$–$\hat{5}$ (F–D♭–C in F minor at bars 11 and 13; and C–A♭–G in C, the dominant of F, at 15 and 17). However, when Brahms reaches the actual dominant, G, in bar 19, this motive appears on different scale degrees, ♮$\hat{3}$–$\hat{1}$–♯$\hat{7}$ or B♭–G–F♯. It is reiterated at the same pitches in the following measure, but its harmonic foothold has now been loosened. Ostensibly, the cello figure, D–E♮–F♯, continues the dominant scale begun in the previous bar

---

[26]Schoenberg, *Style and Idea*, p. 402.

and thus still implies the region of G. But in the absence of a firm harmonic root our ears tend to hear the descending motive in its original function: it becomes $\hat{8}$–♭$\hat{6}$–$\hat{5}$, supported by a bass ascending through $\hat{3}$–$\hat{4}$–$\hat{5}$, in B minor. When both voices have converged on F♯, and when that pitch is solemnly repeated in unison in bar 21, the shift of aural perspective is complete. Then, in a still more rapid shift, Brahms reinterprets the F♯ as the leading tone to the true dominant. It rises to G, whence the three-note motive steps in and guides us firmly back to the tonic in C minor.

Schoenberg justly observes that "the harmony of this . . . section competes successfully with that of many a Wagnerian passage. Even the most progressive composers after Brahms were carefully avoiding remote deviation from the tonic region in the beginning of a piece. But this modulation to the dominant of a minor region on B, and the sudden, unceremonious and precipitate return to the tonic, is a rare case."[27] Especially rare is the sheer terror—I can think of no better term—this passage can evoke in a listener. In bars 19–21 Brahms leads us to the edge of an abyss, and, indeed, makes us lean far over. Then he pulls us suddenly back onto the *terra firma* of C minor.

In the recapitulation Brahms actually does plunge us briefly into the chasm, for at the end of 1a (bars 143ff.) the half cadence is repeated a half step, rather than a whole step, below the dominant, thus bringing us face-to-face with the infamous F♯. In the next bar (147), Brahms quietly but firmly resolves the F♯ to B minor, which now leads logically back to the tonic through D major and G⁷ (bars 150–51). Thus the "sore" F♯ and the B minor that once seemed so frighteningly remote are reintegrated into the familiar context of C minor.

The harmonic expansion of 1b may compete with Wagner's devices, but unique to Brahms—and especially to the op. 51 style—is the turbulent combination of richness and intensity with which the rest of the movement unfolds. The second group has a "paired-theme" design much like that of op. 34:

theme:	2a	2b	2a'	2b'	2c
bar:	33	37	41	49	62

The earlier work seems positively bloated by comparison with the streamlined second group of op. 51.

The whole group is built from the continuous reinterpretation of a few motivic fragments. The descending arpeggio figure of 2a (bars 33–34) becomes 2b, first in inversion (bar 37), then in its original form (39–40). Both these forms intermingle in 2b': the ascending arpeggio appears in diminution at 49–53, then continues underneath the descending one (whose rhythm is now dotted) in 54–56. Besides the arpeggio motive Brahms exploits one other principal idea, the furtive ascending stepwise third, which appears in the second two bars of 2a

[27]Schoenberg, *Style and Idea*, pp. 402–3.

EXAMPLE 31: Brahms, String Quartet, op. 51, no. 1, I, harmonic reduction.

(35–36) and clearly derives from the ur-motive of the quartet, the C–D–E♭ of bar 1. At 2a′ this figure appears simultaneously (like the arpeggio in 2b′) in both its original and inverted forms, and its agitated eighth-note rhythms carry over into 2b′.

Even more clearly than in the Allegretto, the nervous motivic work is sustained here by a fluid harmonic structure. The first a b pair floats in the region of E♭ minor, beginning over an ostinato dominant pedal, moving to its mediant (G♭) at bars 37–38, then back to the dominant at 40. The second thematic pair, a′ b′, greatly extends the harmonic compass. Instead of remaining on the dominant of E♭ minor, the third and fourth bars of 2a′ repeat the initial two-bar pattern up a fourth, in A♭ minor (bars 43–44). The viola here becomes the bass and begins a four-bar chromatic ascent from the third of A♭ minor, C♭, up to G. This line transports above it an astonishing series of harmonies that lead 2b′ into remote regions. Defying verbal description, this progression can best be represented by a reduction of the basic voice-leading (ex. 31).

By bar 49 Brahms has reached the distant climes of D major, which shifts quickly to D minor. Then, in the most hair-raising of the chromatic side-slippings, the dominant of D suddenly explodes outward: at bars 52–53 the A splits, as it were, into B♭ and A♭, thus forming a dominant seventh of the real second-group key, E♭. But the longed-for resolution is not yet at hand, for Brahms prolongs the dominant of E♭ by extending the arpeggios of 2b′ and then by introducing a new theme, 2c, at bar 62, which likewise hovers on the dominant. Only at bar 75 do we get at last a firm cadence; and even here our satisfaction at the sweet major chord is instantly snatched away by the ominous return of the main theme in the minor mode.

During the expansion of 2b′, Brahms adds yet another combustible ingredient—metrical conflict—to a cauldron already seething with harmonic and motivic activity. At bar 58 the upper and lower parts slip out of alignment, as the violins displace the descending arpeggio pattern by a quarter note. After three measures the arpeggios subside, and the second violin and cello pulsate quietly in the two conflicting $\frac{3}{2}$ meters. (The viola chords support the second violin.) The entrance of 2c above this enigmatic accompaniment produces one of the most unusual effects in all of Brahms, for this theme seems to drift outside any metrical framework (see Appendix, ex. M, p. 192). Our ears cannot easily shape or organize it. When the pulsating bi-metrical accompaniment ceases in bar 67, a duple meter begins to emerge in the violin arabesques. A $\frac{4}{4}$ (or $\frac{2}{2}$) pattern becomes explicit at bar 70, where accompaniment and figuration at last move together. The first violin's stepwise descent to E♭ in bars 73–75 firmly restores the original $\frac{3}{2}$ meter. In this process, the F on the last beat of bar 74 remains deliciously ambiguous: we understand its function as an upbeat to the E♭, yet still tend to hear it as a downbeat within the preceding duple metrical pattern.

As in the Allegretto, then, Brahms has deliberately withheld melodic expansion in the second group—and, indeed, in the exposition as a whole. In both movements the potentially tuneful second themes remain metrically and harmonically unstable. The development section of the first movement also remains, like that of the third, without any real lyrical fulfillment. One could easily imagine a handsome melodic transformation of the main theme along the lines of the transformation in the op. 26 development. In fact, Brahms's second movement, the Romanze, seems to offer (or at least promise) just such a tune, as the jagged outlines of the C-minor theme soften into a luxuriant D♭ major. But within the first-movement development the theme appears only in broad sequences, which explore its harmonic rather than melodic capabilities.

IV

Ivor Keys has observed that the main theme of the quartet's first movement "constantly summons a storm, as it were, to drown any incipient songs." Like a number of critics, Keys finds the op. 51 style too consistently ungracious and harsh on the ear. He complains, "Grittiness is certainly in evidence in this quartet, and in its first movement a high proportion of what can most kindly be called non-melodic work. . . . There is a shortage of telling melody combined with a good deal of sheer ungainliness."[28] Indeed, op. 51 demands a good deal from the listener; it is uncompromising in the way that artistic milestones often are. Charles Rosen has suggested that Beethoven's *Hammerklavier* Piano Sonata, op. 106, is hard to listen to largely because of its obsessively concentrated style, a style that marked a turning point for its composer.[29] Brahms's C-Minor Quartet seems to me a similar kind of work.

In Brahms, however, song is never submerged for long. Indeed, a song of 1873, "Regenlied" (op. 59, no. 3), resurfaces in 1878–79 to inspire one of Brahms's most lyrical compositions, the Violin Sonata in G Major, op. 78. Brahms wrote this sonata, as well as two of his other most genial works, the Second Symphony and the Violin Concerto, during his summer vacations at

---

[28]Keys, *Brahms Chamber Music*, pp. 30–31.

[29]Rosen, *Classical Style*, p. 434.

EXAMPLE 32: Brahms, Violin Sonata, op. 78, I.

Lake Worth in Pörtschach. As he himself implied, the lovely natural surround-ings seem to have had an effect on these compositions: "Here the melodies are flying so thick that one must be careful not to step on one."[30] In op. 78 he proves that the newly won thematic-harmonic-formal integration can generate a work as serene and melodious as the quartet is anxious and tuneless.

Despite their different moods, these two chamber works have in common prominent cross-movement thematic relationships. The outer movements of op. 78 share, of course, the dotted "Regenlied" motive,[31] and in the piano ara-besque at the close of the finale (bar 162) there is more than a hint of the opening theme from the first movement. Still more striking is the literal reappearance, in the finale, of the main theme from the Adagio, which enters quite suddenly in its original key (E♭ major) at the point where we expect a return of the second theme in D minor (bar 84). The direct reminiscence rings rather hollow here, despite the skill with which Brahms proceeds to weave the Adagio theme seam-lessly into its new environment. Brahms uses the technique to much better effect in the finales of the Third Symphony and the Clarinet Quintet, op. 115, where the opening theme does not reappear suddenly, but emerges gradually to dominate the closing moments. The success of op. 78 lies not in such high-level procedures, but in the utter limpidity of its thematic process. This is especially evident in the first movement, which represents the height of Olympian tran-quility in the art of developing variation.

The violin sets forth a handful of motives from which this splendid tapestry will be spun (ex. 32), especially by the flexible development of their rhythmic aspects. The piano merely punctuates the first nine measures with discreet chords, allowing the motivic exordium to unfold freely, even asymmetrically. Motives p and q appear together only once, articulating an octave descent from the high D to the D above middle C. Motives p and r appear twice in succession and climb back up to the octave. The melodic and harmonic goal, D major, is expressed by motive s, which is given a one-bar tail and then repeated (in varied form) with a three-bar tail.

---

[30]Reported in Alfred von Ehrmann, *Johannes Brahms: Weg, Werk und Welt*, p. 287.

[31]On the motivic relationships between song and sonata, which encompass more than just the dotted-rhythm motto, see Hans Hollander, "Der Melodische Aufbau in Brahms' 'Regenlied' Sonate."

EXAMPLE 33: Brahms, Violin Sonata, op. 78, I, rebarring.

   As in a number of the Brahms sonata forms we have examined, the opening section of op. 78 has an A B A' structure, in which the central segment begins a kind of development. In the C-Minor Quartet the development is primarily harmonic; here, as in the piano quintet, it is metrical, indeed polymetrical (ex. 33). The violin part, whose rhythm is based on p, reshapes the notated $\frac{6}{4}$ meter into $\frac{3}{2}$ (bar 11), then spills over the bar line in what we hear as an extra measure of $\frac{3}{4}$, whose rhythm recalls r. This pattern begins again in the second half of bar 12, now completely overriding the notated bar lines. At bar 14 the theme settles into a "normal" $\frac{3}{2}$ pattern.

   Underneath the irregularly expanding violin theme, the piano provides a continuous flow of eighth notes whose arpeggio patterns suggest yet another subdivision of the notated meter. The six notes within each slur are grouped by contour as 3 + 3; the slurred groups themselves fall into a larger pattern of 3 (in bars 11–13). The piano thus implies a broad meter of $\frac{18}{8}$ ($\frac{12}{8}$ + $\frac{6}{8}$), which becomes reduced to $\frac{12}{8}$ when the violin settles into a steady $\frac{3}{2}$ pattern at bar 14. This polymetrical relationship between the instruments, one of the most complex in all of Brahms, is further complicated by the actual grouping of pitches in the piano—regardless, that is, of their registral placement and contour. In bar 11, for example, the first group in the right hand comprises F♯–B–F♯–B–F♯–B. This arrangement suggests a 2 + 2 + 2 division of eighth notes within the slur, and thus projects something of the notated $\frac{6}{4}$ meter.

   In the C-Minor Quartet, the metrical-rhythmic aspects of the B section were

EXAMPLE 34: Brahms, Violin Sonata, op. 78, I.

kept simple, as if compensating for the complex harmonies. Here the inverse holds true: the B section moves to an easily understood III, or B major, thereby allowing the listener to concentrate on (and perhaps unravel) the metrical density. As in op. 51, where the disorienting, remote B minor is safely confined within the tonic boundaries of the A and A' segments, so in op. 78 is the metrical confusion flanked by passages of relative clarity, especially the lucid texture of the first nine bars.

The large second group of the violin sonata is a virtual paradigm of the fluent style of developing variation in which each theme grows naturally, almost spontaneously, from the preceding one. Theme 2a (bar 36) is constructed by elegant modification of motives s and r. The stable rhythms, whereby the once empty downbeats and strong beats are filled in, and the square-cut phrase structure of (2 + 2) + (2 + 2) bars effectively disperse the rhythmic-metrical urgency of the first group, thereby reflecting the function of 2a as a stable element within the sonata form.

Initially stable, at least: after eight measures 2a yields to another theme, 2b, by means of a particularly subtle use of the linkage technique (ex. 34). Bar 43 presents a conventional half cadence (to the dominant of the dominant), which Brahms then repeats at the same pitches to initiate the next idea. Even the harmonic content of bar 43 is carried over, except for the bass E on the first beat. The principal alterations involve rhythm—with some surprising results. The dotted rhythm of the figure C♯–B–E evens out to three quarter notes in bar 44 (a hint of the rhythm of s), and Brahms decorates the E–A fifth with an F♯ appoggiatura and a descending A-major arpeggio. The latter modification brings about motive q. This motive, not heard for some time, has actually reconstituted itself!

At bar 48, Brahms extends 2b by continuing the hemiola rhythm and ascending scale of the preceding bar. In another act of motivic self-regeneration, the A–E fourth in the violin in the first half of bar 49 is transformed by the piano into A–E–F♮, which clearly recalls motive s as heard in theme 2a (bar 36). The revived s is treated sequentially, then subsides in bars 53–54 into pairs of quarter notes. From this figure Brahms now elicits p in its initial form, then q. We have thus returned to the opening material; once again, familiar motives seem to have created themselves out of neutral, ostensibly non-thematic figures.

We might expect the exposition to close with the firm establishment of D major and the tranquil return to the opening theme, but the extraordinarily fertile thematic process of op. 78 has not yet run its course. After the cadence in bar 60, the violin moves immediately to the third degree, F♯, beneath which Brahms shifts to the key of B major—familiar to us from theme 1b, where it also followed quite suddenly upon a D chord (D⁷ of bars 9–10). Here Brahms constructs yet another theme, 2c, out of the basic motives. The ubiquitous r rhythm is joined to a figure clearly derived from p (the second-group form, as in bar 36). After a brief canon between piano and violin, motive p—apparently encouraged by the idea of imitation—strikes out on its own (bar 64), leading gradually back to the dominant key area. To celebrate the return, p spontaneously generates still another theme, 2d (bar 70). In the transition, p has been traded back and forth between bass and upper voice; now, in both voices, the two statements of p happily take their places side by side. The exposition at last unravels in bars 77–81. For the first time there is a distinct absence of motivic activity: the even quarter-note scales and bass pedal are intentionally athematic.

In the G-Major Violin Sonata, developing variation seems to have at last become a fully continuous process, one capable of generating an entire sonata exposition. The extraordinary combination of lyricism and developing variation can, I think, be traced back to works such as the A-Major Piano Quartet, op. 26, and "Die Mainacht," in which the thematic, harmonic, and formal procedures are suffused with song. From the expansive, even unbuttoned, mood of op. 78 the tight-lipped op. 51 style seems remote indeed. Yet, as I have tried to show, both works are really generated by similar techniques—by a sophisticated, rapid motivic development and a fluid thematic discourse. Even more remarkable is that both styles have common roots in Brahms's earliest sonata structures, especially the F-Minor Sonata, op. 5, and the B-Major Trio, op. 8. Already in these works his impulse is clear: to build a sonata structure by the continuous variation of brief motives. But the young Brahms was not capable of, or interested in, the sort of "development" we have been examining in his later works. In the early sonata and trio he alters only the mood, the outward demeanor of his motives, for which purpose he skillfully employs the techniques of thematic transformation.

We might say that the extreme chromaticism and harmonic virtuosity of the op. 51 style build on the *harmonic* inheritance of the early transformations, such as the exotic color changes in the second group of op. 5. Op. 78 seems to assume the thematic or *motivic* legacy: its harmonic language is not especially remarkable, but the purely horizontal dimension unfolds with a sophistication and flexibility that Brahms himself was never to surpass. Together the C-Minor Quartet and G-Major Violin Sonata show how far Brahms's compositional powers—actually his powers to realize his fundamental compositional tendencies—had developed by the 1870s.

5

Symphony, 1877–1885

I

The preceding chapters have concentrated primarily on the exposition of Brahms's sonata forms, and only on certain isolated aspects of the development and recapitulation. Given the goal of this study—to examine the role of developing variation—such selective analysis is inevitable, for it is within the exposition (and at several other important moments, such as the retransition) that Brahms is most original and compelling; it is here that the principle of developing variation is most in evidence and that we can trace an evolution in Brahms's compositional style and technique.

On the highest level, Brahms's treatment of sonata form remains fundamentally conservative throughout his career. His recapitulations are, as a rule, less adventurous than many of Haydn, Mozart, and Beethoven: they rarely deviate from the course charted by the exposition. Too extensive a divergence would, of course, undermine the basic function of the sonata recapitulation, which is resolution through restatement. Most listeners have little difficulty in accepting and appreciating Brahms's recapitulations, which, after all, provide a second chance (third, if the exposition has been repeated) to assimilate the complex developmental processes.

The development section itself is more problematic for both the composer and the listener. Here Brahms tends to abandon the progressive techniques of developing variation for such traditional classical procedures as imitative counterpoint, exact sequence, thematic fragmentation, and rapid modulation. After an exposition that has already "developed" its material so fully and effectively, these devices can (and often do) sound mechanical. For example, the exposition of the first movement of the G-Major Violin Sonata, op. 78, pours forth its motivic material (as we have seen) with marvelous spontaneity and fluency.

These qualities are less evident in the development section (especially bars 107–34), where there is something labored about the way the same motives are paraded before us in imitation, sequences, and remote modulations. The development in the other first movement we examined in Chapter 4—that from the C-Minor String Quartet, op. 51—is more persuasive: it relaxes rather than intensifies the already frighteningly intense motivic work of the exposition. Here Brahms makes skillful use of broad sequences, which calmly carry the main theme through a rich series of harmonies. Unlike many of Brahms's developments, this one is extremely taut.

As we have seen, Brahms will occasionally focus a development section around a broad, lyrical thematic transformation, which—especially in a lengthy development—can provide a welcome contrast to the more standard developmental techniques. Although Brahms avoids such expansive moments in op. 51, he continues to plant splendid metamorphoses in later works. Perhaps the finest are those in the *Tragic Overture*, op. 81 (bars 210ff.), and the first movements of the C-Major Piano Trio, op. 87 (165ff.), the A-Major Violin Sonata, op. 100 (137ff.), and the Clarinet Quintet, op. 115 (98ff.).

The basic conservatism of Brahms's sonata structures has led several commentators to suggest an irreconcilable dialectic between the higher-level form and the local thematic-motivic processes. Klaus Velten, Arno Mitschka, and Carl Dahlhaus all claim that the "static-architectonic" principle of sonata form comes into direct conflict with the tendency of Brahms's music to unfold developmentally—as pure *Gedankenentwicklung*.[1] Velten seems genuinely disappointed that Brahms is not more "progressive" on the higher level. And Christian Schmidt sternly advises the critic or analyst that any "attempt to mediate between the individual events [*Einzelereignissen*] and the arrangement of the whole [*Gesamtdisposition*] will not succeed."[2]

In this chapter I hope to show, nevertheless, that developing variation, defined as a flexible principle rather than a rigid set of techniques, can indeed influence the higher-level sonata structure of a movement and even the design of a four-movement work as a whole. Brahms's most ambitious endeavors are found not in the chamber works, but in his more massive sonata-form statements, the symphonies, which were all completed within a single decade, 1876–85. Of particular interest for our study of the relationship between developing variation and sonata procedures are the Adagio of the Second Symphony and the overall structure (as well as certain aspects of the individual sonata movements) of the Third.

[1] See Carl Dahlhaus, "Brahms und die Idee der Kammermusik," pp. 559–60; Velten, *Schönbergs Instrumentation*, pp. 79–81; and Mitschka, *Sonatensatz*, pp. 315–16.

[2] Schmidt, *Verfahren*, pp. 183–84.

II

Sonata principles do not normally play a significant role in Brahms's slow movements.[3] The majority of his Andantes and Adagios have either a ternary or a theme-and-variations structure. But in several instances, most notably in the last three symphonies, the basic A B A plan of a slow movement reveals a strong sonata-form influence. These *Mischformen* are less schematic and more flexible than many first movements. One senses that, outside the bright spotlight of the first-movement position, Brahms felt freer to give rein to his compositional imagination and tendencies.

The structure of the Adagio of the Second Symphony (1877) is easily described: a full sonata-style exposition with primary and secondary key areas (B and F♯) and a closing theme; a brief development; a recapitulation from which the second group is omitted, but into which is inserted another, "secondary," development;[4] and a coda based on the closing idea. The design is hardly revolutionary, but utterly remarkable is the fluency with which themes are created, and the way they actually seem to generate the larger form. The Adagio is one of Brahms's greatest studies in "musical prose." We recall that Schoenberg coined that term to characterize Brahms's "direct and straightforward presentation of ideas, without any patchwork, without mere padding and empty repetitions." Few movements are less padded than this one.

The first twelve bars (ex. 35), which last a full eighty seconds at this tempo, are among the most elusive—impressionistic, it might be said—in all Brahms. Themes remain only fragmentary, avoiding closure and mutating instead into new ideas; every cadence is side-stepped; harmonic areas, including the tonic and dominant, are implied but never established; and the metrical framework evades the authority of the bar line. The cellos present four separate ideas, of which the first three (1a, 1b, 1c) are related in their use of a descending scale. A fifth idea acts as a cadential figure.

Theme 1a takes shape as a twofold descent from the dominant note F♯, first to a mysterious B♯, then to the tonic B♮. In the bassoons, scales rise in contrary motion, from F♯ and B♮ (not shown in ex. 35). The movement begins in utter obscurity, on the dominant and on the notated fourth beat. As in several of the other metrically displaced themes already examined, here—at the very opening—the listener cannot possibly be aware of the real location of the bar line, because the accompaniment (unison and octave F♯'s in the horns, tuba, and low strings) sounds only on the fourth and second beats, which (as in op. 34) are thus perceived as the first and third.

The harmonic and metrical clouds begin to disperse with theme 1b, which

---

[3]See the discussion in Mitschka, *Sonatensatz*, pp. 221–33. Mitschka's accounts of the two slow movements treated in this chapter, from the Second and Third Symphonies, are less cogent than many of his other analyses.

[4]On "secondary developments," see Rosen, *Sonata Forms*, pp. 104–8, 276–80.

EXAMPLE 35: Brahms, Symphony No. 2, op. 73, II, theme and bass only.

also begins on the fourth beat but moves to a clear downbeat in bar 3, where there is also a strong tonic root. Theme 1b ornaments the descending scale of 1a with upper neighbor notes and a more detached articulation (and the introduction of the subdominant). Now, however, the descent occurs only once, as 1b yields to the twofold cadence figure in bars 4–5. (There is an element of "poetic" symmetry in the way theme 1a and the cadence figure, each built from two little phrases, balance each other around the single phrase of 1b.)

The cadence figure refuses to fulfill its ostensible function. Instead of resolving to the tonic, F♯ remains entrenched in the bass, and still another theme (1c) appears over a new iii⁶ chord. The metrical framework established by 1b and the cadence figure begins to dissolve again, because the first two beats of bar 6 remain disconcertingly devoid of rhythmic activity. The cellos sustain a solitary D♯; its supporting first-inversion harmony enters only on the second beat. The new thematic idea, 1c (built like 1a and 1b as an embellished descending scale), begins only with the upbeat to the third beat of the bar—almost as if it has waited to absorb or contemplate the new chord before venturing forth. Like the first theme, 1c articulates a twofold descent coinciding with the notated second and fourth beats.

After two bars, 1c yields to a new disjunct two-note figure, outlining B major, then C♯ (V/V). The eighth-note upbeat B is then placed up an octave and descends into what we recognize as a cadence figure related rhythmically to the

EXAMPLE 36: Brahms, Symphony No. 2, op. 73, II.

one in bars 4–5. It is now aimed at the dominant but, as before, resolution is thwarted by a deceptive cadence—here to a still more startling D major. Brahms enhances the harmonic evasion with a characteristic thematic device, the linkage technique, whereby the would-be cadence becomes a "new" idea; the E♯–F♯ figure of bar 10 serves both to suggest (not make) a cadence and initiate theme 1d. Like themes 1a, 1c, and the first cadence figure, theme 1d is allowed a double statement, then made to disappear. The pause on D major in bar 12—one could hardly call it a cadence—is followed by the first appearance of the violins and a restatement (with no harmonic preparation) of the opening theme (1a').

The entrance of 1a' suggests the first real "poetic" return of the movement; but in fact it serves only to mark a new paragraph in the musical prose, which then continues on its developmental course. As before, 1a' gives way to 1b' (bar 14) and to the first cadence figure (bar 16); but now the latter appears only once, then generates yet another new continuation. The pitches of its characteristic upbeat motive, B–E (also the upbeat to 1b), are taken up by the horn and elaborated into a four-part fugato (1e, bar 17). The final bars of this enigmatic passage move toward the long-expected dominant, F♯; but just as it is reached on the last beat of bar 27, the strings reintroduce theme 1b in C♯ major, the dominant of the dominant.

Brahms delays the arrival of F♯ by a magnificent fulfillment of the once fragmentary theme 1b (ex. 36). In its previous appearances (bars 2 and 14), 1b has yielded after one bar to the cadence figure. Now it is repeated in sequence a fourth higher, then begun again on the high F♯, where at last it breaks away from the descending-scale pattern and pushes still higher, to A♯ (bar 30). The theme then subsides through two bars, sinking to the A♯ two octaves below. To sustain this climax, Brahms avoids resolving the C♯ harmony to F♯ on the last beat of bar 29. Instead, the bass moves up by half step to C×, then D♯. The harmonies then move back through the circle of fifths to C♯ and, eventually, F♯. These progressions are in themselves unremarkable, but the effect is overwhelming because they provide the long-delayed dominant and underpin an apotheosis that has been denied to all previous thematic fragments. This moment reflects the great economy of Brahms's post-1870 style: the fulfillment is no longer a broad melody, as in the development sections of the F-Minor Sonata and A-Major Piano Quartet, but a brief, intense climax.

The second theme, 2a at bar 33, resolves the harmonic tension and is, appropriately, the most "poetically" constructed statement of the movement so far; it has a clear, symmetrical phrase structure of 2 + 2 bars (grouped into 4 + 4).

After another brief climax the closing theme appears (2b, bar 45), at first undulating quietly above a C♯ pedal. This time there is to be no resolution to F♯, for in bars 48–49 the theme pushes directly into the turbulent B minor of the development section. As Tovey observes, we expect this "quiet and naive" theme "to remain in its key and round off this section formally. A child may say the word that makes history; and so this unpretentious theme startles us by moving, with a rapid crescendo, into distant keys, and blazing out in a stormy fugato."[5]

Tovey has conveyed our sense of surprise at the outburst but has not emphasized sufficiently the ingenuity of Brahms's formal procedure, whereby the closing theme seems literally to generate the development. The tranquil three-note scale figure of 2b becomes transformed all at once into the agitated "fugato" motive. (The "fugato" is really only free two-part imitation.) There are, of course, numerous classical precedents for using a cadential theme as the first idea of the development section—for example, the first movements of Haydn's G-Minor Quartet, op. 74, no. 3; Mozart's E♭ Symphony (K.543); and Brahms's own piano quintet. But in these (as in most) instances, the theme appears only for a few bars, serving to extend the cadence and modulate to a new key area, where an earlier subject from the exposition is taken up. In Brahms's symphony, however, the entire development section is built from theme 2b, and it issues from that theme as suddenly and "prosaically" as the ideas of the exposition grew from one another. In other words, the thematic procedure of developing variation has been raised to the higher level of the formal structure: it engenders not only local thematic elements, but larger segments as well.

The recapitulation emerges from the development by a similar but even more dramatic process (see Appendix, ex. N, pp. 193–94). At bar 55, only six bars into the development, the imitative texture dissolves abruptly into a diminished-seventh chord, sustained *tremolando* by the strings. The three-note

---

[5]Donald F. Tovey, *Essays in Musical Analysis, 1: Symphonies*, p. 100.

motive drifts among the woodwinds, isolated and cut off from its customary contexts—theme 2b and the "fugato." In bar 57 the winds' motive is suddenly overlaid by theme 1a in the violins; on the dominant of G major the theme appears in its full, twofold form. As if rejecting this key, another diminished-seventh chord interrupts in bar 59, again setting the three-note motive adrift. At bar 62 the main theme makes another attempt, now on the dominant of E. The tonality is not yet right, but the theme now pushes its way forcefully toward the tonic in "three amazing chromatic steps," as Tovey says, through the dominants of A, B♭, and, finally, B (bars 64–65). The statement of 1a in bars 65–66 seems to be a test run, almost as if the theme cannot yet believe it has arrived home. The actual recapitulation begins on the last beat of bar 67.

As in several of the other sonata forms we have examined, Brahms here approaches the recapitulation obliquely, withholding any clear dominant preparation. Now, however, that harmonic procedure is joined to a thematic process whereby the main theme actually seems to regenerate itself before our very ears. It is not simply the gradual emergence of 1a that grips us, but the association of 1a with the three-note motive. When Brahms superimposes the two ideas at bar 57, and then again at 62 and 65 (see the boxes in ex. N), we immediately understand their relationship: the three-note motive is a simple rhythmic variant of the ascending third that appears in dotted rhythm as counterpoint to 1a. This recapitulation plays tantalizingly with our normal concept of musical process, for the main theme is in a sense reborn here from a motivic element that it had itself created at the beginning of the movement. The ascending third, which sounds new when it appears in 2b (bar 45), has thus gradually reestablished its original context. Furthermore, once the three-note motive has done its work, it retires: it disappears precisely at the actual moment of recapitulation in bar 67.

The motive's triplet rhythm (or $\frac{12}{8}$ metrical framework) continues, however, to penetrate the recapitulation of most of the first group (1a, 1b, 1c). Brahms omits the repetition of 1a, 1b, and the cadence figure that followed 1d in the exposition (bars 12–16), moving instead directly into the fugato, 1e (bar 80). Still further surprises and modifications are in store, for the fugato dissolves after only two entries. The bold B–E fourth in the brass and lower strings at bar 86 seems to call for a reconsideration of the fugato's basic motive. As if obeying the stern summons, the full orchestra reinterprets the motive as the opening of 1b, which bursts out in the minor mode, ornamented by swirling sextuplets. This impressive secondary development is formally analogous to the lyrical fulfillment of 1b in bars 30–32 of the exposition. The theme has once again swelled outward, now into anguish rather than song.

A dramatic half cadence to V ushers in the closing theme 2b (bar 92), which is also greatly modified. (Theme 2a is omitted; this movement, as I have said, is not a traditional sonata form, but a freer *Mischform*.) No longer presenting the "naive" image of diatonic tranquility it did in the exposition, 2b now churns with the chromatic turbulence of the preceding secondary development. Only gradually does the agitation subside and yield to the last, coda-like appearance of 1a (bar 97; see Appendix, ex. O, p. 195). Brahms here associates the three-note motive with the main theme even more clearly than in the development section: the rising third in the bassoons and cellos (bars 95–96) becomes transmuted a bar later into the familiar dotted rhythm (see boxes in ex. O). Underneath the final return of the theme, we hear the profoundly significant triplet rhythm, now only a final, faint echo of the movement's most powerful developmental idea.

In this Adagio, then, Brahms has fashioned a splendid image of how the principle of developing variation can permeate—can seem actually to generate— all levels of a sonata structure. The individual themes unfold by progressive modification of a brief idea, as in 1a, which first descends from F♯ to B♯ and then repeats but alters the gesture to descend to the tonic B. The higher-level succession of themes is governed by the same principle: 1b, and then 1c, explore the musical essence (the descending scale) of 1a. And just as the themes grow from each other, so do the segments of the sonata form. The tail of the exposition (theme 2b) engenders the development section; the recapitulation coalesces gradually out of the development; and the last motive in the recapitulation (the three-note figure) gives rise to the coda.

This movement is deeply, densely Brahmsian, as I have tried to show. Not surprisingly, then, it was slow to win favor, even comprehension, among his admirers. Hermann Levi, for many years a friend and champion of Brahms, wrote to Clara Schumann in 1879, "In the next concert I shall do Brahms's Second. I have not yet been able to make the Adagio my own; it leaves me cold."[6] As he had with the Piano Quartet, op. 25, Eduard Hanslick grumbled that "the ingenious working-out of the themes seems more significant than the themes themselves."[7] He reported too that "because of this the Adagio had less effect on the public than the other three movements." Tovey remarks that "the opening melody was considered very obscure by contemporary critics."[8] Listeners simply could make no sense of "rhythms that expand as irregularly as those of the slow movement."

But, as usual, Tovey also puts his finger on what was probably the real source of Levi's, Hanslick's, and the audiences' discomfort: "It is never the complexity of Brahms that makes him difficult for us; it is simply his originality. And this slow movement is intensely original." The individuality, and the great triumph, lie in Brahms's integration of his most characteristic compositional impulses. He has in this movement wedded his beloved (and essentially conservative)

---

[6]Cited in Berthold Litzmann, *Clara Schumann: Ein Künstlerleben nach Tagebüchern und Briefen*, 3: 399.

[7]Eduard Hanslick, *Concerte, Componisten, und Virtuosen der letzten fünfzehn Jahre, 1870– 1885*, p. 226.

[8]Tovey, *Essays in Musical Analysis*, 1, p. 99.

sonata principles to those flexible and diverse procedures we have called developing variation.

III

Although the Third Symphony (1883) is Brahms's shortest, it is also perhaps his most ambitious, striving more than any other for a coherence that extends beyond individual movements. The reappearance of the opening theme of the first movement at the very end of the finale has always been perceived and appreciated by listeners. What has never been sufficiently recognized, however, is that this remarkable return is but one manifestation of a dense network of thematic, harmonic, and formal processes spanning the work. The return is satisfying precisely because it represents the ultimate mingling and resolution of these different currents. As might be expected, Brahms continues to rely strongly on sonata principles and on the various methods of developing variation. In the Third Symphony, however, these techniques not only shape the separate movements, but inform the work as a whole.

To summarize: the key relationships among the movements project onto a higher level the tonal plan characteristic of "orthodox" (to use Tovey's term) sonata forms. The outer two movements are in F major and minor, the inner two in C major and minor. At the same time, Brahms exploits over the large span a special tonal relationship, that between the pitches A♮ and A♭, and between certain of their affiliated tonalities (F major and minor, A major, and A♭ major). The two notes clash at the very opening; their conflict unfolds on different structural levels and is resolved only in the coda of the final movement.

On a more local level, the three sonata-form movements of the Third Symphony draw upon the methods of developing variation we have examined in the C-Minor Quartet, the G-Major Violin Sonata, and the Adagio of the Second Symphony. Especially compelling from this viewpoint are the exposition of the first movement and the moments of recapitulation in the first two movements. In the Third Symphony these procedures are supplemented on a higher level not only by the tonal plan, but by a thematic-formal process involving the second subject of the Andante. Figure 2 will help clarify the large-scale processes in the symphony.

Let us examine first the large-scale tonal features. Both inner movements lie in the key of the dominant, in C major and minor respectively. This arrangement is not only without precedent in Brahms's other four-movement works, but in those of his classical and romantic predecessors. In most classical sonata-style pieces in the major mode, the subdominant serves as the key of at least one of the inner movements, almost invariably the slow movement. Although the later Beethoven and the early romantics often deviated from this scheme, especially by substituting third- or Neapolitan-related keys, none wrote a four-movement work with the plan of Brahms's Third.

Brahms is clearly attempting something special; indeed, I think that by

MOVEMENT	I				II			III			IV			
	Exp.	Dev.	Rec.	Coda	("Second group") Exp.	Rec.	Coda	Alleg.	Trio	Alleg.	Exp.	Dev.	Rec.	Coda
"SONATA" PLAN	F		F	(C)	C			c		c	(c) f		(F) f	F
A♮ / A♭ CONFLICT	F A (A♮–A♭–A♮) (A♭)		F D (A♮)			F / D♭ triads	plagal cadence	plagal cadence	A♭	plagal cadence	f (A♭)		F f (A♮) (A♭)	F (A♭)
"MISSING" THEME					X	?					X (A♭)		X (A♭)	X (A♭)

FIGURE 2: Brahms, Symphony No. 3, op. 90.

placing the two central movements in C, he is attempting to create, in the larger dimensions of the whole symphony, an analogy to the classical second group or second key area. It is probably for this reason—to impart a higher-level tonal direction—that in the first movement Brahms avoids a strong dominant where we most expect it: as a key in the second group and as a harmony in the retransition. The second group stays resolutely in A (major and minor); and in the retransition the tonic F is approached directly from an augmented-sixth harmony. C major *does* appear, however, in the coda, from bar 183 on. Here Brahms presents the main theme over the dominant C. (The "motto" of the symphony also appears on C for the first time, as C–E♭–C.) This is followed (in bars 195ff.) by a passage with repeated V^7 chords.

The first movement ends in the tonic, of course, but the subsequent Andante, in C major, can be said to carry over the strong dominant sonorities of the preceding coda. The Allegretto, in C minor, prolongs and inflects the C major of the Andante, and then links up with the finale even more clearly than the Andante does with the first movement. For the finale begins on the pitch C with an inscrutable, unaccompanied theme that lies uneasily between the preceding C minor and the new tonic-to-be, F minor. Because of the prominent B♮'s and E♭'s, C minor might still be heard as tonic here. (From this aural perspective the D♭'s would be Neapolitan inflections.) Only when the texture expands out into real parts at bar 5 does it become clear that C is functioning as the minor dominant of F minor (although there is never a firm cadence to F). The tonic minor governs most of the finale. The symphony's true tonic, F major, actually emerges only toward the end of the movement, first in the recapitulation of the second group, then more emphatically at the coda (bar 267). With these large-scale tonal procedures, then, Brahms effectively sustains the harmonic tensions of a traditional one-movement sonata form across an entire symphony.

F minor plays a significant role not only in this sonata-type design, but also in the other tonal process of the symphony, centered on the relationship between A♮ and A♭. As has often been observed, most articulately by Roger Sessions, Brahms brings these two pitches into conflict at the very beginning of the symphony.[9] The harmonies underpinning the F–A♭–F motto move from F major to a diminished-seventh chord built on the tonic root, and back to F major. The main theme enters on the last chord; the motto moves into the bass. The A♮ and A♭ now clash more forcefully: the minor third of the motto at bar 4 contradicts the preceding A♮ in the melody and succeeds in deflecting the harmony toward the tonic minor. Nor will the troublesome A♭ be easily displaced. It remains part of the harmony when the bass motto returns to F at bar 5, and even audaciously ushers in its own lower fifth, D♭. The A♭ and D♭ retreat gradually

[9]See Roger Sessions, *The Musical Experience of Composer, Performer, Listener*, p. 47. See also Schoenberg's discussion of the relationship between the motto and the movement's key areas, in his *Theory of Harmony*, p. 164.

over the next dozen bars, and the first theme group at last subsides into an F-major cadence—its first—at bar 15.

As Sessions points out, the subsequent transition and arrival at the second key area (bars 15–35) extend the A♮–A♭ influence over a wider area, expanding the tonal processes that are so compressed at the opening. In bars 19–21 the motto appears securely in F major as A–C–A, but an F–A♭–F statement overlaps with the last note. Here the A♮–A♭ idea becomes still more prominent by affecting the voice-leading: the bass A♮ of bar 21 drops directly to the A♭ of bar 22, which now resolves as a dominant to D♭ major. The tonal digression is broader than in the opening bars, for the D♭ appears in the bass and governs not just a single bar but an entire eight-bar phrase (23–30).

The A♭–D♭ matrix begins once again to dissolve as Brahms introduces the second key area with two more overlapping statements of the motto. Over the last note of F–A♭–F in the double bass (bar 29), the woodwinds begin a statement on C♯–E–C♯: the D♭ has been respelled and reharmonized as the third of A major, but the A♭ has vanished. Soon (in bar 49) the C♯/D♭ is also removed, dropping down to C♮ as the mode turns to minor for the remainder of the exposition.

Brahms rekindles the A♮–A♭ conflict at the opening of the recapitulation, always an important spot for dramatic reinterpretation in his sonata structures. At bars 120–24 the opening chords are enriched or expanded. The A♭ of the motto is harmonized not with the original diminished-seventh chord, but with a bold A♭⁷; the motto's last pitch, F, then appears as part of the resolution, D♭ major.

The Andante, in C major, does not concern itself directly with the A♮–A♭ relationship. Its exposition has an orthodox tonal design, I–V; the recapitulation remains in the tonic. However, the bold juxtaposition of F and D♭ triads in bars 75–76 (the developmental extension of the second group) brings the pitch conflict back to our consciousness. The series of plagal cadences that closes the movement does so even more emphatically. In the first cadence (bars 128–29) the tonic alternates with a simple IV, or F-major, triad. In the second (bar 130), Brahms replaces the subdominant with a warm flatted sixth, or A♭. In bars 132–34 this A♭ harmony is transformed into the minor subdominant, which resolves back to the tonic. In the final bars of this movement, then, Brahms reminds us gently (at the original pitch level) of the important A♮–A♭ relationship.

The Allegretto seems to recall these plagal sonorities in bars 24ff. Over a tonic (C) pedal Brahms introduces a minor subdominant, which at first subsides onto the tonic but then (in bar 29) becomes F major, thus again adumbrating the central pitch conflict. The Trio section of this movement is in VI, or A♭ major, a key area that serves to keep the crucial A♮–A♭ issue in our ears, even in the realm of the symphony's "dominant," C.

The tonal drama resumes center stage in the finale. The A♭ dominates, of course, in the F-minor first group and especially in the mysterious chorale in A♭ major that interrupts the first group at bars 18–19, almost as if to warn us solemnly of the pitch (and related key areas) still be be dealt with. And it is at the return of this chorale theme in the development section (bar 149) that Brahms brings the A♮–A♭ struggle to a climax. The theme appears on the dominant of A minor and moves upward in a remarkable series of harmonic shifts through the regions of C minor (155), D♭/C♯ minor (159), and E minor (163). At bars 167–68 it is wrenched up another half step into F major, and the A♮ is triumphantly asserted above a ⁶₄ chord in bars 169–70. But the victory is short-lived, for in the next measure the major third sinks back to A♭, and the recapitulation is underway in the tonic minor.

Only in the coda is the matter at last settled. At the *poco sostenuto* of bar 267 the key signature sheds three of its flats, and the once restless theme of the finale moves into the major mode in magisterial augmentation. The high A♮ of the transformed theme (bar 269) is appropriately set in relief by its *forte* dynamic and by its placement at the beginning of a slur. At bar 297 only a faint trace of the pitch conflict remains: underneath a fragment of the theme, a tonic chord alternates with D♭ (♭VI), recalling the plagal cadences of the Andante and allowing the conflict to flicker for the last time.

IV

Metrical development plays a large role in the Third Symphony, especially in the first two movements. The opening bars of the first movement pose a kind of metrical problem. Unless he has his eyes on the conductor or on the score, the listener is not likely to perceive any definite meter in the two initial chords, each lasting a full bar. The main theme, entering in the third bar, begins to project a metrical profile. But what meter do we hear? The violins seem to articulate ³₂, that is, a triple rather than duple division of the bar; the fourth beat, normally strong in ⁶₄, remains conspicuously empty. The cellos and violas take no firm position on the matter; their harmony changes only every six beats, offering little clue to the internal rhythmic-metrical articulation. Nor is any meter defined by the "motto," announced by contrabassoons and double basses in broad whole notes. The only hint of the notated ⁶₄—and it really is little more than a hint—comes from the timpani and trombones, which cut off their roll and chord (respectively) on the fourth beat. Not until bar 7 does the duple division of the bar become explicit in all parts: the theme, the motto, and the harmonic voices now move every half bar.

Though relatively uninformative as to compositional process, the autograph of the Third Symphony (located at the Library of Congress) does shed a sidelight on these metrical ambiguities. All the notes held for a full bar were notated by Brahms *not* as dotted whole notes, as given in the Brahms *Sämtliche Werke*, but as two tied dotted half notes (see Figure 3).[10] The first edition of the score also

[10]The score has been published in facsimile by the Robert O. Lehman Foundation, New York. The only place in the first movement where Brahms writes dotted whole notes is in the trombone

FIGURE 3: Brahms, Symphony No. 3, op. 90. Facsimile of first page of autograph manuscript. Reproduced by permission of the Library of Congress, Music Division.

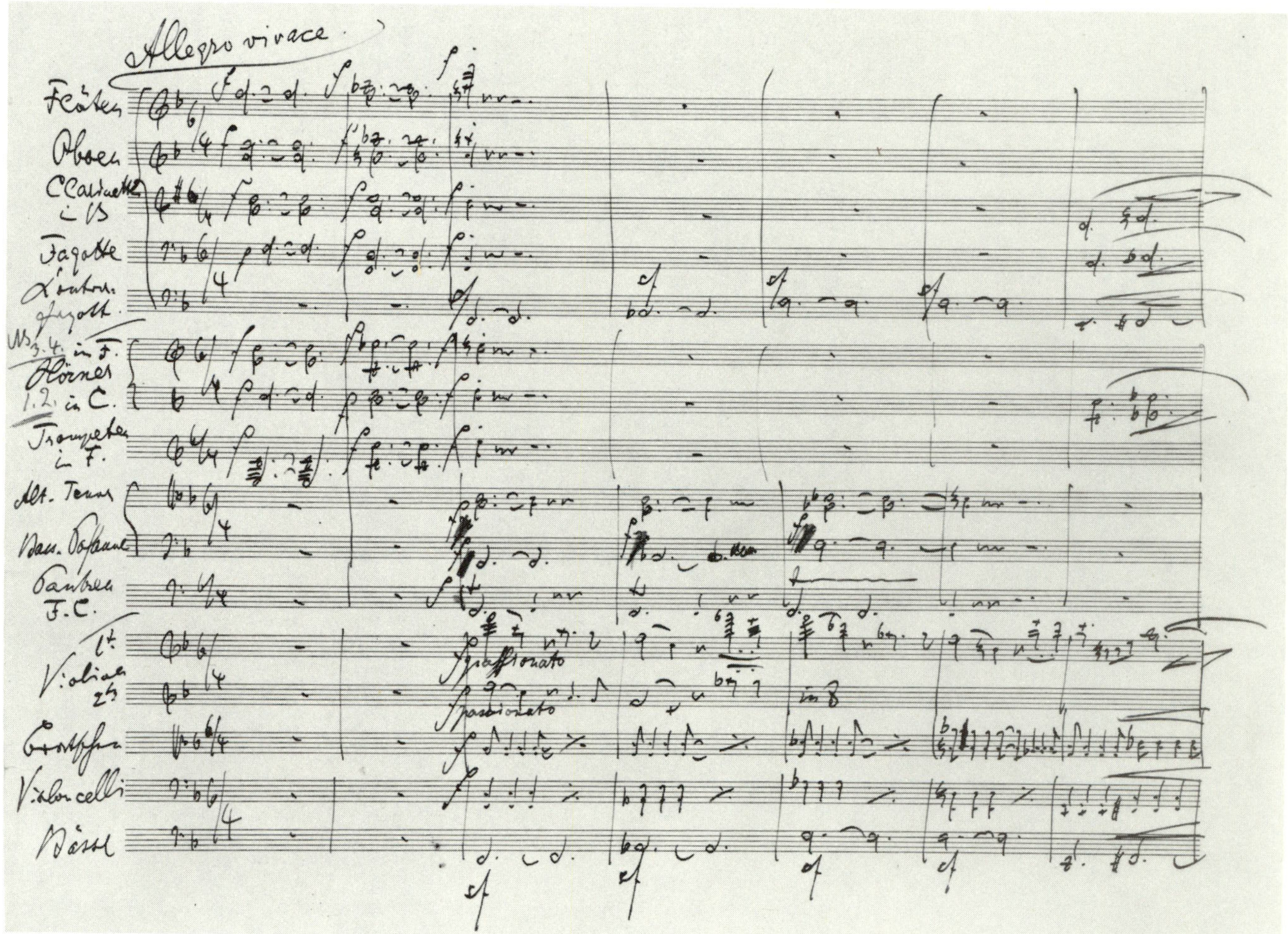

has the tied dotted half notes. The two methods of notation are theoretically equivalent, of course. But the Third Symphony is, to the best of my knowledge, the *only* autograph Brahms notated in this fashion. In other scores in $\frac{6}{4}$ (for example, the first two movements of the D-Minor Piano Concerto) or in $\frac{3}{2}$ (the first movement of the C-Minor String Quartet), all notes that last a full bar are written as dotted whole notes.[11] Why did Brahms alter his notational practice only for this symphony? A conductor would almost certainly beat the opening bars in two, regardless of the notation. Brahms probably intended the tied dotted half notes to provide a written reinforcement of the latent meter and to ensure that conductor and players project something of the tension between the potential duple and triple (and "single") articulations of the bar.

The second group of the exposition raises the duple-triple issue in a different fashion. The new A-major theme (bar 36) is notated in $\frac{9}{4}$, which is heard as an expansion or broadening of the original meter into triple time (and not an inner reordering of the bar, as at the opening). At bar 49 the meter contracts once again to $\frac{6}{4}$.

These matters are brought to a stunning climax at the close of the development section, where the recapitulation may be said to be generated out of a metrical contraction (see ex. 37a). At bar 112 the main theme appears in the somber key of E♭ minor. It now follows its natural tendency to unfold in $\frac{3}{2}$. (The triple division has also been prepared by the preceding three bars.) There are no trombones or timpani to hint at the fourth beat; at first there is no accompaniment at all. The descending scales in dotted rhythms in bars 115–19 make the triple division explicit.

The last two bars of this passage (118–19) are marked *ritardando*; then in bar 120 the recapitulation begins abruptly in the original tempo (Tempo I°). And now the duple $\frac{6}{4}$ is articulated clearly: the strings, not present at the beginning of the movement, firmly divide each bar in two. Brahms's tempo markings ensure that we hear the return not simply as an inner restructuring of the bar—not as a shift from $\frac{3}{2}$ to $\frac{6}{4}$—but as a real truncation or compression. He does not specify how fast the recapitulation is to arrive in proportion to the retransition,

---

and timpani parts in bars 116–19, at the end of the retransition (p. 19 of the autograph). The horns and woodwinds are, however, still notated as tied dotted half-notes (even though the implied meter is now clearly $\frac{3}{2}$!). Figure 2 reveals another interesting temporal aspect of the first movement: Brahms's original tempo was "Allegro vivace," which was changed to "Allegro con brio" before publication (see Brahms, *Briefe an Simrock*, 3: 47). In the Violin Sonata, op. 78, Brahms had indicated a rare "Vivace ma non troppo" for a limpid first movement in $\frac{6}{4}$ meter. But in the weightier symphony, he may have felt that "vivace" would suggest too fast a tempo—velocity rather than energy.

[11] The autographs I have examined (either partially or wholly) for this notational practice include: the D-Minor Piano Concerto, op. 15, in the full score and in the arrangements for four hands, one piano, and for two pianos; the *German Requiem*, op. 45, arranged for four hands; the C-Minor String Quartet, op. 51; the *Alto Rhapsody*, op. 53; the G-Major Violin Sonata, op. 78; and the Fourth Symphony, op. 98. An extremely useful source is Peter Dedel, *Johannes Brahms: A Guide to His Autograph in Facsimile*.

EXAMPLE 37: Brahms, Symphony No. 3, op. 90, I.

but every conductor or reader of the score must (or should) make a decision. One solution is to make a half note of the *ritardando* bars (118–19) equivalent to a dotted half note at the Tempo I°; from the listener's standpoint, the $\frac{3}{2}$ bar will seem to be reduced by a third, to $\frac{2}{2}$ (ex. 37b). Most recorded performances of the symphony follow roughly this practice, although few conductors keep a sufficiently steady tempo throughout bars 118–19 to allow the compression to be felt. Another, more dramatic solution—one that is really more faithful to Brahms's markings (but that I have never heard attempted)—is to slow the tempo at the earlier *ritardando* in bars 110–11, maintain this slower tempo through the *poco sostenuto*, and then slow down still further at the second *ritardando* in bars 118–19. The degree of compression could then be doubled by making a *quarter* note of bars 118–19 equal to a dotted half at the Tempo I°; the aural result is a metrical contraction from $\frac{3}{2}$ to $\frac{2}{4}$ (ex. 37c).[12]

Whatever the means, the recapitulation should be perceived as emerging by a kind of metrical paroxysm, which Brahms reinforces with an equally sudden harmonic compression or elision. (We have already referred above in passing to the avoidance of dominant preparation.) In bars 117–19 the prevailing key, E♭ minor, moves toward its own dominant, B♭; an F pedal point, heard as V/V in E♭ minor, is present throughout. This F has originated as a *thematic* note, the endpoint of the descending scales; but at 118 it begins to function as the *harmonic* bass note of an F⁷ chord. On the last beat of bar 119 this harmony is intensified by an Italian augmented-sixth chord, G♭–B♭–E♮, which resolves on the downbeat of bar 120 to an F-major triad. We still assume this to be functioning as V of B♭, but in fact the F has suddenly asserted itself as the tonic and as the first note of the main theme! In the subsequent violent shift to A♭⁷ and D♭, the harmonic framework seems to rebel against the bold usurpation by F major. Not until the beginning of the transition to the second group (bar 136) is the tonic confirmed.

V

A powerful conjunction of metrical and harmonic processes also generates the recapitulation of the Andante of the symphony. Explosive in the first movement, these processes now become lyrical and fluent. Once again the opening theme poses the "problem," here involving the status of the fourth or last beat of the bar, about which melody and accompaniment disagree (ex. 38). The melody, phrased or slurred within the bar, interprets the fourth beat as a concluding element; but in the accompanying parts, the fourth beat begins a slurred group and thus leads forward into the next bar. There is a harmonic corollary to this rhythmic conflict. The root-position tonic triad, articulated (as expected) on the first beat of bar 1, reappears on the last beat, and on the second beat of bar 2, alternating with a IV triad. We are thereby made aware of the potential ambiguity of the tonic harmony: it can be strong (as I) or weak (as the dominant of IV).

---

[12]For other discussions of proportional relationships of meter or tempo in Brahms, see Epstein, *Beyond Orpheus*, pp. 78–79, 83–86, and 91–95; and Allen Forte, "The Structural Origin of Exact Tempi in the Brahms-Haydn Variations."

EXAMPLE 38: Brahms, Symphony No. 3, op. 90, II.

Throughout the exposition the fourth beat threatens to displace the metrical framework, as happens in the F-Minor Quintet, the C-Minor Quartet, and—more significantly—in the first movement of this symphony, where the last (sixth) beat asserts itself in bars 51–77. At bar 29 of the Andante, in the transition to the second group, stresses on beats 4 and 2 begin to upset our metrical orientation; by bar 34 the notated fourth beat sounds like a downbeat. As in the other pieces we have examined, the accompanying parts fully support the displaced meter by sounding only on beats 4 and 2. By the downbeat of bar 40 the original metrical grid has been restored, only to be obscured again (though not dislocated) by the remarkable second theme (bars 41ff.) This theme sounds nothing like the first one, but it in fact exploits the same kind of rhythmic ambiguity: above the opaque seventh harmonies, the fourth beat is treated both as a forward-leaning upbeat (bars 40–41) and as an element of closure (bar 42).

As in the first movement, these procedures are brought to a climax during the retransition (bar 80; the Andante has no development section proper, only a developmental extension of the second group from bar 71). On the second beat of bar 80 (see ex. 39) the developmental extension comes to a halt on a diminished-seventh chord built on C, above which the clarinet quietly introduces a fragment of the main theme (the first three notes). The metrical profile of the theme is now as hazy as the underlying harmony: the fragment begins on the (notated) fourth beat, and its first note is tied over the bar line. The flute, oboe, and bassoon successively take up this figure over harmonies that shift restlessly but remain rooted on C. In the fourth statement of the theme fragment (bar 84), the eighth-note figure D–B is augmented to two quarter notes; this augmentation delays the final C (of the fragment) until the fourth beat. Simultaneously with that C the flute and oboe begin another statement, which is modified still further: Brahms retains the D–B augmentation but removes the tie across the bar line, thus placing D on the downbeat of bar 85. And when the augmented theme fragment is followed by the second figure of the main theme (G–A–G–A), we suddenly realize that the augmented fragment is standing in for the opening motive—that, in fact, the recapitulation has begun. The phrasing still shows the influence of the preceding retransition, however, for both the melodic voice *and* accompaniment are slurred across the bar line. Originally, only the

EXAMPLE 39: Brahms, Symphony No. 3, op. 90, II.

accompaniment had the aberrant slurring: the melody was phrased normally (see ex. 38); now they are displaced together. Not until the next bar (87) are the proper downbeat and the original phrasing restored.

Let us briefly retrace our steps to examine the harmonic component of this remarkable passage, where Brahms makes good on the promise of the opening bars by exploring the ambiguities of the tonic chord. The entire retransition unfolds over the well-entrenched C pedal. As in the first movement, the tonic pedal has entered *before* the thematic recapitulation, although here too we are not, I think, supposed to recognize the bass as the tonic. In bars 81–84 the strings and brass change harmony on the second beat of each bar, thus moving in the displaced or syncopated framework of the theme fragment. At bar 84, the bar with the augmentation, the harmony settles on a D^7 chord. Then, as the theme fragment at last completes its evolution into the main theme, the D^7 (still with a bass C) shifts suddenly to C major on the second beat of bar 85. Brahms has thus bypassed altogether the dominant of C: as in the first movement, the pedal note simply asserts itself as a tonic when the theme returns. Our surprise is intensified because melody and harmony are not synchronized; the latter continues to move in the displaced metrical pattern of the retransition. The tonic chord thus clashes with the melodic B♮ on the second beat of bar 85.

The whole process by which the recapitulation emerges is so subtle, so carefully drawn out, that one cannot point to a single moment where the return begins. It literally evolves element by element; theme, meter, and harmony coalesce into what we finally understand as the recapitulation. This passage

EXAMPLE 40: Brahms, Symphony No. 3, op. 90, II.

represents perhaps the greatest refinement of Brahms's techniques of developing variation up to 1883.

VI

The recapitulation of the Andante now brings us to consider the higher-level thematic-formal drama of the Third Symphony, for the mysterious second theme of the exposition (bars 41–50) fails to reappear in the recapitulation. In its place (bar 108) comes a new lyrical melody, which Brahms creates through one of his most inspired uses of the linkage technique. The tail of the horns' unobtrusive cadence figure in bar 107 is taken up by the violins in 108 as the beginning of the new theme (ex. 40). In the exposition (bars 22–23) this cadence figure appears twice in succession (clarinet, strings), then yields to an ornamented restatement of the main theme. In the recapitulation Brahms abbreviates the cadence, extracting from its last notes a new thematic idea.

After this theme has run its lyric course, the two-note head motive of the original second theme is heard, much as it was in the exposition (cf. bars 56–62 and 115–21); but the theme of which this motive is an echo seems to have vanished. We have often seen Brahms using the linkage technique as an elegant method of generating new ideas. Here, however, it is put into the service of the larger design of the symphony, for it replaces an earlier theme and thus sets in motion a drama that is resolved only in the finale.

The "missing" theme resurfaces three times in the last movement. The first occurs, quite unexpectedly, near the beginning. The main theme comes to a half cadence on C at bar 18, and we expect further development on the dominant, or in the tonic. Instead, the trombones (not heard since the coda of the Andante) solemnly intone on E♭ the two-note head motive of the Andante's second theme, and the strings and woodwinds enter with the theme in the key of A♭. It appears in its entirety, with an extra statement of the two-note motive inserted between the phrases in bars 22–23. But the character has changed: the original, cloudy seventh harmonies have cleared up to become plain, chorale-like triads.

The original theme had deftly side-stepped cadences; the transformed version closes squarely where it began, on A♭.

But then the theme vanishes. In bars 29–30 the trombones give out one last statement of the two-note motive on E♭; this pitch is then nudged up to E♮ as the full orchestra bursts in, on the dominant of F minor, with a variant of the opening theme. The Andante theme has thus been an inscrutable parenthesis within the first group. Indeed, one could easily remove the chorale and proceed directly from the dominant half cadence of bar 18 to the reappearance of the same chord in bars 29–30; the first group would still display an eminently Brahmsian logic and continuity. And the finale continues to unfold (in a sonata-rondo form) as if unperturbed by the interruption. Further development of the main theme leads at bar 51 to the "orthodox" dominant, where Brahms presents a broad and proper second theme. Too proper, in fact. One suspects that Brahms may have made this theme intentionally square and stodgy to keep us thinking about that other, more memorable second theme, the Andante chorale.

The development section brings back the chorale, and from it Brahms now builds an enormous climax. The development begins innocently enough, by exploring a descending four-note scale derived from the main theme (clarinets, bars 129–31). Brahms initiates a canon on this figure at bar 141, but seven bars later the canon is abruptly halted. After half a bar of terrifying silence, the familiar two-note and triplet motives of the Andante theme appear *forte, ben marcato*, treated imitatively at the distance of a measure. At bar 159 the entries come only a half measure apart, and the stretto reaches a climax as all parts play the triplet figure of the theme simultaneously in bars 167–68.

Here the two great dramas of the symphony merge—those of the A♮–A♭ conflict, and of the missing theme. The tonic major, which asserts the A♮ over the A♭, appears at the same moment that the Andante theme reaches its apotheosis.

But neither story is concluded here. As we saw earlier, the A♮ sinks back to A♭ (F major reverts to F minor) at the beginning of the recapitulation (bars 170–71). The Andante theme, too, seems to lack fulfillment and resolution, for it does not appear in the recapitulation (which begins with the material that had followed the parenthesis at bar 30 in the exposition). Its resolution comes only with the coda, where it appears for the last time (bar 280) in a new cadential form, first in F major, then moving through D major (288) and back to the tonic major. The radiant D major effectively neutralizes the D♭–A♭ axis that has dominated much of the symphony, and, by leading back through the circle of fifths, it is integrated with the tonic, rather than set against it (as were the D♭ and A♭).

The return of the opening theme of the symphony at bar 301 does not so much bring us back to where we began as it affirms how far we have come. Like the chorale theme, the opening theme is now completely at rest. The original harmonic paroxysms—the inflections toward F minor and D♭ major—have subsided into pure F major. The rhythmic and metrical ambiguities are dissipated

EXAMPLE 41: Brahms, Symphony No. 4, op. 98, III.

in the shimmering string tremolos, whose bisection of the bar (in 301, 303, etc.) and gentle syncopation (302, 304) project the notated duple meter (now ¢, of course) easily and comfortably. Although the coda of the first movement had anticipated this moment, it had proved to be only a temporary lull before further development. Now the promise of that first coda is fully realized.

The specific procedures of developing variation that we find in the Third Symphony—the linkage technique, elided or obscured recapitulations, motivic consistency, continuous exploitation of a pitch conflict, metrical displacements—are none of them new in Brahms's music. We have encountered them in most of his mature works from the Piano Quintet, op. 34, on. But what is unique to this symphony, I believe, is the way in which these procedures are put into the service of a larger, coherent four-movement structure. In their local occurrences they create expectations and tensions that are fulfilled (resolved) only at the end of the piece. Indeed, that is what makes the concluding return of the opening theme so satisfying. The return constitutes one of Brahms's most persuasive thematic transformations—this is precisely what it is, altering mood and character while retaining pitch relationships—because it seems genuinely to embody all the thematic, harmonic, metrical, and formal processes that have spanned the symphony since the theme's initial appearance.

VII

To conclude this discussion of how Brahms applies the procedures of developing variation to the symphony, we should look briefly at his fourth and final effort in this medium, which followed after only a short time. Completed in the summer of 1885, the Fourth Symphony, op. 98, was in fact the next sonata-style work Brahms published after the Third, op. 90. (Only solo and choral songs intervene.) As might be expected, then, the E-Minor Symphony shares several large-scale structural features with the F-Major. Brahms makes no attempt to build a hyper-sonata form, but, as in the Third, he exploits a basic tonal relationship—here between E and C—across much of the symphony. Like the A♮–A♭ conflict, this one is presented at the opening (though less boldly), where the famous descending thirds of the main theme outline successive E-minor and C-major triads. There is no actual C-major harmony at this point, except for a brief hint at bar 5, but Brahms fulfills its potential handsomely at the opening of the recapitulation (bar 249). Here the theme appears in rhythmic augmentation, and its fourth note, C, is greeted by the full orchestra with a C-major triad. In technique, if not in spirit, this recapitulation recalls the first movement of the F-Major Symphony, where at the analogous spot A♭ generates extra measures and a modulation to D♭.[13]

The quasi-fanfare that opens the slow movement of the Fourth Symphony carefully outlines a triad we naturally assume to be the tonic. Only when the theme enters, in the fifth bar, do we realize that the piece has been in, or on, ♭VI. The deceiver turns out to be C major, the tonic E major. Thus the E and C are brought into an even more unusual—because non-diatonic—relationship than in the first movement. And the C♮, D♮, and G♮ of the ♭VI region continue to color the melodic and harmonic structures of this unique Andante. Like the slow movement of the Third Symphony, this one concludes with non-dominant cadences that recall the pervasive tonal relationship (bars 114–18).

As if acceding to the tonal pressure applied delicately in the first movement, and more heavily in the Andante, the third movement of the Fourth Symphony falls into the key of C major—and then does not hesitate to inflect in its fourth measure toward A minor by moving through E minor (the minor dominant). The finale returns firmly to the realm of E minor, but near the end, especially in variations 27 and 28 (bars 217–32) and the coda (from 253), the tonic again confronts C.

As in the Third Symphony, the movements of the Fourth are linked by certain high-level thematic processes. The chain of descending thirds which forms the first theme is clearly, if briefly, recalled by the woodwinds between the first and second themes of the scherzo (bars 48–51). And, as Schoenberg and other commentators have observed, the 28th and 29th variations in the finale prominently display the same series of descending thirds. Brahms also goes beyond mere thematic allusion, however, for he actually interrupts the coda of the scherzo to offer a preview of the finale. In the last statement of the main theme (bar 311), the original pause (of bars 5–6) is expanded into a grotesque parody of the forthcoming chaconne theme. An exact transposition of the first five notes of that theme, A–B–C–D–E♭, is subjected to enormous registral displacement (see ex. 41). When the finale begins—after about a minute— Brahms sets about restoring dignity and logic to the theme. He returns it to a single register and completes it by raising the sharped fourth to a fifth and resolving that pitch to the tonic. He then pays tribute to the resuscitated theme by proceeding to build an entire variation movement from it.[14]

---

[13]For a detailed and sensitive analysis of motivic process and phrase structure in the first movement of the Fourth Symphony, see Dunsby, *Structural Ambiguity in Brahms*, Chapter 4.

[14]An entry in Brahms's pocket calendar for 1885 reading "IV. Symphonie. Finale und Scherzo" suggests he may have composed the fourth movement before the third (see Kalbeck, *Johannes Brahms*, 3: 445). As in the F-Minor Sonata, op. 5 (discussed in Chapter 2), Brahms would then have "planted" the fragmentary reference after the complete theme had already been composed. The "pre-hearing" of the chaconne theme has been remarked in Walker, *Study*, pp. 76–77.

The last two movements of the Fourth Symphony are unique in Brahms's instrumental oeuvre. None of his other scherzos or scherzo-substitutes has the energy and sparkle of the third movement; and no other finale (of a multi-movement, sonata-style work) is cast as a chaconne. Indeed, these movements are so strongly profiled that they tend to draw our attention away from the higher-level tonal and thematic design of the work. The individual movements of the Third Symphony are somewhat more conventional in style and more uniform in tone, and they thus more readily invite our contemplation and comprehension of the larger "sonata" and tonal-thematic processes. The Third Symphony is clearly weighted toward its finale, which serves as a climax and resolution of these processes. But both symphonies, together with the Adagio of the Second, show how impressively Brahms rose to the symphonic occasion: how in the period from 1877 to 1885 he was able to put at the service of massive symphonic structures the compositional principles he had developed in his piano, chamber, and vocal music for 25 years.

6

The Late Style, 1886–1896

I

The Third and Fourth Symphonies are Brahms's last great large-scale instrumental compositions. His final orchestral work, the Double Concerto, op. 102 (summer 1887), does not seem to build on the achievements of the symphonies. Their real inheritance is to be found in the smaller chamber works written in the interim—the Cello Sonata in F, op. 99; the Violin Sonata in A, op. 100; the Piano Trio in C Minor, op. 101 (all from summer 1886); and the Violin Sonata in D Minor, op. 108 (drafted the same summer). Here we find the extreme conciseness and economy that characterize his late creations.

Brahms's close friends and perceptive critics the Herzogenbergs were quick to notice precisely these features. Upon receiving opp. 100 and 101 from the composer, Heinrich wrote Brahms:

> Your last chamber-music pieces proved a positively royal gift. . . . They are constructed in the plainest possible way from ideas at once striking and simple, fresh and young in their emotional qualities, ripe and wise in their incredible compactness. . . .
>
> We had a foretaste in the 'cello sonata [op. 99], and now the violin sonata and trio seem to us the perfect development of this new drift. No one, not even yourself, can say what it will lead to; let us hope it will clear the field and leave the giants in possession. Smaller men will hardly trust themselves to proceed laconically without forfeiting some of what they want to say.[1]

[1]Johannes Brahms, *Herzogenberg Correspondence*, pp. 302–3.

In these pieces, and in the later sonata-style chamber works, Brahms reduces the dimensions but increases the density of "what he wants to say." He seems to focus his attention—and thus ours as well—more on individual movements than on the *Gesamtdisposition*. Instead of attempting high-level tonal, thematic, and formal designs (except, to some extent, in the Clarinet Quintet, op. 115), he refines the more local procedures of developing variation and continues to reassess their relationship to sonata techniques. Movements tend to be very short: the entire four-movement D-Minor Sonata, op. 108, takes just over twenty minutes to perform, for example.

Our impression of compactness is due not only to the absolute duration, however, but also to the severe economy of thematic material. This aspect of Brahms's "new drift" is already evident in the Fourth Symphony, whose main theme is derived from a single motive—really just an interval—that appears in descending form as a third, and in inversion as a sixth. This theme seems astonishingly restricted when compared with the Adagio of the Second Symphony or the first movement of the Third, which display a profusion of thematic material.

In the F-Major Violoncello Sonata, Brahms manages to blend the economy of the Fourth Symphony with the flexibility of the Second and Third. The result is, as Schoenberg demonstrated, a theme that expands immediately and rapidly by the free reinterpretation of a fourth (C–F). The sonata also shows what effect this headlong style of developing variation can have on the sonata form, for Brahms abandons his preferred (though not his exclusive) first-group design, A B A', in favor of a more economical theme-counterstatement plan (roughly A A'). He may well have felt that the demands of such speedy motivic development on the listener would be great enough—even Schoenberg found the theme difficult to grasp at first—without the additional distraction of contrasting B material. Like the new thematic economy, this formal scheme appears in a more conservative state in the Fourth Symphony, where the main theme extends eighteen measures and is then repeated with ornamentation (A A'), blending into the transition to the second group at about bar 33. This first group may strike us as rather pallid, especially because the theme is subjected to decoration rather than genuinely developing variation. But in his next opus, the cello sonata, Brahms enriches a similar design with extraordinary imagination.

As we saw in the Schoenberg analysis, the sonata theme consists of two phrases (a and b) of four and five bars respectively. At bar 9 a counterstatement begins, in which phrase a is expanded to twice its original length (see schematic superimposition, ex. 42). The first two motives (C–F, Ab–G) are repeated together an octave lower. The third, however, is pulled apart. Its initial figure (D–C) is isolated and twice repeated, almost as if stuttering; the continuation (C–Bb–G) is fleshed out with neighbor notes. Brahms also enriches the supporting harmonies. The original bass line of bars 1–2, F–D–Bb–C, harmonized with I–vii°$^6_5$/V–vii°^{7}/V–V, now appears in the top line of the piano; the descent is filled in as F–Eb–Db–C–B♮–C and supports new F^7 and Db harmonies. (The texture

EXAMPLE 42:   Brahms, Violoncello Sonata, op. 99, I.

proves to be re-invertible, for the descending line is put back in the bass at bars 11–12.)

In the counterstatement, phrase B retains its original length and blends into the transition at bar 22; but it is developed from within with even greater fluidity than phrase A. The original jagged dotted rhythms become smooth, sweeping legato arches. Brahms now saturates phrase B with the basic interval/motive, the fourth, by inserting an A into the original leap from F to D (compare bars 5 and 17 in example 42) and a D into the leap from C to G (bars 6 and 18). The theme thereby becomes a succession of ascending fourths (C–F, A–D, G–C, D–G, etc.).

II

Each of Brahms's late chamber works probes in its own way these flexible procedures of developing variation. Perhaps the most sophisticated and compelling piece, from this point of view, is the Clarinet Sonata in F Minor, op. 120, no. 1 (1894), one of the last pair of sonata-form works Brahms was to complete. In the first movement Brahms returns to a double-theme structure, similar in kind to the tripartite first groups we have examined during this study, but considerably more ambitious. Instead of A B A', the design of the first 52 bars (see Appendix, ex. P, pp. 196–97) might be represented as A B A' B' A"; these symbols, however, can scarcely convey the fluency with which A and B material are

EXAMPLE 43: Brahms, Clarinet Sonata, op. 120, no. 1, I.

interwoven, nor the considerable formal ambiguities Brahms generates. The formal functions of A and B are reexamined at every stage.[2]

Set out in stark octaves by the piano, A (bars 1–4) seems at its first appearance almost more an introductory flourish—an *intonazione*—than a proper theme. It unfolds impulsively and irregularly by the successive "liquidation" of a brief motive (bracketed in ex. 43). This motive leaps up a fourth and descends stepwise through a third. Its initial interval is then reduced to a third, and the motive appears sequentially in truncated form and in diminution, as C–E♭–D♭, B♭–D♭–C, and finally F♭–A♭–G♭, resolving to the tonic F. The tonality of the unharmonized theme remains ambiguous until the last F: we might be hearing D♭ major, B♭ minor (suggested especially by the G♭ in bar 4), A♭ major, or F minor. But above (and just before) the thematic F of bar 5, the clarinet enters with a solidly triadic theme (B) that establishes the key of F minor.

The clarity of the new theme seems to confirm our first suspicions about A: it has been a freely rhapsodic introduction for the piano. Unlike A, theme B takes shape as a conventional eight-bar period, divided cleanly into 4 + 4. Furthermore, it is harmonized by conventional, predictable progressions in F minor and moves to a half cadence on the dominant (bar 12). This half cadence seems to portend a consequent phrase, a complement to the first eight bars of B. To our surprise, this function is assumed by a return of A material, played by the clarinet (A', bar 13). As in its first appearance, the basic motive of A moves downward in sequence and in diminution (bars 15–16). The once-impulsive introductory theme assumes the decorum befitting a consequent phrase, arranging itself in four tidy bars, then appearing again in ornamented form. But in this second statement (bar 18), A' begins to assume its former role. At bar 20 it is extended, evolving into a rhythmically augmented, but exact, reiteration of bars 3–4. The subsequent appearance of B' at bar 25 confirms the introductory status of the last eight bars of A'.

Like B, B' begins with a full eight-bar statement moving to the dominant (bar 32). Now, however, the last four measures are repeated and modified to lead to A♭, the dominant of D♭. Our sonata-form sensibilities tell us that the second group has arrived, but on some level we also perhaps expect the reappearance of

[2]For a detailed but disappointingly myopic analysis of the first movement, see Schmidt, *Verfahren*, pp. 23–99.

A in its guise as a consequent to B. Brahms ingeniously fulfills both expectations by presenting a much transformed, but recognizable, A as the first theme of the second group (A″, bar 38). The basic motive appears in the bass in broad half notes, over which the top voice of the piano sets forth the same scale fragment that concludes the original A theme in bars 4–5: A♭–G♭–F. The G♭ that was a mysterious intruder in F minor is now easily assimilated into D♭ major. Like the opening A, A″ is begun by the piano alone. The clarinet enters in bar 39, at first simply arpeggiating the bittersweet notes of a ii⁷ chord (in D♭), then (in bars 43–44) directly quoting the basic motive of A. This allusion confirms for the listener the connection of the D♭-major theme with A.

I have suggested that A″ serves both as a consequent to B and as a second theme in its own right. It also acts in its original capacity, as an introduction, for the half cadence to A♭ at bar 52 is followed by a genuinely new theme in C minor, the minor dominant of F.

What is so remarkable in this exposition is not simply that Brahms is able to derive so much from the laconic A material—Haydn and Beethoven were also, after all, masters at such thematic economy—but the utter fluency with which he continually transforms the formal status of A. It is at one moment a grand rhetorical prelude, then a perfectly natural answering phrase to another theme, then a stable theme in its own right; in each of these roles it still retains one or more of its other functions. This thematic-formal fluency represents a style of developing variation still more sophisticated than that manifested by the G-Major Violin Sonata, op. 78. There, short lyrical fragments are continually re-grouped in new combinations, but the basic thematic-formal structures, such as the A B A′ first group, remain firmly intact. In the clarinet sonata even these formal units yield to the procedures of developing variation; they are at every moment reexamined and reinterpreted.

The most impressive reinterpretation in the sonata comes at the formal juncture we have so often seen Brahms exploit for such purposes, the retransition-recapitulation (see ex. 44). At bar 130, theme A appears in F♯ minor. At the opening of the movement, both the pitch structure and bare texture of this theme avoided establishing a tonality. Now, however, its key is projected unambiguously: the theme is richly harmonized, and its first three notes outline an F♯-minor triad. In this robust form, theme A clearly functions as the culmination of the development section; but because of its past history, it may also be expected to assume an introductory role.

The theme moves to a half cadence on its dominant (C♯) in bar 134, reiterating the familiar concluding three-note scale figure, E–D♮–C♯. The harmony underneath the last note is respelled as D♭ major; it appears in first inversion, with F♮ in the bass. In the next bar (137) the chord adds a dominant seventh, spelled as B♮. Then in bar 138, the bass F suddenly presents itself as the tonic root, and the recapitulation is underway with theme B. We now realize that the D♭ ⁶₅ chord in bar 137 has functioned as a German sixth (in an unusual inversion), which bypasses the real dominant to which it is supposed to resolve, C major.

EXAMPLE 44: Brahms, Clarinet Sonata, op. 120, no. 1, I.

Two aspects of this passage directly recall procedures in the first and second movements of the Third Symphony. One is the avoidance, actually the circumvention, of dominant preparation for the tonic. The other is the way in which the tonic root slips in early, but avoids being perceived as the tonic until the recapitulation is upon us. In the clarinet sonata, however, these older procedures are enhanced by the shadowy role of theme A, which Brahms "recapitulates" in the development section, outside the tonic key. The theme has, in a sense, fulfilled its original destiny. As an introduction at the beginning of the movement, it stood partially outside the exposition; now, as the climax of the development, it lies literally outside the formal recapitulation.

We are also reminded of the two earlier F-minor works, the Sonata, op. 5, and the Quintet, op. 34, in which Brahms similarly incorporates the A segment of a tripartite opening group into the retransition. In op. 5 the retransition subsumes or replaces both the A and B segments; the tonic return and recapitulation coincide with A' (bar 138; see Appendix, ex. A). The elision is skillful, but also a bit too expedient: Brahms really seems to be seeking a way to avoid presenting A twice (as A and A') in his recapitulation. In op. 34, the elision is much more exciting; the recapitulation bursts in with the B theme, which is harmonically, melodically, and metrically unsettled (bar 166).

In both the piano sonata and the quintet, material from theme A appears in fragmentary form, and on the dominant; there is no doubt that we are hearing a retransition. Even in the more sophisticated Third Symphony, where there is no dominant preparation, the thematic material is unstable, pressing toward resolution. In the clarinet sonata, Brahms refines these procedures to generate still greater thematic-harmonic-formal ambiguity. Theme A appears in its entirety and, indeed, in a *more* stable form than at the opening of the movement. And it is this illusion of stability, together with our recollection of the introductory status of A and the smooth harmonic elision, that make the entrance of the recapitulation so effective.

The formal ambiguity in this sonata is very different from that often encountered in the sonata forms of the greatest classical master of ambiguity, Haydn. Brahms does not intend a witty, deceptive recapitulation. Rather, the retransition-recapitulation functions as one stage in the very sober, continuous reexamination of the A material. Although he does not abandon the larger sonata superstructure, Brahms tends to dissolve some of its local boundaries by making the exposition, development, and recapitulation all serve as successive reinterpretations of the thematic material. Early in this study we saw that one of Brahms's first sonata forms, the first movement of op. 5, could be heard as a somewhat clumsy set of discrete character variations on a motive. In the clarinet sonata, one of Brahms's very last sonata structures, the form has once again in a sense broken down into a set of "variations." But now awkward discontinuity has been replaced by the most sophisticated and fluent techniques of developing variation.

III

In Chapters 3 and 4, I suggested that after the large chamber works of his first maturity (1861–65), Brahms turns temporarily away from sonata forms and toward the Lied—and a particular kind of prose-like poetic text—as testing grounds for the procedures of developing variation that are to appear in his later instrumental music. After his final chamber pieces, song again becomes an important medium; and the texts, taken from the Bible, are now fully prosaic. The *Four Serious Songs*, op. 121, of May 1896, represent Brahms's final meditations on the art of developing variation. (The eleven posthumously published Chorale Preludes, op. 122, are, of course, superb "variations" on their respective chorale tunes; but they do not explore the thematic and formal principles that have been treated in this study.) In the third song, "O Tod, wie bitter bist du," the compositional techniques worked out over a lifetime seem to be distilled to their essence. And, most remarkably, they shape not only the musical structure, but also the spiritual meaning of the work.

The text comprises verses 1 and 2 of Chapter 41 of Ecclesiasticus, from the Apocrypha. As in the *German Requiem*, Brahms uses the Martin Luther translation:

1. O Tod, wie bitter bist du, wenn an dich gedenket ein Mensch, der gute Tage
   und genug hat und ohne Sorge lebet und dem es wohl geht in allen Dingen
   und noch wohl essen mag!
2. O Tod, wie wohl tust du dem Dürftigen, der da schwach und alt ist, der in
   allen Sorgen steckt und nichts Bessers zu hoffen noch zu erwarten hat!

1. Oh death, how bitter is the thought of you to a man who has a good life and
   sufficient possessions and who lives without sorrow; and who is fortunate
   in all things and may still eat well.
2. O death, how well you serve the needy man, who is feeble and old, who is
   beset by all sorrows and has nothing better to hope for or to expect.

EXAMPLE 45: Brahms, "O Tod," op. 121, no. 3.

We are given two contrasting viewpoints—two variations, as it were—on
death: it is dreaded by the healthy and happy man, and welcomed by the broken
and needy one. Brahms articulates the distinction most obviously by means of
the change of mode from minor to major in bar 18. And, as has often been pointed
out, the two aspects of death are conveyed as musical transformations of a single
theme: the harsh descending thirds of the first *"O Tod"* become at the end (bar
31) blissful ascending sixths (ex. 45). This is one of Brahms's most profound
thematic transformations—a transfiguration, really. As in the earliest works we
have examined, the piano sonatas and the op. 8 Trio, the basic motivic content
is preserved but endowed with new expressive qualities. In altering the contour
but retaining the interval of the third, Brahms manages to combine two of his
most characteristic compositional impulses, his lifelong tendency to thematic
transformation and his late proclivity for themes with highly restricted intervals.

Even more than the metamorphosis of the opening theme at the end of the
Third Symphony, this one embodies the musical processes by which the song
has unfolded. As Schoenberg demonstrates in his well-known analysis in
"Brahms the Progressive," it is only the last stage in a complex motivic development involving the interval of a third (see Appendix, ex. Q, pp. 198–99).[3] With
the letters a through f, Schoenberg labels the different motive forms that Brahms
derives by continuous variation of the interval in the first twelve bars of the
song. The interval first appears in descending, disjunct form (a) in the voice, and

---

[3]See Schoenberg, "Brahms the Progressive," in his *Style and Idea*, pp. 431–35.

in imitation in the bass of the piano. Motive form b, a rising disjunct third, is the retrograde of a. At bar 3 we have c, which is a filled in by a passing note; c+, which occurs in the fifth and sixth phrases (bars 8–9), appears first as an augmentation, then as a retrograde, of c. Motive-form d is the inversion of a, an ascending sixth, which occurs at bar 6 and again, of course, at the end of the song.

On two extra staves beneath the music, Schoenberg shows how the intense repetition and imitation of motive a creates a chain of descending thirds, forming a seventh, which he labels e. And f represents a large-scale augmentation of motive-form b, the ascending third, in the bass of bars 8–11.

After thus dissecting the song, Schoenberg remarks, "The sense of logic and economy and the power of inventiveness which build melodies of so much natural fluency deserve the admiration of every music lover who expects more than sweetness and beauty from music."[4] Indeed, there is much more than sweetness and beauty in Brahms's wonderful song; but there is also more than Schoenberg's somewhat restricted analysis reveals.

Schoenberg focuses only on Brahms's treatment of a single interval—one that, moreover, is likely to be prevalent in any tonal work of the common-practice period. In response to the proliferation of thirds displayed in Schoenberg's analysis, Brahms might have remarked, "Any fool could compose like that!" But of course, neither Brahms nor Schoenberg—neither composer nor analyst—was a fool. And by expanding on Schoenberg's insights, as we have often done in the course of this study, we can see how developing variation affects not only the motivic-intervallic process in this song, but also the metrical, harmonic, and even the larger formal processes.

As in several of Brahms's large instrumental works, meter becomes in this brief song a powerful tool of developing variation. Schoenberg himself remarks that the individual phrases of the song constantly vary in length, but he does not elaborate on the remarkably fluid metrical structure generated by the asymmetry.[5] I believe we tend to hear the first five phrases of the song (I retain Schoenberg's numbering of the "phrases," as in example Q) as indicated in example 46, where I have rebarred the music so that analogously accented words or pitches appear on downbeats.

No sooner is the $\frac{3}{2}$ meter established by the double statement of *"O Tod"* than it is disrupted by the implicit $\frac{4}{2}$ meter of the twofold *"wie bitter."* The first *"wie bitter"* (phrase 2) concludes on the third beat of the real bar 3, thereby usurping the upbeat that should be occupied by the next *"wie,"* if the second phrase of the song were to be parallel to the first. We thus hear *"wie bitter"* as a metrical expansion from $\frac{3}{2}$ to $\frac{4}{2}$. With the addition of *"bist du,"* the second *"wie bitter"* moves more firmly and more quickly toward a downbeat, thereby restor-

[4]Schoenberg, *Style and Idea*, p. 435.

[5]Schoenberg, *Style and Idea*, p. 440.

EXAMPLE 46: Brahms, "O Tod," op. 121, no. 3, metrical analysis.

ing the original triple meter. In phrase 4 the metrical framework seems to contract still further, from $\frac{3}{2}$ to $\frac{2}{2}$, and even to a single-beat measure, $\frac{1}{2}$.

The irregular metrical plan is further complicated by the canonic imitation between voice and piano beginning at bar 5 (see circled cross and dotted lines in ex. Q). Here the two quarter-note B's of the piano sound like upbeats, but so do the first two E's of the imitative response by the voice.

No notation can accurately capture the listener's experience of such a fluent passage, of his wavering between metrical orientation and disorientation. But however he chooses to organize the meter, there is no mistaking the general effect of explosion at the first *"bitter."* After the regular, controlled statements of *"O Tod,"* the voice leaps spasmodically up an augmented octave from the low C to a high C♯. At *"bitter"* the meter responds with a correspondingly violent shift—an aftershock, one might say, of the opening up of a fault in the line.

This flexible metrical development finds a larger-scale expression in the actual change to duple meter at bar 18. Here, in what amounts to a reversal of the earlier contractions, meter and sentiment seem to expand together. The notated $\frac{3}{2}$ and implied $\frac{2}{2}$ and $\frac{1}{2}$ meters of the first part of the song, in which upbeats and downbeats fall, so to speak, uncomfortably close to each other, are broadened to a more genial $\frac{4}{2}$ (notated by Brahms as ₵). The feminine rhythms at *"wohl"* and *"du"* further soften the impact of the downbeats.

In the final section of the song (bar 31; see Appendix, ex. R, p. 200), Brahms reinstates the original triple meter but abandons the asymmetry of the opening. At *"wie wohl"* he retains the gesture of textual and sequential repetition—like *"wie bitter,"* this phrase is repeated a minor third lower—but he now expands and regularizes the sequence into a pair of genuinely parallel three-bar statements (bars 33–35, 37–39). The triple meter is thus unequivocally articulated, and all metrical development and tension have been laid to rest.

Although his analysis implies that the basic interval, the third, affects the

EXAMPLE 47: Brahms, "O Tod," op. 121, no. 3, harmonic-motivic reduction.

harmony of the song, Schoenberg does not discuss the remarkable relationship between motivic and tonal processes. The interlocking thirds produce at the opening a bold harmonic series, E minor–C major–A minor–F♯ major–E minor. This progression can, of course, be labeled in E minor as i–VI–iv–V/V–i⁶. But it is made to seem anything but ordinary by the way in which the triads are starkly juxtaposed, especially when the leap of an augmented octave, from C to C♯, dramatizes the shift from A minor to F♯ major. The sevenths outlined horizontally by the voice (B–C) and the bass (F♯–E)—these are shown as e in Schoenberg's analysis—also prevent our hearing any conventional harmonic progression.

And when the F♯–E seventh is expressed vertically in the F♯ dominant-seventh chord in bar 3, this too fails to resolve properly. Underneath the E, the piano moves by step to hollow-sounding octaves on G and B, thus shaping a weak, first-inversion tonic. As the voice descends to B, the piano merely sustains, stirring only to replace the E the voice has abandoned. If the sudden shift from A minor to F♯ major has conveyed the intense anguish of *"bitter,"* this remarkably unsatisfactory cadence projects the resignation and despair that follow. With these harmonic procedures (and the simultaneous metrical explosion discussed above) Brahms has, I think, captured a typical progression of human emotion: an angry outburst of resentment followed by a tired expression of acceptance.

The ubiquitous third stimulates still more impressive harmonic effects in the transition to the final *"O Tod"* (see ex. 47 and ex. R). In bars 24–26 the harmony settles on A major (IV). Over the bass A in bar 27 the right hand of the piano plays an ascending third, C♯–D♯–E (this would be Schoenberg's motive c +); the chord takes on a dominant seventh (F×) as the voice reverses the motive at *"und nichts Bessers"*; the A⁷ chord then behaves as a German sixth, resolving on the downbeat of bar 28 to a ⁶₄ chord in C♯ minor. The motivic dialogue between piano and voice is repeated on the same pitches over this new harmony. In bar 29 the ascending motive, C♯–D♯–E, is reharmonized yet again; now the bass moves as well, descending in contrary motion through G♮–F♯–E. We expect a C♯-minor chord over that final E on the third beat of bar 29, but Brahms astonishes us by harmonizing the two outer E's with a remote A-minor triad.

Having wrenched us into a new harmonic region, Brahms calmly moves toward a half cadence on the dominant of E minor. We now await, presumably, a grim *da capo* of the opening sentiments, much as in the return of bars 13–17; but what actually follows is the grandest harmonic-motivic and expressive effect of the song.

At the fermata of bar 30, the upper part of the piano has played a prolonged 4–3 suspension over the dominant B; the pitches are, of course, E–D♯, the first two notes of the by-now-familiar third motive E–D♯–C♯. No C♯ is present, however: we assume it has been eradicated by the powerful C♮ of the A-minor chord. But as the *"O Tod"* theme enters in the tonic major, instead of the anticipated minor, Brahms recommences, then completes (and continues) the motivic third at the top of the piano accompaniment (bar 31); here is a subtle example of linkage technique, used to end one phrase and begin another.

In the final segment, the harsh progressions generated by thirds and sevenths at the beginning of the song become purely diatonic and comprehensible, as I–vi–IV–ii–vii°–IV⁶, etc. And the F♯–E seventh, so ambiguous in the horizontal and vertical dimensions of bars 1–3, becomes perfectly lucid in bars 36–39. The vocal line leaps from E down to F♯, but then leads that F♯ smoothly down to the tonic E; the seventh is thus safely embedded, and resolved, within an octave. And the harmonic F♯⁷ chord, which failed to resolve properly in bar 3, now moves purposefully through the circle of fifths: it is ii⁶₅, then (with an A♯) V⁷/V, leading to V and I.

The conclusion of the song can be said to epitomize all that is original and compelling in the musical techniques of Brahms examined in this study. The E-major statement of *"O Tod"* is, as we have said, a heightened transformation, a transfiguration that results from continuous harmonic, motivic, and metrical development, and is at the same time closely bound up with the meaning of the words, the progression from *"bitter"* to *"wohl."* Brahms prepares this transformation with a highly characteristic device, the familiar linkage technique: the E–D♯ figure of the 4–3 suspension is taken over and completed as E–D♯–C♯.

And what of the form? Brahms does not simply create a two-part song from the two verses of his text, although there is the vestige of such a plan (bars 1–17, 18–40). A more precise representation along these lines might be A B A   A' C A". But I think the successive development and reinterpretation of material are really too profound to allow of any such procrustean designation. Elements of the first *"O Tod"* are explored, leading to an exact return at bars 13–17. Then the pace of development increases—mode, meter, and contour are changed—as the theme moves outward in new directions. The final return to *"O Tod"* is particularly splendid because we expect another literal return (as at 13–17), but get a transfigured one.

This is surely one of Brahms's greatest "recapitulations," serving both as a final stage in the development of material and as a satisfactory rounding-off. The immediate preparation for it equals any of Brahms's retransitions in skill and power. Brahms thus achieves in "O Tod" what is perhaps an ideal balance between continuous development and stable recapitulation.

7

Epilogue: Developing Variation
in Early Schoenberg, 1892–1905

I

The analysis of "O Tod" in "Brahms the Progressive" remains Schoenberg's single most comprehensive discussion of any Brahms piece; he accounts for 25 of 40 bars, more than in any other analysis. As I suggested in Chapter 1, Schoenberg tends to focus on local compositional techniques rather than larger structural or formal issues, and on themes only a few bars long rather than entire movements or works. The other analyses in "Brahms the Progressive," such as his parsing of the Andante theme from the String Quartet, op. 51, no. 2, deal with no more than a dozen bars of music; in the 1931 radio talk, he confines his discussion of the F-Major Violoncello Sonata, op. 99, likewise to the main theme.

It is perhaps not surprising, then, that in Schoenberg's own early music the influence of Brahms's methods of developing variation is to be felt most profoundly on the level of the individual theme. Schoenberg's earliest sonata-style works, such as the String Quartet in D of 1897, tend to be formally *more* conservative than Brahms's; but within a few years the younger composer far outstrips Brahms in formal complexity: *Verklärte Nacht*, op. 4 (1899), and the String Quartet in D Minor, op. 7 (1904–5), both reinterpret sonata principles in ways that go well beyond the Brahms aesthetic.[1] Despite their radical difference in outward appearance, however—and despite the rapid evolution in style—the works of Schoenberg's first decade do share certain basic compositional tech-

---

[1] For formal analyses of *Verklärte Nacht*, see Richard Swift, "1/XII/99: Tonal Relations in Schoenberg's *Verklärte Nacht*" and Philip Friedheim, "Tonality and Structure in the Early Works of Schoenberg," pp. 112–39. I return to the quartet below.

niques with those of Brahms. Several produce their thematic and motivic material by distinctly Brahmsian procedures of developing variation, displaying many of the same devices that Schoenberg was later to write about in Brahms's music.

Most of the music Schoenberg composed in the 1890s lies in manuscript in various locations, still awaiting editing and publication.[2] The only early works to appear in print so far are the D-Major String Quartet of 1897, the Three Piano Pieces of 1894, and the Six Pieces for Piano Four Hands of 1896. (See Bibliography for details.) The chronology of the works of this period is difficult to establish, since Schoenberg did not date many of the songs, instrumental pieces, fragments, and sketches. It is too early, then, to be able to form a clear, rounded picture of Schoenberg's stylistic development.

Some fine preliminary work in this area has been done by Ulrich Thieme, in his 1979 Inaugural-Dissertation, *Studien zum Jugendwerk Arnold Schönbergs*. Thieme carefully and sensitively analyzes much of the unpublished music (some of which is conveniently reproduced in facsimile), as well as the published works. Thieme's account accords well with (and, of course, draws upon) Schoenberg's own views on his formative years. Thieme divides this period into three segments: "autodidactic beginnings," up to 1895; a phase characterized by the influence of Brahms and Dvořák, from 1895 to 1897; and a final phase of "coming to grips with" [*Auseinandersetzung mit*] Wagner and Strauss, 1898–99. The work that adopts Brahmsian thematic-motivic procedures most thoroughly, Thieme suggests (and attempts to demonstrate), is the *Serenade für kleines Orchester* of September 1896.[3]

Thieme's impressive survey of Schoenberg's *Jugendzeit* does not, however, do full justice to the powerful, pervasive Brahms influence, which pre-dates 1895 and extends considerably after 1897. Indeed, one of Schoenberg's earliest surviving musical utterances shows the unmistakable profile of Brahms. In his informative "Notes on the Four String Quartets" of 1949, Schoenberg recalls that "at about the age of 18" he attempted the first movement of a symphony, whose main theme he recalls as in example 48.[4]

---

[2]The principal locations are the archives of the Arnold Schoenberg Institute in Los Angeles, the Nachod Collection at North Texas State University, the Pierpont Morgan Library, and the Library of Congress. The entire contents of the Nachod collection have recently been published in facsimile (in poor reproductions) in Arnold Schoenberg, *The Arnold Schoenberg-Hans Nachod Collection*. There is still no thorough inventory of Schoenberg autograph sources. It is best to use the early catalogue by Josef Rufer, *The Works of Arnold Schoenberg*, in conjunction with that of Jan Maegaard, *Studien zur Entwicklung des dodekaphonen Satzes bei Arnold Schönberg*, 1. For an inventory of the early songs, see Walter Bailey, "The Unpublished Songs of Arnold Schoenberg: c. 1893–1900," Appendix I, pp. 110–18; and Leonard Stein, "Toward a Chronology of Schoenberg's Early Unpublished Songs."

[3]Ulrich Thieme, *Studien zum Jugendwerk Arnold Schönbergs*, pp. 94–107. See also the sensitive discussion of Brahmsian procedures in Musgrave, "Schoenberg and Brahms," pp. 242–370. For a stylistic analysis of the early songs, see Bailey, "Unpublished Songs," pp. 30–109.

[4]Arnold Schoenberg, "Notes on the Four String Quartets," pp. 35–36.

EXAMPLE 48: Schoenberg, symphony theme, ca. 1892.

There is, alas, no manuscript source for this symphony. But if Schoenberg's recollection of its date is correct—he was eighteen in 1892—this theme is one of the first we have (aside from the early violin duets). Schoenberg reports that "Mozart, Brahms, Beethoven and Dvořák were my models at this time." He suggests no priority of influence among this distinguished group, but the theme betrays an impressive grasp of Brahms's thematic principles. The last two bars are clearly borrowed from the main theme of Brahms's *Tragic Overture*, op. 81, and the preceding measures grow toward that quotation in an evolutionary manner we have often observed in Brahms's themes. Indeed, this A-minor theme is almost a miniature paradigm of developing variation. The germ or basic idea is the tonic-defining third A–C, presented in the first bar. From this the theme climbs across five bars toward F; D is added, somewhat tentatively, on a weak beat in bar 2. The three-note succession A–C–D is repeated in diminution, now placing D firmly on the downbeat of bar 3. E is introduced, like D, on a weak beat. Then, in bar 4, the arpeggiated A-minor triad summarizes the theme's progress and, as before, places the new high note on a strong beat. In its last bar the theme reaches F.

The theme virtually constructs itself by the continuous reinterpretation and expansion of a small motive. The process is, to be sure, almost painstakingly "organic." But even the later Schoenberg, the discerning commentator on Brahms's themes, might have admired the flexible phrase structure and metrical design. The five bars divide asymmetrically into three phrases of 1½ + 1½ + 2. The "conventional" two-bar phrase completes the whole thematic process, resolving the tension created by the two less regular phrases. The first two phrases articulate respectively the first two notes of the structural ascent, C and D; the last accelerates the pace, presenting both E and F in short succession.

It is indeed remarkable that the young, largely self-taught Schoenberg should have understood the inner workings of Brahms so well. The Three Piano Pieces of 1894, which appropriate the distinctive piano style of Brahms's late pieces, show that Brahms continued to cast a broad shadow over Schoenberg's instrumental compositions. (The collections opp. 116–19 had only recently been published, in 1892–93.) And the first, in C♯ minor, exploits a very familiar Brahmsian device, metrical displacement (see Appendix, ex. S, p. 201): although notated in $\frac{2}{4}$, the music unfolds as if in $\frac{6}{8}$. As in so many of the Brahms examples discussed earlier in this study, the listener cannot possibly be aware of the dislocation, since the written meter is not established at the outset. Only in bars 9–10 do we become aware of a conflict: the $\frac{6}{8}$ pattern begins an eighth note "early," on the downbeat of bar 10. In bars 14–15, where the displaced $\frac{6}{8}$ has been reestablished, the right hand plays a hemiola (a $\frac{3}{4}$ pattern) above the left-hand accompaniment, which remains in $\frac{6}{8}$. Such metrical complexities, piling ambiguity upon (or within) ambiguity, even outdo Brahms, their obvious model.

As Schoenberg himself admitted, the String Quartet in D major of 1897 is "strongly under the influence of Brahms and Dvořák."[5] The folk-like, pentatonic themes of the first and last movements point clearly enough to the Bohemian composer, but the inner movements are distinctly Brahmsian in conception. Like Brahms, Schoenberg substitutes for the traditional scherzo a brief, haunting Intermezzo (see Appendix, ex. T(a), p. 202). Indeed, he seems to have had a specific Brahms movement in his ear, the third movement of the B♭-Major Quartet, op. 67 (see ex. T(b)). In both pieces the viola plays a plaintive, triple-time melody to a pulsating accompaniment *con sordini*.

Schoenberg's own third movement is a set of variations, a formal design Brahms often included in his multi-movement works. The theme has a brooding quality reminiscent of Brahms; also Brahmsian is the way in which the phrase structure of the variations adheres quite rigidly to that of the theme, while the harmony is progressively intensified from within.

Of course, resemblances or borrowings of this general kind tell us little about the important structural principles of either Brahms's or Schoenberg's music. On several occasions Schoenberg himself voiced disapproval of music historians' efforts to trace this kind of stylistic influence, and of fledgling composers' attempts to learn their craft only by writing "in the style of" older masters. Both groups concentrate too much on surface qualities and are unable to do justice to the musical "idea" or essence, according to Schoenberg:

> To listen to certain learned musicians, one would think all composers did not bring about the representation of their *vision*, but aimed solely at establishing a style— so that musicologists should have something to do. As far as I myself am concerned, I allow that one can try to detect the personal characteristics of the finished work from the score, from its more or less remarkable figures or turns of phrase. But to overlook the fact that such personal characteristics follow from the true characteristic idea and are merely the symptoms—to believe, when someone imitates the symptoms, the style, that this is an artistic achievement—that is a mistake with dire consequences! A sensitive ear hears characteristics, even invisible ones, where the deaf sees at most style.[6]

This distinction between "style" and "idea" runs throughout Schoenberg's writings and, of course, furnished the title for his collection of essays. By "idea"

---

[5] Schoenberg, "Notes," p. 36. See also Reinhard Gerlach, "War Schönberg von Dvořák Beeinflusst?"

[6] Arnold Schoenberg, "Why No Great American Music?" in his *Style and Idea*, pp. 177–78.

EXAMPLE 49: Schoenberg, String Quartet, 1897, I.

Schoenberg presumably means not only the basic shape or *Grundgestalt* from which a composition should grow logically, but also the technique or method by which it is developed. When composers (or musicologists) seek inspiration in the work of an older master, they should take care to appropriate (or discuss) not the "symptoms" of his work, but its essential principles, its "true characteristic idea."[7]

For much of his D-Major Quartet—to say nothing of the Piano Pieces—Schoenberg seems to be adopting the symptoms of Brahms, rather than his fundamental compositional procedures. (The same might be said about many of the early, unpublished Lieder.) The first group of the first movement is, to be sure, motivically and rhythmically economical, drawing most of its material from the unison theme of the first four bars. But it is in the second theme (in the key area of B major, or VI) that Schoenberg reveals a deeper understanding of the principles he was later to uncover in Brahms's A-Minor Quartet. Like the Brahms theme, Schoenberg's has an outwardly regular eight-bar structure, which even shows strong traces of a traditional antecedent-consequent design of 4 + 4 bars (see ex. 49). The "antecedent" extends to the half cadence on F♯ in bar 42, the "consequent" to the full (or firmer) closure in that key at bar 46; but within this framework Schoenberg, like Brahms, develops his motive forms fluently from the wistful one-bar idea.

First the one-bar figure is repeated almost exactly (bar 40); only the eighth-note upbeat is changed, from D♯ to C♯. Then real development begins. The F♯ is approached from D♯, and the ascent is compressed within the first half of the bar—that is, within two beats instead of three. The second half of bar 41 presents a new motivic idea (x) comprised of paired, sequentially descending thirds, extending to the second beat of bar 42. This fourth arrival on the pitch F♯ marks off the first half of the theme. But the developmental process will not permit closure. Instead, x generates a related motive form, in which the initial third is

---

[7]On the broader connotations of Schoenberg's "idea," see Charlotte M. Cross, "Three Levels of 'Idea' in Schoenberg's Thought and Writings."

reversed (E–G♯), or (to put it another way) the G♯ upbeat is approached from below instead of above. We are reminded of Brahms's linkage technique, whereby the tail end of one segment (here the antecedent) is repeated or slightly varied to begin a new one.

In the consequent phrase (bars 42–46), Schoenberg continues to develop motive x in a series of one-bar fragments. The interval of a third that concludes each one provides the audible common denominator, even when there is some variation in the rhythm and interval content of the first part of the motive. These concluding thirds, which really extend back into the antecedent, are A♯–F♯ (bar 42), F♯–D♯ (43), A♯–C♯ (the third reversed, bar 44), and E♯–C♯ (inverted, bar 45). As these fragments keep spinning themselves out, we lose any sense of symmetry, any impression that we are hearing a normal consequent. Schoenberg has us guessing where the phrase will end, until in bar 46 a cadential descending second, G♯–F♯, at last brings the evolutionary motivic process (and the thirds) to a halt—just in time to create a tidy eight-bar theme.

If Schoenberg has not quite attained here the elegance and sophistication he so admired in Brahms's themes, he has nevertheless crafted a theme that is eminently Brahmsian in its flexible treatment of motive forms, its exploitation of ambiguity and of the linkage technique, and in its outward decorum, which contains these "progressive" techniques within eight very polite bars.

II

After the D-Major Quartet Schoenberg began to experiment with larger and freer forms, without, however, abandoning the principles of developing variation. He was exposed to the massive creations of Mahler and Strauss; through the influence of his friend and teacher Alexander von Zemlinsky, he also came to appreciate the music of Wagner. "I had been a 'Brahmsian' when I met Zemlinsky," Schoenberg explains. "His love embraced both Brahms and Wagner, and soon thereafter I became an equally confirmed addict."[8]

Verklärte Nacht, op. 4 (1899), thus emerges as a peculiar but compelling hybrid of Wagnerian and Brahmsian principles. Schoenberg himself analyzed the musical results: "In my *Verklärte Nacht* the thematic construction is based on Wagnerian "model and sequence" above a roving harmony on the one hand, and on Brahms' technique of developing variation—as I call it—on the other. Also to Brahms must be ascribed the imparity of measures, as for instance in measures 50–54, comprising five measures, or measures 320–37, comprising [phrases of] two and one-half measures."[9] *Verklärte Nacht*, *Pelleas und Melisande*, and *Gurrelieder* are apotheoses of late romantic musical "styles." As

[8]Schoenberg, "My Evolution," in his *Style and Idea*, p. 80.

[9]Schoenberg, *Style and Idea*, p. 80.

Schoenberg realized, they did not project a sufficiently personal voice, a truly individual *Gedanke*. The first work to achieve that goal was, in his view, the String Quartet in D Minor, op. 7, composed in 1904–5.

> [I] turned in the direction that was much more my own than all the preceding. . . . I combined all the achievements of my time (including my own) such as: the construction of extremely large forms; greatly expanded melodies based on a richly moving harmony and new chord progressions; and a contrapuntal technique that solved problems offered by superimposed, individual parts which moved freely in more remote regions of a tonality and met frequently in vagrant harmonies.[10]

The quartet is cast as a single fifty-minute movement, whose various sections correspond to the traditional divisions of first movement, scherzo, slow movement, and finale. Two development sections are interpolated, before and after the scherzo, and there are brief recapitulations of the primary themes just before and after the slow movement. The finale reviews all the preceding themes and leads into a slow coda in the major mode.

Schoenberg's quartet was roundly hissed at its premiere in 1907.[11] What upset his contemporaries, apparently, was not the extended form—such all-in-one pieces had been written before by Liszt, Strauss, and even Beethoven in the finale of his Ninth Symphony—but the technical "achievements" outlined in the passage cited above. Even Mahler, one of Schoenberg's most sympathetic supporters, was nonplused by the quartet. "I have conducted the most difficult scores of Wagner," he remarked. "I have written complicated music myself in scores of up to thirty staves and more; yet here is a score of not more than four staves, and I am unable to read them."[12]

In a brilliant essay of 1924 entitled "Why Is Schoenberg's Music So Hard to Comprehend?" Schoenberg's former pupil Alban Berg championed the quartet and its composer by elucidating those features that the average listener (not to mention a musician like Mahler) might have found perplexing. Although the analogy has never, to my knowledge, been pointed out, Berg tries to do for Schoenberg precisely what Schoenberg would later try to do for Brahms. The two authors argue from different sides, as it were: Berg demonstrates how Schoenberg is not an utter revolutionary, a destroyer of tradition, while Schoenberg proves that Brahms is not simply a reactionary. But their ultimate critical goal is the same—to show by means of detailed analysis how a great composer can be an innovator without ever abandoning the laws of musical logic and clarity. (The question of influence is delicate here. In his early study with

[10]Schoenberg, "Notes," p. 36.

[11]See Reich, *Schoenberg*, pp. 20–22.

[12]Reported by Schoenberg in "How One Becomes Lonely," in his *Style and Idea*, p. 42.

Schoenberg, Berg would surely have encountered this kind of polemical analysis; but it is also probable that in preparing his radio talk on Brahms in 1933, and later "Brahms the Progressive," Schoenberg turned to Berg's essay as a model of how to promote a maligned composer.)

Berg analyzes harmonic progressions and thematic structure in the first ten bars of the quartet, then discusses the varied recapitulations of these bars throughout the rest of the piece. For our study of developing variation, the last two aspects are the most significant. Berg shows that the opening "theme" (see Appendix, ex. U, p. 204) is actually a contrapuntal aggregate of three fully independent and invertible lines: the melody (which he labels 1), the tremolo arpeggiations in the viola (2), and the stepwise bass line (3). The theme never returns in exactly the same form, Berg explains, "since merely mechanical repetition is foreign even to this early Schoenberg work."[13] Schoenberg varies his material principally by the systematic application of contrapuntal inversion. At the second appearance of the theme, in E♭ minor in bar 30, the original texture is turned on its head: the vertical ordering of the parts becomes 3 (in octaves), 2, 1. At the return to the tonic in bar 65, parts 2 and 3 are varied, and the whole thematic complex is reshuffled to read 2 (a variant in sixteenth notes), 1 (in octaves), 3 (varied by eighth-note triplets). When the theme is recapitulated in D minor just before the slow movement, 38 bars after letter I, we find the following line-up: 3 (a variant in eighth-note triplets, but different from the earlier pattern), 1 (in octaves), 3 (inverted and in eighth-note diminution). At the very last return, the major-mode apotheosis in the coda at letter O, the melody (1) is at last back on top of the texture, while the lower parts play an inversion of 3 in sweet parallel tenths.

Berg gives no historical provenance for Schoenberg's densely contrapuntal textures, nor for his methods of varying the principal material. Another Schoenberg pupil, however, pinpoints the source of these saturated textures, in which there is no "filler," no neutral or insignificant "accompaniment." In 1912 Anton Webern wrote admiringly:

> Schoenberg's art of thematic writing is immensely enhanced in op. 7. It is marvellous to observe how Schoenberg creates an accompaniment figure from a motivic particle, how he introduces themes, how he brings about interconnections between the principal sections. And everything is thematic! There is, one can say, not a single note in this work that does not have a thematic basis. This is unparalleled. If there is a connection with another composer, then that composer is Johannes Brahms.[14]

Also Brahmsian, to my ear and eye, are the kinds of variations the thematic

---

[13]Alban Berg, "Why Is Schoenberg's Music So Hard to Comprehend?" p. 27.

[14]Anton Webern, "Schoenberg's Music," p. 16.

EXAMPLE 50: Schoenberg, String Quartet, op. 7.

components undergo, especially perhaps the triplet variants of 3, the original bass line (for example, at 38 after letter I). This is the type of reinterpretation we have often seen Brahms use at moments of recapitulation—for example, in the Adagio of the Second Symphony or the return to the A' section in "Die Mainacht," where the original eighth-note accompaniment dissolves into shimmering triplet figuration.

The technique of variation that Berg analyzes is close to what Dahlhaus, in his monograph on Brahms's First Piano Concerto, op. 15, calls "developing variation": the recasting of a theme at each separate appearance in the sonata structure. In Chapter 1, I suggested that this higher-level developing variation, although significant, is less essential to our (and Schoenberg's) appreciation of Brahms than an understanding of how his themes unfold and succeed each other on a more local level. Although, as Berg suggests, Schoenberg's music abounds in the former type—virtually nothing recurs untransformed in op. 7—it is not surprising that the quartet's lower-level thematic construction shows even more clearly the influence and the spirit of Brahms's procedures.

We have already examined in detail two Schoenberg themes that develop in Brahmsian fashion, the opening of the early symphony from about 1892 and the second theme from the D-Major Quartet. Let us turn (with Berg) to the principal voice of the first theme in the D-Minor Quartet. Berg asks his readers "to admit the rightness of the first bars of a melody which, contrary to expectation, consists of 2½-bar phrases" (ex. 50a, copied from Berg).[15] In fact, the theme defies expectation even more than Berg acknowledges. The first phrase does not end after 2½ bars: it is not abruptly cut off on the high-D sixteenth note, but (as is implied by Schoenberg's slurring, which Berg fails to reproduce) resolves or settles on the low E. The second phrase, however, also *begins* on this note. There is thus an elision between the two phrases, providing a moment of delicate but deliberate ambiguity. On the one hand we perceive the E as a rather disjunct, but necessary, conclusion to the first phrase; on the other, we (like Berg) hear

---

[15]Berg, "Why Is Schoenberg's Music," p. 22.

EXAMPLE 51: Berg's rewriting of Schoenberg's String Quartet, op. 7.

the E as initiating a parallel phrase on the second degree of the scale—much like the responses beginning on the supertonic in such classical pieces as Beethoven's First Symphony and Brahms's Second. If we hear the E in this double role, we can also experience the Brahmsian linkage technique, whereby the last little figure of the first phrase is taken over, with only a slight variation, to propel the second phrase forward (ex. 50b). Schoenberg himself displays the elision between phrases in his analysis of this theme in *Fundamentals of Musical Composition*. Moreover, he associates the "free rhythmic organization" with Brahms, whose Andante theme from the A-Minor String Quartet is analyzed in the same musical example.[16]

Not only do the metrical and phrase structure recall Brahms, but the theme develops with Brahmsian velocity. After the two initial phrases, Schoenberg abandons the rhythmic pattern he has established; in shorter note values and less regular rhythms the theme ascends quickly to the high B♭ (bar 7) and then to high F (bar 8). Berg suggests that bar 7 constitutes a highly varied, compressed repetition of bars 3 to 5—he presumably means they both share the ascent from low E to high A (to which the B♭ is then an appoggiatura)—but admits that "the listener, who has not quite grasped the rhythm of the initial phrase, is sure to lose his way."

To help this perplexed individual, Berg rewrites the theme in a more easily graspable form (see ex. 51), precisely as Schoenberg does with Brahms's Andante theme (see Chapter 1, ex. 3). Berg explains, cheekily:

Here the dissymmetry of the original has in fact been disposed of, in favour of a two-bar structure which will satisfy even the densest listener. The motivic and rhythmic evolution proceeds nice and slowly, dodging any opportunity of variation. Since the

---

[16]See Schoenberg, *Fundamentals*, Example 111 a and b (p. 140), and the commentary on p. 138.

listener might conceivably stumble over 16ths in a quick Alla breve movement, they are dispensed with entirely. . . . The 8th-note motion remains constant and the harmony changes only every half-bar. There may still be a chance, however, that even this mutilated theme will not be understood, so a literal repeat in the principal key follows right on its heels. This should guarantee a general intelligibility bordering on outright popularity, and the matter will be clinched by removing all polyphony and substituting the simplest accompaniment imaginable.[17]

Berg's ingeniously vulgar revision of Schoenberg's theme actually carries further—to an absurd extreme—a process of regularization begun by the composer himself. Schoenberg's sketches for op. 7 (now at the Schoenberg Institute) reveal his concern for the very same issue Berg raises, the proper structure and pacing of the theme. As he began work on the quartet, Schoenberg jotted down, but quickly broke off, a draft of the main theme. Beneath the first sketch he then wrote out the full theme much as we know it, provided it with a bass line, and sketched some inner parts. A facsimile of the two drafts is given as figure 4, and a transcription of the first as example 52.

In retrospect the first, fragmentary draft has to strike us as an accelerated, compressed version of the theme in its final form. Schoenberg must have realized that it develops too fast, too soon—even for the most intelligent listener. In the second bar this early version of the theme ascends to the high A, a point reached much more gradually and logically in the final version, where the first phrase goes only as far as F (the third of the tonic triad), and the second, parallel phrase (bars 3–5) completes the triadic outline with A. Indeed, in the first draft there *is* no parallel phrase: the second phrase abandons the opening rhythm and soars impatiently up to the high B♭ and F. In the final version this climactic rise is again less frantic, occurring only at bars 7 and 8, where it is comfortably spread out over two bars. A comparison of the two themes at this point reveals how Schoenberg expanded and slowed up the ascent. The figure in bar 5 of the first draft (ex. 53a) becomes "padded" with repetition of the G♮–B♭–A–G♯ figure in bar 8 of the final version (ex. 53b). Similarly, the opening phrase of the theme, which has no parallel response in the first draft, is provided with an immediate sequential repetition in the final version.

The first draft is in one sense too fast and compressed; in another sense it is too slow. After attaining the high A in only two bars, the theme drops to B♭, where it sits stodgily for almost another two full bars. Its subsequent sprint up to the high B♭ and F seems an embarrassed effort to compensate for the delinquency. Thus in the first draft the development is at first too rapid, then virtually non-existent, then once again too hasty. The final version is more purposeful, logical, and even-tempered: each ascent (D to F, E to A, B♭ to F) is spread over at

---

[17]Berg, "Why Is Schoenberg's Music," p. 24.

FIGURE 4: Schoenberg, String Quartet, op. 7. Facsimile of two drafts of main theme. Reproduced, by permission, from page "Sk 5" of the sketchbook of 1904–5 in the archives of the Arnold Schoenberg Institute, Los Angeles.

EXAMPLE 52: Schoenberg, String Quartet, op. 7, transcription of first draft for main theme.

EXAMPLE 53: Schoenberg, String Quartet, op. 7, comparison of first draft and final version.

least two bars. The climax of bars 8–9 is thus carefully prepared, rather than impulsively attacked.

We recall that Berg considers the final rise to this climax (bar 7) a "variation" of bars 3–5. Whether or not our ear hears it as such, we do perceive the low E of bar 7 as a point of reference: we understand that we are hearing a roughly parallel statement of the previous phrase that began on that pitch (in the last half of bar 3). In the first draft, however, the final ascent begins somewhat arbitrarily from the B♭, where the theme has been idling for two bars; we are thus much less likely to hear any connection or parallel with what has preceded.

In one of the rare instances where Schoenberg writes in some technical detail about his own compositional process, he describes how another theme underwent revisions much like those of op. 7. In the essay "Heart and Brain in Music," he reproduces seven sketches for two of the main subjects of the Chamber Symphony, op. 9, composed in 1906, shortly after the quartet.[18] Especially re-

---

[18]Schoenberg, *Style and Idea*, pp. 58–60 (ex. 3).

vealing are the preliminary drafts of the cello theme at rehearsal number 2. In its rapid ascent and wide leaps, this theme bears a resemblance to the principal idea of the quartet (and both probably owe their origin to the athletic themes of Richard Strauss). We need not examine its genesis in detail here—the reader can follow that process in Schoenberg's examples—except to note that, much as in op. 7, the first attempts develop too fast: they climb too swiftly and introduce contrasting rhythms too soon. The final form moderates the evolutionary process. All this is noted by Schoenberg himself, who writes, "There was at hand from the start a sufficient amount of motival forms and their derivatives, rather too much than too little. The task, therefore, was to retard the progress of development in order to enable the average good listener to keep in mind what preceded so as to understand the consequences. To keep within bounds and to balance a theme whose character, tempo, expression, harmonic progression, and motival contents displayed a centrifugal tendency: this was here the task."[19] Schoenberg thus verbalizes (and demonstrates in another work) precisely the concerns we have found in the drafts of the op. 7 theme.

III

In "National Music," an essay written in 1931, Schoenberg attempted to explain the ways in which he had inherited the venerable tradition of German music. "My teachers," he says in an often-quoted statement, "were primarily Bach and Mozart, and secondarily Beethoven, Brahms, and Wagner."[20] He then lists what he learned from each of these masters. Among the techniques he absorbed from Bach are contrapuntal thinking and "the art of producing everything from one thing." From Mozart came inequality of phrase lengths and "co-ordination of heterogeneous characters to form a thematic unity." Brahms, we are told, taught Schoenberg:

1. Much of what I had unconsciously absorbed from Mozart, particularly odd barring, and extension and abbreviation of phrases.
2. Plasticity in moulding figures; not to be mean, not to stint myself when clarity demands more space; to carry every figure through to the end.
3. Systematic notation.
4. Economy, yet richness.

The theme of the op. 7 Quartet can be seen to epitomize all these Brahms influences. We have examined its uneven barring and phrase structure (no. 1). We might also note how, like Brahms, Schoenberg prefers to contain irregular,

[19]Schoenberg, *Style and Idea*, pp. 60–61.

[20]Schoenberg, *Style and Idea*, p. 173.

shifting metrical divisions within a standard, and thus "systematic," notation (no. 3). The qualities under no. 4 perhaps speak for themselves: the theme is economical yet rich in both its horizontal and vertical dimensions, in its developmental unfolding and in its polyphonic density. And a comparison of the sketch and the final version has shown us the idea expressed in no. 2—that the richness not be too overwhelming, too compressed; that an idea be allowed to expand slowly, even with a certain amount of repetition, "when clarity demands more space."

Thus, by the time he reaches compositional maturity, Schoenberg no longer apes the "symptoms" of Brahms, but has genuinely absorbed Brahms's true characteristic ideas, especially the flexible principles of developing variation. As might be expected, it is Schoenberg himself who best expresses how, despite its apparent innovation, his music has its roots deep in the past. In the same essay, "National Music," he explains, "I immediately imitated everything I saw that was good. . . . For if I saw something, I did not leave it at that; I acquired it, in order to possess it; I worked on it and extended it, and it led me to something new. . . . I am convinced that eventually people will recognize how immediately this 'something new' is linked to the loftiest models that have been granted us."

As we have seen in this study, Brahms also drew extensively upon the "lofty models" of his past (and present)—upon Beethoven, Schubert, Schumann, and Liszt. Like Schoenberg, Brahms did not simply appropriate "styles"—his music does not sound like the music of these composers—but rather worked on and "possessed" certain fundamental compositional principles. From such procedures as thematic transformation, metrical displacement, the linkage technique, and continuous motivic reinterpretation, he created a unique and compelling musical language.

"He would have been a pioneer if he had simply returned to Mozart," Schoenberg said of Brahms. "But he did not live on inherited fortune; he made one of his own."[21] The latter statement could be applied to Schoenberg himself. For that is how a musical tradition is, or should be, perpetuated and continually revitalized. Powerful figures like Brahms and Schoenberg do not merely inherit a tradition. They labor to make it their own and thereby to create something new.

[21]Schoenberg, "Brahms the Progressive," in his *Style and Idea*, p. 439.

Appendix of Longer Musical Examples

EXAMPLE A: Brahms, Piano Sonata, op. 5, I, bars 1–144. From Johannes Brahms, *Sämtliche Werke*, by permission of Breitkopf & Härtel, Wiesbaden.

EXAMPLE B: Brahms, Piano Trio, op. 8 (original version), I, bars 80–165. From Johannes Brahms, *Sämtliche Werke*, by permission of Breitkopf & Härtel, Wiesbaden.

EXAMPLE C: Brahms, Piano Quartet, op. 25, I, bars 229–65. From Johannes Brahms, *Sämtliche Werke*, by permission of Breitkopf & Härtel, Wiesbaden.

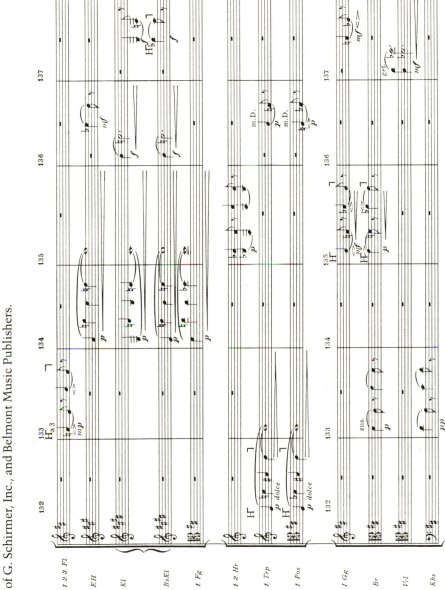

EXAMPLE D: Brahms, Piano Quartet, op. 25, I, bars 132–37, orchestrated by Schoenberg. Examples D and E copyright © 1940 G. Schirmer, Inc. Copyright renewed 1967 by Belmont Music Publishers. Used by permission of G. Schirmer, Inc., and Belmont Music Publishers.

EXAMPLE E: Brahms, Piano Quartet, op. 25, I, bars 48–52, orchestrated by Schoenberg.

EXAMPLE F: Brahms, Piano Quartet, op. 26, I, bars 137–51. From Johannes Brahms, *Sämtliche Werke*, by permission of Breitkopf & Härtel, Wiesbaden.

EXAMPLE G: Brahms, Piano Quintet, op. 34, I, bars 200–12. From Johannes Brahms, *Sämtliche Werke*, by permission of Breitkopf & Härtel, Wiesbaden.

EXAMPLE H: Brahms, Piano Quintet, op. 34, I, bars 82–100. From Johannes Brahms, *Sämtliche Werke*, by permission of Breitkopf & Härtel, Wiesbaden.

EXAMPLE I: Brahms, "Die Kränze," op. 46, no. 1, bars 43–58. From Johannes Brahms, *Sämtliche Werke*, by permission of Breitkopf & Härtel, Wiesbaden.

EXAMPLE J: Brahms, "Die Schale der Vergessenheit," op. 46, no. 3, bars 1–40. From Johannes Brahms, *Sämtliche Werke*, by permission of Breitkopf & Härtel, Wiesbaden.

EXAMPLE K: Brahms, String Quartet, op. 51, no. 1, III, bars 1–44. From Johannes Brahms, *Sämtliche Werke*, by permission of Breitkopf & Härtel, Wiesbaden.

EXAMPLE L: Brahms, String Quartet, op. 51, no. 1, I, bars 1–26. From Johannes Brahms, *Sämtliche Werke*, by permission of Breitkopf & Härtel, Wiesbaden.

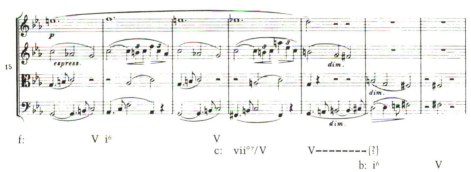

EXAMPLE M: Brahms, String Quartet, op. 51, no. 1, I, bars 62–78. From Johannes Brahms, *Sämtliche Werke*, by permission of Breitkopf & Härtel, Wiesbaden.

EXAMPLE N: Brahms, Symphony No. 2, op. 73, II, bars 50–64. From Johannes Brahms, *Sämtliche Werke*, by permission of Breitkopf & Härtel, Wiesbaden.

EXAMPLE O: Brahms, Symphony No. 2, op. 73, II, bars 94–104. From Johannes Brahms, *Sämtliche Werke*, by permission of Breitkopf & Härtel, Wiesbaden.

EXAMPLE P: Brahms, Clarinet Sonata, op. 120, no. 1, I, bars 1–55. From Johannes Brahms, *Sämtliche Werke*, by permission of Breitkopf & Härtel, Wiesbaden.

EXAMPLE Q: Schoenberg's analysis of Brahms's "O Tod," op. 121, no. 3. Reprinted by permission of Faber and Faber, Ltd., from *Style and Idea*, edited by Leonard Stein.

EXAMPLE R: Brahms, "O Tod," op. 121, no. 3, bars 26–40. From Johannes Brahms, *Sämtliche Werke*, by permission of Breitkopf & Härtel, Wiesbaden.

EXAMPLE S: Schoenberg, Piano Piece, 1894, bars 1–23. Used by permission of Belmont Music Publishers, Los Angeles, California 90049. Copyright 1968 by Belmont Music Publishers.

EXAMPLE T: (a) Schoenberg, String Quartet, 1897, II, bars 1–9.
(b) Brahms, String Quartet, op. 67, III, bars 1–8.

(a)   **Andantino grazioso**

(b) **Agitato (Allegretto non troppo)**

EXAMPLE U: Schoenberg, String Quartet, op. 7, bars 1–10.

Bibliography of Works Cited

Abraham, Gerald. *A Hundred Years of Music.* 4th ed. London: Duckworth, 1974.

Adorno, Theodor W. *Philosophy of Modern Music.* Translated by Anne G. Mitchell and Wesley V. Blomster. New York: Seabury, 1973.

Bailey, Walter B. "Schoenberg's Published Articles: A List of Titles, Sources, and Translations." *Journal of the Arnold Schoenberg Institute* 4 (1980): 155–91.

————. "The Unpublished Songs of Arnold Schoenberg, c. 1893–1900." M.A. thesis, University of Southern California, 1979.

Bent, Ian. "Analysis." In *The New Grove Dictionary of Music and Musicians*, 1: 340–88. London: Macmillan, 1980. 20 vols.

Berg, Alban. "Why Is Schoenberg's Music So Hard to Comprehend?" 1924. Reprinted in *Schoenberg, Berg, Webern: The String Quartets* [see separate entry], pp. 20–30.

Berlioz, Hector. *The Memoirs of Hector Berlioz.* 2d ed. Translated by David Cairns. New York: Knopf, 1969.

Bozarth, George. "A Brahms Cadenza by Moscheles." Letter in *The Musical Times* 121 (1980): 14.

————. "The *Lieder* of Johannes Brahms—1868–71: Studies in Chronology and Compositional Process." Ph.D. dissertation, Princeton University, 1978.

————. "The *Liederjahr* of 1868: Brahms Research and Modern Musicology." Paper (unpublished) given at International Brahms Congress, Detroit, 1980.

Brahms, Johannes. *Johannes Brahms Briefe an J. V. Widmann, Ellen und Ferdinand Vetter, Adolf Schubring.* Edited by Max Kalbeck. (His Briefwechsel, 8.) Berlin: Deutsche Brahms-Gesellschaft, 1915.

————. *Johannes Brahms Briefe an P. J. und Fritz Simrock.* Edited by Max Kalbeck. 4 vols. (His Briefwechsel, 9–12.) Berlin: Deutsche Brahms-Gesellschaft, 1919.

————. *Johannes Brahms im Briefwechsel mit Joseph Joachim.* Edited by Andreas Moser. 2 vols. (His Briefwechsel, 5–6.) Berlin: Deutsche Brahms-Gesellschaft, 1908.

————. *Johannes Brahms im Briefwechsel mit Karl Reinthaler, Max Bruch, Hermann*

Deiters, Friedr. Heimsoeth, Karl Reinecke, Ernst Rudorff, Bernhard und Luise Scholz. Edited by Wilhelm Altmann. (His Briefwechsel, 3.) Berlin: Deutsche Brahms-Gesellschaft, 1908.

—— . *Johannes Brahms: The Herzogenberg Correspondence*. Edited by Max Kalbeck. Translated by Hanna Bryant. New York: Dutton, 1909.

—— . *Letters of Clara Schumann and Johannes Brahms, 1853–1896*. Edited by Berthold Litzmann. 2 vols. 1927. Reprint, New York: Vienna House, 1973.

—— . *The N. Simrock Thematic Catalog of the Works of Johannes Brahms*. Edited with an introduction by Donald M. McCorkle. New York: Da Capo, 1973.

—— . *Opus 24, Opus 23, Opus 18, Opus 90*. Facsimile edition, includes Symphony No. 3. New York: Robert Owen Lehman Foundation, 1967.

Colles, H. C. *Symphony and Drama, 1850–1900*. (Oxford History of Music, 7.) London: Oxford University Press, 1934.

Cross, Charlotte M. "Three Levels of 'Idea' in Schoenberg's Thought and Writings." *Current Musicology* no. 30 (1980): 24–36.

Czesla, Werner. "Motivische Mutationen im Schaffen von Johannes Brahms." In *Colloquium Amicorum: Joseph Schmidt-Görg zum 70. Geburtstag*, edited by S. Kross and H. Schmidt, pp. 64–72. Bonn: Beethovenhaus, 1967.

Dahlhaus, Carl. *Arnold Schönberg: Variationen für Orchester, op. 31*. Munich: Fink, 1968.

—— . "Brahms und die Idee der Kammermusik." 1973. Reprinted in *Brahms Studien* 1 (1974): 45–57.

—— . "Issues in Composition." In his *Between Romanticism and Modernism: Four Studies in the Music of the Later Nineteenth Century*, translated by Mary Whittall, pp. 40–78. Berkeley and Los Angeles: University of California Press, 1980. (Original German edition, 1974.)

—— . *Johannes Brahms: Klavierkonzert nr. 1, d-moll, op. 15*. Munich: Fink, 1965.

—— . "Musikalische Prosa." 1964. Reprinted in his *Schönberg und Andere: Gesammelte Aufsätze zur neuen Musik*, pp. 134–45. Mainz: Schott, 1978.

Dedel, Peter. *Johannes Brahms: A Guide to His Autograph in Facsimile*. Ann Arbor: Music Library Association, 1978.

Downs, Philip. "Beethoven's 'New Way' and the *Eroica*." 1970. Reprinted in *The Creative World of Beethoven*, edited by Paul Henry Lang, pp. 83–102. New York: Norton, 1971.

Dunsby, Jonathan M. "Schoenberg and the Writings of Schenker." *Journal of the Arnold Schoenberg Institute* 2 (1977): 26–33.

—— . *Structural Ambiguity in Brahms: Analytical Approaches to Four Works*. Ann Arbor: UMI Research Press, 1981.

Ehrmann, Alfred von. *Johannes Brahms: Weg, Werk und Welt*. Leipzig: Breitkopf & Härtel, 1933.

Epstein, David. *Beyond Orpheus: Studies in Musical Structure*. Cambridge, Mass.: MIT Press, 1979.

Forte, Allen. "The Structural Origin of Exact Tempi in the Brahms-Haydn Variations." 1957. Reprinted in *Johannes Brahms: Variations on a Theme of Haydn*, edited by Donald M. McCorkle, pp. 185–200. New York: Norton, 1976.

Friedheim, Philip. "Tonality and Structure in the Early Works of Schoenberg." Ph.D. dissertation, New York University, 1963.

Friedlaender, Max. *Brahms's Lieder: An Introduction to the Songs for One and Two Voices*. Translated by C. Leonard Leese. London: Oxford University Press, 1928.

Gal, Hans. *Johannes Brahms: His Work and Personality*. Translated by Joseph Stein. New York: Knopf, 1963.

Geiringer, Karl. *Brahms: His Life and Work*, 2d ed. New York: Oxford University Press, 1947.

Gerber, Rudolph. "Formprobleme in Brahmsschen Lied." *Jahrbuch der Musikbibliothek Peters* 39 (1932): 23–42.

Gerlach, Reinhard. "War Schönberg von Dvořák Beeinflusst? Zu Arnold Schönbergs Streichquartett D Dur." *Neue Zeitschrift für Musik* 133 (1972): 122–27.

Giebeler, Konrad. *Die Lieder von Johannes Brahms: Ein Beitrag zur Musikgeschichte des 19. Jahrhunderts*. Münster: Kramer, 1959.

Goehr, Alexander. "Schoenberg's *Gedanke* Manuscript." *Journal of the Arnold Schoenberg Institute* 2 (1977): 4–19.

Gombrich, E. H. *Art and Illusion: A Study in the Psychology of Pictorial Representation*. Princeton: Princeton University Press, 1960.

Gülke, Peter. "Über Schönbergs Brahms-Bearbeitung." 1975. Reprinted in *Arnold Schönberg*, edited by Heinz-Klaus Metzger and Rainer Riehn, pp. 230–42. Munich: Text & Kritik, 1980.

Hancock, Virginia. "Brahms and His Library of Early Music: The Effects of His Study of Renaissance and Baroque Music on His Choral Writing." D.M.A. dissertation, University of Oregon, 1977.

Hanslick, Eduard. *Concerte, Componisten und Virtuosen der letzten fünfzehn Jahre, 1870–1885*. Berlin: Allgemeiner Verein für Deutsche Literatur, 1886.

———. *Music Criticisms 1846–99*. Rev. ed., translated and edited by Henry Pleasants. Harmondsworth: Penguin, 1963.

Hauptmann, Moritz. *The Nature of Harmony and Metre*. Translated by W. E. Heathcote. London: Sonnenschein, 1888. (Original German edition, 1853.)

Henschel, George. *Personal Recollections of Johannes Brahms: Some of His Letters to and Pages from a Journal Kept by George Henschel*. Boston: Badger, 1907.

Herttrich, Ernst. "Johannes Brahms—Klaviertrio H-Dur Opus 8, Frühfassung und Spätfassung: Ein analytischer Vergleich." In *Musik, Edition, Interpretation: Gedenkschrift Günter Henle*, edited by Martin Bente, pp. 218–36. Munich: Henle, 1980.

Hill, William G. "Brahms' Op. 51—A Diptych." *Music Review* 13 (1952): 110–24.

Hofmann, Kurt. *Die Erstdrucke der Werke von Johannes Brahms*. Tützing: Hans Schneider, 1975.

Hollander, Hans. "Der melodische Aufbau in Brahms' 'Regenlied' Sonate." *Neue Zeitschrift für Musik* 125 (1964): 5–7.

Jenner, Gustav. *Johannes Brahms als Mensch, Lehrer, und Künstler: Studien und Erlebnisse*. Marburg: Elwert, 1905.

Joachim, Joseph. *Letters from and to Joseph Joachim*. Selected and translated by Nora Bickley. London: Macmillan, 1914.

Jonas, Oswald. *Introduction to the Theory of Heinrich Schenker: The Nature of the Musical Work of Art*. Translated and edited by John Rothgeb. New York: Longman, 1982.

Kalbeck, Max. *Johannes Brahms*. Rev. eds. 4 vols. Berlin: Deutsche Brahms-Gesellschaft, 1913–22.

Kalib, Sylvan. "Thirteen Essays [by Heinrich Schenker] from the Three Yearbooks *Das*

Meisterwerk in der Musik." 3 vols. Ph.D. dissertation, Northwestern University, 1973.

Keller, Hans. "The Chamber Music." In *The Mozart Companion,* edited by H. C. Robbins Landon and Donald Mitchell, pp. 90–137. New York: Norton, 1969.

————. "K. 503: The Unity of Contrasting Themes and Movements." *Music Review* 17 (1956): 48–58, 120–29.

Keys, Ivor. *Brahms Chamber Music.* Seattle: University of Washington Press, 1974.

Kirby, Frank E. "Brahms and the Piano Sonata." In *Paul A. Pisk: Essays in His Honor,* edited by John Glowacki, pp. 163–180. Austin: University of Texas Press, 1966.

Klein, Rudolf. "Die konstruktiven Grundlagen der Brahms-Symphonien." *Österreichische Musikzeitschrift* 23 (1968): 258–63.

Lamberton, Elizabeth Jean. "Brahms's Piano Quintet, Op. 34, and Duo-Piano Sonata, Op. 34 *bis*: A Critical Study." M.A. thesis, University of British Columbia, 1978.

Litzmann, Berthold. *Clara Schumann: Ein Künstlerleben nach Tagebüchern und Briefen.* Rev. ed. 3 vols. Leipzig: Breitkopf & Härtel, 1920.

Longyear, Rey. *Nineteenth-Century Romanticism in Music.* 2d ed. Englewood Cliffs, N.J.: Prentice-Hall, 1973.

McCorkle, Donald M. "Five Fundamental Obstacles in Brahms Source Research." *Acta Musicologica* 48 (1976): 253–72.

MacDonald, Hugh. "Thematic Transformation." In *The New Grove Dictionary of Music and Musicians,* 19: 117–118. London: Macmillan, 1980. 20 vols.

Maegaard, Jan. *Studien zur Entwicklung des dodekaphonen Satzes bei Arnold Schönberg.* 3 vols. Copenhagen: Hansen, 1972.

Mason, Colin. "Brahms' Piano Sonatas." *Music Review* 5 (1944): 112–18.

Mason, William. *Memories of a Musical Life.* New York: Century, 1902.

May, Florence. *The Life of Johannes Brahms.* 2d ed. 2 vols. London: Reeves, 1948.

Meyer, Leonard B. *Explaining Music: Essays and Explorations.* Berkeley and Los Angeles: University of California Press, 1973.

Mitschka, Arno. *Der Sonatensatz in den Werken von Johannes Brahms.* (Inaugural-Dissertation, Mainz.) Gütersloh: [n.p.], 1961.

Musgrave, Michael G. "Schoenberg and Brahms. A Study of Schoenberg's Response to Brahms's Music as Revealed in His Didactic Writings and Selected Early Compositions." Ph.D. dissertation, University of London, 1980.

Nagel, Wilibald. *Die Klaviersonaten von Johannes Brahms: Technisch-ästhetische Analysen.* Stuttgart: C. Grüninger, 1915.

Newcomb, Anthony. "The Birth of Music Out of the Spirit of Drama: An Essay in Wagnerian Formal Analysis." *19th-Century Music* 5 (1981): 38–66.

Newman, William S. "A 'Basic Motive' in Brahms's *German Requiem.*" *Music Review* 24 (1963): 190–94.

————. *The Sonata Since Beethoven: The Third and Final Volume of a History of the Sonata Idea.* 2d ed. New York: Norton, 1972.

Nüll, Edwin von der. "Strukturelle Grundbedingungen der Brahmsschen Sonatenexposition im Vergleich zur Klassik." *Die Musik* 22:1 (1929): 32–37.

Ophüls, Gustav. *Brahms Texte.* Berlin: Simrock, 1897.

Orel, Alfred. "Ein eigenhändiges Werkverzeichnis von Johannes Brahms: Ein wichtiger Beitrag zur Brahms Forschung." *Die Musik* 29:2 (1937): 529–41.

Pascall, Robert J. "Formal Principles in the Music of Brahms." Ph.D. dissertation, Oxford University, 1973.

―――. "Some Special Uses of Sonata Form by Brahms." *Soundings* 4 (1974): 58–63.

Ratz, Erwin. *Einführung in die musikalische Formenlehre: Über Formprinzipien in den Inventionen und Fugen J. S. Bachs und ihre Bedeutung für die Kompositionstechnik Beethovens*. Vienna: Österreichischer Bundesverlag, 1951.

Ravizza, Victor. "Konflikte in Brahms'scher Musik: Zum ersten Satz der C-Moll Sinfonie, Op. 68." *Schweizer Beiträge zur Musikwissenschaft* 2 (1974): 75–90.

Reich, Willi. *Schoenberg: A Critical Biography*. Translated by Leo Black. New York: Praeger, 1971.

Réti, Rudolf. "Formale Erläuterungen zu Arnold Schönbergs Klavierstücken." *Der Merker* 2 (1911): 715–17.

―――. *The Thematic Process in Music*. New York: Macmillan, 1951.

―――. *Tonality, Atonality, Pantonality: A Study of Some Trends in 20th-Century Music*. London: Rockliff, 1958.

Riemann, Hugo. "Die Taktfreiheiten in Brahms' Liedern." *Die Musik* 12:1 (1912): 10–21.

Rosen, Charles. *The Classical Style: Haydn, Mozart, Beethoven*. New York: Viking, 1971.

―――. "Influence: Plagiarism and Inspiration." *19th-Century Music* 4 (1980): 87–100.

―――. *Sonata Forms*. New York: Norton, 1980.

Rufer, Josef. *Composition with Twelve Notes Related Only to One Another*. Translated by Humphrey Searle. London: Rockliff, 1954. (Original German edition, 1952.)

―――. *The Works of Arnold Schoenberg: A Catalogue of His Compositions, Writings and Paintings*. Translated by Dika Newlin. London: Faber, 1962.

Sams, Eric. *Brahms Songs*. Seattle: University of Washington Press, 1972.

Schauffler, Robert H. *The Unknown Brahms, His Life, Character and Works; Based on New Material*. New York: Crown, 1933.

Schenker, Heinrich. ["Analysis of the First Movement."] Translated by Elliot Forbes and F. John Adams, Jr. In Ludwig van Beethoven, *Symphony No. 5 in C Minor*, pp. 164–82. New York: Norton, 1971.

―――. *Harmony*. Edited by Oswald Jonas. Translated by Elisabeth Mann Borghese. Cambridge, Mass.: MIT Press, 1973.

―――. Schmidt, Christian M. *Verfahren der motivisch-thematischen Vermittlung in der Musik von Johannes Brahms dargestellt an der Klarinettensonate f-moll, op. 120, 1*. Munich: Katzbichler, 1971.

Schoenberg, Arnold. *The Arnold Schoenberg-Hans Nachod Collection*. Edited by John A. Kimmey, Jr. Detroit: Information Coordinators, 1979.

―――. *Fundamentals of Musical Composition*. Edited by Gerald Strang and Leonard Stein. London: Faber, 1967; New York: St. Martin's Press, 1970.

―――. *Johannes Brahms: Klavierquartett G-Moll, Op. 25, für Orchester gesetzt*. Edited by Rudolf Stephan. (His *Sämtliche Werke*, 26.) Mainz: Schott; Vienna: Universal, 1972.

―――. *Letters*. Selected and edited by Erwin Stein. Translated by Eithne Wilkins and Ernst Kaiser. New York: St. Martin's Press, 1965.

―――. *Models for Beginners in Composition*. New York: G. Schirmer, 1942.

―――. "Notes on the Four String Quartets." In *Schoenberg, Berg, Webern: The String Quartets* [see separate entry], pp. 35–51.

———. "The Orchestral Variations, Op. 31: A Radio Talk." *The Score* 27 (1960): 27–40.

———. *Preliminary Exercises in Counterpoint*. Edited by Leonard Stein. London: Faber, 1982.

———. *Six Piano Pieces for Four Hands, 1896*. Los Angeles: Belmont, 1973. Reprinted in his *Sämtliche Werke*, vol. 5, pp. 79–92. Mainz:Schott; Vienna: Universal, 1973.

———. *Stil und Gedanke: Aufsätze zur Musik*. Edited by Ivan Vojtech (His Gesammelte Schriften, 1.) Frankfurt: Fischer, 1976.

———. *String Quartet in D Major, 1897*. Edited by Oliver W. Neighbour. London: Faber, 1966.

———. *Structural Functions of Harmony*. Rev. ed. Edited by Leonard Stein. New York: Norton, 1969.

———. *Style and Idea: Selected Writings of Arnold Schoenberg*. Edited by Leonard Stein. New York: St. Martin's Press, 1975.

———. *Theory of Harmony*. Translated by Roy E. Carter. Berkeley and Los Angeles: University of California Press, 1978.

———. *Three Piano Pieces, 1894*. Los Angeles: Belmont, 1968. Reprinted in his *Sämtliche Werke*, vol. 4, pp. 75–83. Mainz: Schott; and Vienna: Universal, 1968.

Schoenberg, Berg, Webern: The String Quartets. A Documentary Study. Edited by Ursula von Rauchhaupt. Hamburg: Deutsche-Grammophon, 1971.

Schubring, Adolf. "Schumanniana Nr. 8. Die Schumann'sche Schule: IV. Johannes Brahms." *Neue Zeitschrift für Musik* 56 (1862): 93–96, 101–4, 109–12, 117–19, 125–28.

———. "Schumanniana Nr. 12. Ein Deutsches Requiem . . . von Johannes Brahms." *Leipziger Allgemeine Musikalische Zeitung* 4 (1869): 9–11, 18–20.

Schumann, Robert. *On Music and Musicians*. Edited by Konrad Wolff. Translated by Paul Rosenfeld. New York: Norton, 1969.

Schwejda, Donald M. "An Investigation of the Analytical Techniques Used by Rudolf Réti in *The Thematic Process in Music*." Ph.D. dissertation, University of Indiana, 1967.

Sessions, Roger. *The Musical Experience of Composer, Performer, Listener*. Princeton: Princeton University Press, 1950.

Sittard, Josef. *Geschichte des Musik- und Concertwesens in Hamburg vom 14. Jahrhundert bis auf die Gegenwart*. Altona: Reher, 1890. Reprint, Hildesheim and New York: Olms, 1971.

Solomon, Maynard. "On Beethoven's Creative Process: A Two-Part Invention." *Music and Letters* 61 (1980): 272–83.

Stahmer, Klaus. *Musikalische Formung in soziologischem Bezug, dargestellt an der instrumentalen Kammermusik von Johannes Brahms*. Kiel: [n.p.] 1968.

Stein, Jack. *Poem and Music in the German Lied from Gluck to Hugo Wolf*. Cambridge, Mass.: Harvard University Press, 1971.

Stein, Leonard. "Toward a Chronology of Schoenberg's Early Unpublished Songs." *Journal of the Arnold Schoenberg Institute* 2 (1977): 72–80.

Stuckenschmidt, Hans H. *Schoenberg: His Life, World, and Work*. Translated by Humphrey Searle. London: Calder, 1977.

Swift, Richard. "1/XII/99: Tonal Relations in Schoenberg's *Verklärte Nacht*." *19th-Century Music* 1 (1977): 3–14.

Thieme, Ulrich. *Studien zum Jugendwerk Arnold Schönbergs: Einflüsse und Wandlungen*. Regensburg: Bosse, 1979.

Tovey, Donald F. *Beethoven*. London: Oxford University Press, 1945.

———. "Brahms's Chamber Music." In his *Essays and Lectures on Music*, pp. 220–70. London: Oxford University Press, 1949.

———. *Essays in Musical Analysis, 1: Symphonies*. London: Oxford University Press, 1935.

———. *Essays in Musical Analysis, 3: Concertos*. London: Oxford University Press, 1936.

———. *Essays in Musical Analysis (Supplementary Volume): Chamber Music*. London: Oxford University Press, 1944.

———. "Franz Schubert." In his *Essays and Lectures on Music*, pp. 103–33. London: Oxford University Press, 1949.

Urbantschitsch, Viktor. "Die Entwicklung der Sonatenform bei Brahms." *Studien zur Musikwissenschaft* 14 (1927): 265–85.

Velten, Klaus. "Das Prinzip der entwickelnden Variation bei Johannes Brahms und Arnold Schönberg." *Musik und Bildung* 6 (1974): 547–55.

———. *Schönbergs Instrumentation Bachscher und Brahmsscher Werke als Dokumente seines Traditionsverständnisses*. Regensburg: Bosse, 1976.

Walker, Alan. *A Study in Musical Analysis*. London: Barrie and Rockliff, 1962.

Webern, Anton. "Schoenberg's Music." In *Schoenberg, Berg, Webern: The String Quartets* [see separate entry], pp. 15–19. (Original German edition, 1912).

Webster, James. "Schubert's Sonata Form and Brahms's First Maturity (II)." *19th-Century Music* 3 (1979): 52–71.

Westafer, Walter. "Overall Unity and Contrast in Brahms's *German Requiem*." Ph.D. dissertation, University of North Carolina, 1973.

Wilke, Rainer. *Brahms, Reger, Schönberg Streichquartette: Motivisch-thematische Prozesse und formale Gestalt*. Hamburg: Wagner, 1980.

Winklhofer, Sharon. *Liszt's Sonata in B Minor: A Study of Autograph Sources and Documents*. Ann Arbor: UMI Research Press, 1980.

Wörner, Karl. *Das Zeitalter der thematischen Prozesse in der Geschichte der Musik*. Regensburg: Bosse, 1969.

Index of Brahms's Works

(Boldface indicates a more extended analysis)

General Index